# Patterns of Japanese Policymaking:
## Experiences from Higher Education

# Westview Replica Editions

This book is a Westview Replica Edition. The concept of Replica Editions is a response to the crisis in academic and informational publishing. Library budgets for books have been severely curtailed; economic pressures on the university presses and the few private publishing companies primarily interested in scholarly manuscripts have severely limited the capacity of the industry to properly serve the academic and research communities. Many manuscripts dealing with important subjects, often representing the highest level of scholarship, are today not economically viable publishing projects. Or, if they are accepted for publication, they are often subject to lead times ranging from one to three years. Scholars are understandably frustrated when they realize that their first-class research cannot be published within a reasonable time frame, if at all.

Westview Replica Editions are our practical solution to the problem. The concept is simple. We accept a manuscript in camera-ready form and move it immediately into the production process. The responsibility for textual and copy editing lies with the author or sponsoring organization. If necessary we will advise the author on proper preparation of footnotes and bibliography. We prefer that the manuscript be typed according to our specifications, though it may be acceptable as typed for a dissertation or prepared in some other clearly organized and readable way. The end result is a book produced by lithography and bound in hard covers. Initial edition sizes range from 400 to 600 copies, and a number of recent Replicas are already in second printings. We include among Westview Replica Editions only works of outstanding scholarly quality or of great informational value, and we will continue to exercise our usual editorial standards and quality control.

# Patterns of Japanese Policymaking:
## Experiences from Higher Education
### T. J. Pempel

The author of this study of policymaking in postwar Japan
contends that the prevailing perceptions of the subject advanced to date are inadequate. Professor Pempel identifies
three distinct patterns of policymaking within Japan's current
system of hegemonic pluralism. One of these, "policymaking by
camp conflict," is associated with broad, highly emotional,
ideological issues that polarize political forces and that are
resolved only after widely publicized battles in the Diet, the
media, and the streets. A second pattern, "incremental policymaking," involves nonideological problems that are settled
largely through bureaucratic procedures almost totally removed
from public scrutiny. A third pattern, "pressure group policymaking," pits a limited number of special interest groups
against one or more government agencies; this process is less
conflictual and public than camp conflict, but more visible
and antagonistic than incremental policymaking.

These patterns are examined both theoretically and empiri-
cally and are thoroughly tested in the areas of university administration, enrollment expansion, and specialization in
higher education. The results have import for Japan scholars
and will be of interest also to students of comparative education and public policy.

T. J. Pempel, associate professor of government at Cornell
University, is currently engaged in an investigation of the
Japanese state bureaucracy and in a project on comparative
public policy in Japan, France, West Germany, Britain, and the
United States.

## Studies of the East Asian Institute
## of Columbia University

This volume is included in the Studies of the East Asian
Institute of Columbia University. The institute was established in 1949 to prepare graduate students for careers dealing with East Asia and to aid research and publication on
East Asia during the modern period. The Studies of the East
Asian Institute were inaugurated in 1962 to bring to a wider
public the results of significant new research on modern and
contemporary East Asia.

# Patterns of Japanese Policymaking:
## Experiences from Higher Education

### T. J. Pempel

Westview Press / Boulder, Colorado

*A Westview Replica Edition*

*This book is included in the Studies of the East Asian Institute, Columbia University*

Published in 1978 in the United States of America by
   Westview Press, Inc.
   5500 Central Avenue
   Boulder, Colorado  80301
   Frederick A. Praeger, Publisher


Library of Congress Catalog Card Number:  78-15846
ISBN:  0-89158-270-3


Printed and bound in the United States of America

For my parents

Agnes F. Pempel
and
the late Thomas D. Pempel

# Contents

# Tables and Figures

## Tables

## Figures

# Acknowledgments

I owe a great debt to many individuals and institutions for help in completing this work. The greatest intellectual debts are to Peter Katzenstein, Kitamura Kazuyuki, Theodore Lowi, Mizuno Kunitoshi, James Morley, and Nagai Michio. The bulk of the financial support for my research in Japan was provided by the U.S. Education Commission through a Fulbright Fellowship. The East Asian Institute at Columbia University and the China-Japan Program at Cornell University provided additional financial help plus office space, administrative assistance, and an environment conducive to research and writing.

In addition to those named above, I would like to thank Douglas Ashford, George Z.F. Bereday, John C. Campbell, Gerald Curtis, David Mozingo, Herbert Passin, William Steslicke, Sunada Ichirō, Sidney Tarrow, Terasaki Masao, Norman Uphoff, and Herschel Webb for various comments and suggestions during the writing and rewriting stages.

While in Japan, I received invaluable help from the Ministry of Education, the National Diet Library, and the National Institute for Educational Research.

I would also like to thank the dozens of individuals who took time out from busy schedules to allow themselves to be interviewed for one or another phase of the research.

Laurie Ann Schlansky, Tammy Thompson, and Yvonne Yung all provided important research assistance. Mervyn Adams supplied yeoman help in the editorial work.

Alice McDowell Pempel, by refusing to become a captive to my research and by the excited pursuit of her own, provided me with an invaluable oasis and a constant sense of perspective.

# 1. Introduction

How do governments formulate policies to regulate behavior in their societies?  By whom are the
decisions made, through what structural arrangements,
and in response to which of the many demands and
pressures extant in the society; how do these differ
from problem to problem, and from regime to regime?
Such questions have been at the heart of political
science through its long evolution, for it is in
grappling with such questions that abstractions such
as liberty, equality, authoritarianism, corporatism,
capitalism, oppression, and democracy take on tangibility, concreteness, and visibility.
     This is a book about policymaking in Japan since
World War II.  It contends, among other things, that
the dominant perceptions of the subject advanced to
date are inadequate.  Much of the present writing,
for example, implies that there is some single,
clearly identifiable policymaking process in Japan.
Usually this is seen to revolve around a ruling triumvirate of the conservative Liberal Democratic Party
(LDP), big business circles, and the senior echelons
of the national bureaucracy.  All three are seen to
rule the country in combination--the three legs of a
tripod, each serving as an equally critical support.[1]
Other arguments see singularity in policymaking as the
consequence of the country's alleged dominance by
class conflict or monopoly capital.[2]  Parallel to both
is a perspective that argues that little takes place
in Japanese politics without a struggle by, and great
attention to, the interests of the relatively autonomous political factions within the LDP.[3]  Similarly
prevalent and complementary are interpretations of
Japanese policy formation that assert the alleged
uniqueness of a process peculiar to Japan.  This last
is variously seen as the result of its feudal heritage, its alleged dominance by an emperor system, or
various cultural peculiarities.[4]  Such perceptions of
uniqueness are often reinforced by the prevalence

1

throughout the literature of vernacularisms which at least implicitly convey a lack of parallel to behavior in other societies: _ringisei_, _hanashiai_, _nemawashi_, _keiretsu_, _oyabun-kobun_, _giri-ninjo_, and the like.

If claims for the existence of some singular, and perhaps uniquely Japanese, pattern of policymaking are at best partly convincing, it will not do to swing blindly to alternative positions, alleging either that Japan's policymaking is just like that of all other political systems, or conversely that each and every policymaking situation is so unique that it defies categorization. Perhaps at some high level of abstraction it makes sense to analyze all policymaking as essentially the same in terms such as input-output, satisficing, operational environment, or feedback loops.[5] But such a level inevitably forces one into a factual and practical vacuum, which blurs significant distinctions and obscures important empirical differences. Individual case studies, by way of contrast, though providing important contributions to the study of Japanese policymaking as well as they have elsewhere, all too frequently rely extensively on sui generis explanations, making them of little more value for systematic understanding of complex realities than the oversimplifications and often tautological models they seek to correct.

This book argues for an intermediate-level paradigm. It examines in detail the way in which the Japanese government has, since the end of World War II, formulated state policy in three distinct areas of higher education: control of political activities and disruptions on campus; the shift from general and humanistic educational content to specialized and technical education; and finally the expansion in the overall number of students enrolled in higher educational institutions. These three cover some of the most significant areas where higher education interacts with politics and government. They also provide the basis for more analysis than is possible from any single case study, and yet more hard information and detail than is possible in a purely theoretical work.

On the basis of detailed examinations of the processes by which policy was formulated in these three areas, the book finds little to confirm and much to challenge in existing interpretations of how policy is made in Japan. First of all, there is tremendous variation and little homogeneity in the processes involved. Furthermore, there are numerous instances where little, if any, evidence emerges of business or LDP influence; nowhere is there any evidence whatever that intra-LDP factional considerations were critical. Class conflict, a feudal heritage, the emperor system, and monopoly capital are similarly limited in ability to provide useful explanations. Beyond this, the study shows that most instances of policy formation can be explained with little reliance on any purported uniqueness in Japanese behavior. Far more insight seems possible by examining Japanese behavior in a comparative rather than a culturally specific context.

At the same time, the three are not seen to be entities unto themselves. There is form in Japanese policymaking. The key focus of the book is the isolation of three ideal typical patterns of policymaking, labeled variously "policymaking by camp conflict," "incremental policymaking," and "pressure group policymaking." Which of these three patterns is more likely to occur in any single situation is seen to be a function of the combined interplay between the nature of the issue involved and varying political structures. Certain issues in Japan, as elsewhere, are highly charged emotionally, others are not; some are extremely broad in their intended scope, others are quite narrow and specific; finally, some issues are composed of numerous component parts which can be isolated and dealt with separately while others demand a holistic, yes-or-no solution. Understanding these three critical components takes one a long way in understanding the policymaking process that results when any particular issue arises in government. Beyond this, two essential structural factors influence the process, namely legal requirements and the political resources of the groups and individuals most directly interested in and affected by the issue. Chapter 2 will detail this basic framework for the analysis of differences in policymaking process. It will suggest as well that policy outcomes result from a combination of the issue involved and the process by which it is formulated.

If this book is primarily about policymaking, it is also about policy itself. Although at the present stage in our knowledge of political science it hardly seems necessary to justify a study of policy outcomes as well as policymaking processes, a word on the subject may be useful. In the study of Japanese politics, as more generally throughout the discipline of political science, attention has all too frequently been devoted to political processes at the expense of analyzing political outcomes. Power and influence are clearly manifest in the process of making official decisions; one can learn a great deal about the politics of any society by investigating the way it reaches decisions. At the same time, just as it is

3

only partially correct to describe the complex inner
workings of a particular watch or a television set
without their respective purposes, adequacy, and impact, so too it is necessary to do more than convey a
picture of the inner mechanics of specific policymaking processes in Japan.  The policies themselves,
their broader societal meaning, and their consequences should also be assessed to provide the political
and normative breadth needed to make meaningful statements about "the politics" of a particular country.[6]
     Public policy is more than simply the residual
of the process whereby it is formulated, and increasingly there has been a recognition of the need to
undertake empirical studies of the policies of various states as well as of their policymaking processes.[7]  It will not do to assert with Schumpeter that
one can label a nation-state "democratic" on purely
procedural grounds.[8]  It strains the use of terms to
suggest that, so long as "free elections" are the
basis for selecting policymakers, any actions they
take and any policies they pursue are ipso facto
"democratic."  Similarly, it is important to go beyond process to the investigation of policy content
itself and to analyze not only how policymakers do
what they do, but to look as well at what it is they
choose to do.
     At the same time, in examining outcomes it will
not do to imply, as certain students of public policy
have, that policymaking processes are largely irrelevant.[9]  Outcomes are a legitimate and important subject for political inquiry.  But it is intellectually
and politically intolerable to suggest that political
systems are inherently similar just because similar
policies emerge.  It is important whether such policies emerge as a consequence of actions by a benevo-
lent despot, an isolated technocratic elite, or open
conflict and confrontation.  Health policy may be
comparable in all three, for example, but the political significance, the balance of power, the channels
of public access, and ultimately the lives of the
citizenry are inevitably quite different under the
three in ways that an investigation of public policy
and potential outcome alone would not clarify.[10]
Thus, the study of policymaking cannot and should not
be isolated from the study of public policy.  At the
same time, the study of public policy requires attention to the processes of policy formation.  Hence,
this study will discuss both.
     Finally, a few brief words should be said about
the three areas being investigated, all of which fall
within the functional area of higher education.  The

4

choice of three issues within a single functional
area makes it difficult to claim that patterns dis-
covered are inherently generalizable across the universe of Japanese policymaking.  In the abstract it
might have been better to have chosen three issues
from a wider array of possible areas.  Yet there is
a wholeness and unity to the area of higher education (or any other area) that would be lacking in
cases chosen randomly from disparate areas such as
foreign policy, labor policy, budgetmaking, agricultural policy, or defense policy, for example.  By
concentrating attention on a single functional area,
the most affected and involved political forces remain potentially the same, as do such things as their
ideological and cultural values and their political
resources.  One can more easily compare the differences in reaction of a single ministry, such as the
Ministry of Education, on several different issues of
higher education, for example, than one can try to
generalize about "governmental" or "bureaucratic"
actions from a diversity of agencies organized to
deal with a range of functionally unique problems.
This is one important merit in a study of policymaking and issues within a single functional area.  Further, by relating to broad hypotheses and propositions formulated about policymaking and by dealing
with three discrete subareas of higher education, it
is possible to steer clear of the "barefoot empiri-
cism" and dangerous atypicality of the single case
study.  Whether the patterns suggested capture all or
most instances of Japanese policymaking is both impossible to claim and irrelevant to demand.  The study
of the subject is simply too underdeveloped at present.  Yet familiarity with the secondary literature
on Japanese policymaking suggests broader applicability of the patterns and numerous parallels in other
functional areas.  As such it should be at least sug-
gestive well beyond the area of higher education.

     As noted, the study deals with three specific
areas of higher educational' policy: university administration, specialization and differentiation, and,
finally, enrollment expansion.  While educators would
hardly accept any implication that these three areas
encompass the full range or even necessarily the most
important aspects of higher educational policies, the
three do touch on dimensions of higher education of
major political concern: who is educated; in what
subjects and in what manner; and under whose overall
supervision?

     These problems have become critical in Japan, as
well as in all the industrial democracies of Western

Europe and North America. As the occupational base
of these countries has shifted from predominantly agricultural and light industrial to heavier industry,
technology, and the service sectors, a university education has increasingly become the sine qua non for
individual success and influence. Where higher education was once available only to the offspring of
the most socially prominent and economically advan-
taged families in society, it has become increasingly
available, if not to all at least to increasing proportions of these societies. In 1960, for example,
only four of twenty-two OECD countries had enrollment
rates of more than 10 percent; by 1970 all but four
did.[11] Increasingly these countries are forced to
face the political, not simply educational, question
of whom to educate. Is there to be an inevitable
trend toward universal higher education, as there
once was such a trend in elementary school and later
high school? Or are restrictions to be established?
If so, on what groups and with what justifications?

Furthermore, education is becoming an increasingly important political and social issue. Higher
education enrollments now approach or exceed one-
quarter of the age cohort in several societies, including Japan, with expenditures for education ac-
counting for 5 percent or more of GNP in most industrial nations. Moreover, 20-45 percent of government
expenditure is allocated to education in all industrial societies, with higher education taking ever-
larger proportions of these figures. At the same
time, higher educational background plays an integral role in the individual's eventual career, and
the business, scientific, and technical worlds are
increasingly demanding specific types of research and
student training. As a result of all these things,
governments in all industrialized countries are beginning to recognize that it is politically and socially expensive to leave the choice of the subjects
studied completely to individual student or faculty
preference. More and more, funds are being allocated
to encourage particular courses of study and to "produce" particular types of graduates, usually with an
eye toward manpower management and presumed occupational needs.

Governments have always been somewhat concerned
over the activities of faculty and student members on
campuses, most particularly when such activities take
the form of antigovernmental protest activities. But
in addition to trying to control antigovernmental activities, the state has become more broadly concerned
with insuring the "correct" administration of univer-

sity campuses as these campuses have come to play an increasingly important economic and social role. Few university administrations have been inclined to flaunt university autonomy at the expense of government funds and access to the higher echelons of power; few governments have been willing to let them try. There has instead developed a growing symbiosis between university and state, in which each tends to see itself as the more benefited, but in which government controls have unquestionably increased. University administration in this sense has become a key political problem in a wide range of societies.

Hence, all three questions under investigation-- enrollment expansion, specialization and differentiation, and finally university administration--have become central political, as well as educational, problems in most industrialized societies. Higher education is no longer, if ever it was, of concern only to those involved in making its administration more rational, more liberal, or more godly. Sociologists, economists, social engineers, politicians, and technologists all have legitimate and specific areas to investigate in higher education. Its wide impact clearly makes it a public policy issue of valid concern to political scientists.

For the student of Japan, higher education has been at least as politically charged. As will be examined subsequently, many higher educational issues have been injected into the Japanese political world during various periods since World War II, ranging from such rather pedantic problems as the issuance of university charters to the more headline-dominating activities of student radicals. The range and variety of important higher educational issues in postwar Japan thus command the attention of the political scientist interested in understanding how public policy in an area of political significance has been formulated under different problematic conditions within Japan, and with what political as well as educational results.

# 2. Framework for Analysis

Using such diverse terms as "decision-making," "lawmaking," and "political process," modern political scientists from Burgess and Bentley through Truman, Almond, and Easton have devoted a great deal of attention to the means by which important political determinations are made. To date there have been two dominant modes of analysis regarding this problem: the case study of a single decision, and the more sweeping theories aimed at isolating patterns common to some universe of policymaking situations. Because these two approaches have too often gone forward in isolation from one another, both in general political analysis and in the study of Japanese politics, there has been an intellectually frustrating gap between theory and reality, between purportedly universalistic verities and the particularities that often seem to defy them. This study aims at a middle level of analysis, in an effort to bridge this chasm by presenting empirical material and theoretically significant patterns simultaneously. More than one case is examined in detail and more than one overarching pattern of policymaking is isolated, and the cases and the patterns are related directly to one another. Throughout, an effort is made as well to reconcile the two with existing theories and empirical findings. The approach taken is neither purely inductive nor purely deductive; rather it draws on both methods in the hope of mutual stimulation and reconciliation.

This is done through the construction and application of three "pure types," a method with intellectual roots in both Platonic "ideal forms" and Weberian "ideal types." The three are constructed on the basis of inductive propositions derived from existing case studies, combined with broader generalizations about Japanese policymaking and policymaking in the abstract. As with Platonic or Weberian types, they are abstractions from reality with a theoretical integrity of their own that is unlikely to be mirrored

9

absolutely and perfectly in any real situation.  The
three patterns serve instead as theoretical maps
against which realities may be compared.  By highlighting certain central relationships and thereby
providing a somewhat oversimplified theoretical abstraction, such ideal types act as lenses through
which any particular case can be examined, suggesting fundamental questions or relationships worthy of
exploration.  In addition, the method allows one to
analyze the degree to which any particular case ac-
cords with the abstract type or shows gaps between
expected and actual behavior.  To the extent that a
close mesh is found, the applicability of the pattern is reconfirmed; to the extent that it does not,
the most basic areas in which the pattern must be
reevaluated are revealed.  In short, the method provides a theoretical structure for research but is
flexible enough to accommodate new and unexpected
findings.

These three patterns are seen as the consequence
of both structural and functional features.  In all
political systems certain fixed structural constraints
operate as a bias for or against certain processes and
aid or impede certain policy possibilities.[1]  Like-
wise, in different functional areas inherent constraints arise from the nature of the issue and problem involved.  Such structural and functional constraints serve as external determinants of both process and policy.  As such they shape policymaking
processes and public policy itself.

Attention to both structural and functional explanations of policymaking and public policy has a
long tradition within political science.  Structural
explanations all begin from the perspective that
something essential about the context of the political relationships within which policy is formulated
accounts for the major variations in process and policy.  In one typical genre, the cultural or social
basis of politics is the starting point in the identification of a presumed commonality among all major
examples of policymaking.  Hence, there are studies
of policymaking in Britain, France, Africa, Eastern
Europe, or some other geographical area; or of the
politics of Anglo-Saxon, Iberian, or Mediterranean
societies.  Alternatively, the stress is on economic
or technological constraints, with the result an
analysis of policymaking or policy in capitalist vs.
socialist economies; in industrial, industrializing,
or "postindustrial" societies; or in "the welfare
state" or "urban society."  Still other structural
constraints are seen to be inherent in pluralism,

10

authoritarianism, or militarism. Regardless of the specific characteristics, all such explanations emphasize some structurally defining context or condition(s) within which policymaking takes place and which limits both process and outcomes.

Analysis which presumes some such structural limitations is in many ways similar to that which begins by examining functional limitations. Both presume inherent constraints upon policy formation, and subsequently upon policy choice. Both treat policymaking processes as largely constrained. But while structural analysis begins by assuming that such constraints are constant regardless of the issue involved, functional analysis presumes that the constraints are inherent in certain types of issues and that these constraints are constant over different political structures.

Much functional analysis argues that there is an inherent logic within some single functional arena, such as foreign policy, housing policy, transportation policy, or budgeting, which in turn is seen as the prime contributor to the most meaningful differences in policymaking processes. Problems of budgeting, for example, are seen to involve top civil servants and politicians almost exclusively, a premium on maximization of the budgetary share allotted to one's organization, a willingness on the part of all actors to work toward a "reasonable" compromise in dividing the national tax pie, and the like.[2] Foreign policy, by way of contrast, is assessed as a process of maximizing the national domestic and security interest through the use of economic and military means with the stakes frequently involving the lives and deaths of hundreds or thousands of individuals, the sovereignty of the state, or the national way of life.[3] Consequently, there is a thrust toward intra-elite agreement and minimization of externally exploitable differences of opinion. Thus, the mechanisms and problems involved in formulating some single category of policy, such as defense, are usually presumed to be roughly comparable over time within single societies, and from one society to the next, while these are seen as inherently different in critical ways from policymaking toward other categories of issues such as health care or urban redevelopment. Functional policy categories thus emerge as the key determinants of the significant variations in policymaking.

More sophisticated but intellectually akin to interpretations based on straightforward functional limitations are those which begin analysis of political processes with some typology of political issues. Such typological categories are seen to define the different political constraints within which different types of issues must inevitably be resolved. Thus, the key intellectual problem becomes one of identifying the relevant categories of issues. In all cases, however, the analysis follows lines transcending such clear functional categories as tax policy, foreign policy, or social welfare policy.

On the basis of two variables, the likelihood of official coercion and the degree to which such coercion is applied through individual conduct as opposed to an "environment of conduct," for example, Lowi has suggested a fourfold categorization of all political issues: regulative, distributive, contituent, and redistributive.[4] Zimmerman, refining Lowi's categories, comes up with five modified categories of issues.[5] Riker meanwhile has validated an important distinction between zero-sum and non-zero-sum political situations which establish separate patterns of political interaction among political actors. For him a key concern is the presence or absence of disaggregable payoffs in political situations.[6] Froman, in two separate works, suggests the importance of differentiating between issues which are "areal" (affecting the entire political community) and those which are "segmental" (affecting specific segments of the community more than others).[7] Others have suggested the utility of differentiating between "strategic" and "tactical" issues, issues which involve "symbolic" or "material" satisfaction of political demands, and policies which would require adaptation to the environment as opposed to those which would seek to control the environment.[8] Appealing as any such categorization may be, there rarely has been sufficient empirical testing of the suggested categories to insure uniform acceptance of their relevance for all policymaking situations. Consequently, although there is some recognition of the fact that characteristics internal to the issue at hand may constrain policymaking, no single schema or set of variables has yet been demonstrated to have sufficient breadth or empirical relevance to dominate alternative approaches.

Still, the logic inherent in both structural and functional explanations is intuitively appealing. Broad external structural constraints do exist on the types of policymaking and the types of policies that emerge in any single society. Countries with planned economies ipso facto exclude market mechanisms, such as variations in the interest rate, as a possible tool

of fiscal policy; coalition governments generally find
it more difficult to promote far-reaching policies of
change than hegemonic governments; a technologically
competent and honest civil service is more able to
deal adequately with the complexities of urban redevelopment than an inexperienced and venal one; a society with a participant political culture will handle political problems from a different perspective
and with different results than an exclusionary one;
and most political analysts versed in the history and
culture of a particular country or geographical area
can provide convincing evidence for the unique aspects of its politics.

Similarly, there is an appeal to the notion that
functional constraints exist, and that not all issues
are comparably resolved. The participants, the
stakes, and the technical problems involved in administrative reform are quite different from those involved in social welfare. Effectiveness in politics
almost inevitably demands some degree of specialization, and few individuals or groups can be specialists in everything; the result is that their relative
influences will differ from one issue to the next.
It is certainly difficult to imagine military solutions to educational problems; few teachers would be
effective strategists in warfare itself, and not
many more would fare well in the Byzantine politics
of weapons procurement. Issues which at time "t"
are highly conflictual, broad in scope, and redistributive of major social benefits are unlikely to
have completely changed their nature by "t+1," and
they are certainly likely to be dealt with differently from issues which are compromisable, narrow,
and purely distributive.

Both perspectives thus inform this study. It
will be argued that certain features of contemporary
Japanese politics broadly shape both policymaking and
public policy. Some of these seem unique to Japan;
others have parallels in most other highly industrialized pluralist democracies. In all cases, however, their influence is rather general and pervasive
throughout Japanese politics, affecting most policymaking and most public policy in essentially comparable ways. Similarly, certain features of higher
education as a problem area provide a comparable
shaping to process and policy. Again, some of these
elements are peculiar to Japanese higher education;
others are common to higher education in a wide range
of other industrialized societies. Both such compar-
abilities affect policymaking possibilities, though
it will be argued  they are even more important in

the shaping of policy choices and possibilities than process per se.

In the assessment of processes of policy formation it is essential to look not simply at the constants in structure and function but at their variations as well. Some structural features of Japanese politics provide a general and uniform effect on all areas of policymaking; others are more variable in their impact. Similarly, while elements of higher education may have their own inherent logic and may shape policymaking processes and policy outcomes in common directions, there are different components of higher educational issues that differ widely from one another, despite their common inclusion in the category "higher education." Thus, in addition to the simple set of structures which leads to a single undifferentiated "policymaking in Japan" or the functional logic which leads to a "policymaking in higher education," there remains a wide range of policymaking processes which can be isolated only by a sensitivity to the variations rather than the constants in both the structures of Japanese politics and the characteristics of issues that emerge under the common rubric "higher education." The analysis of these variations and their consequences forms the core of this study.

Five such variables are seen as critical. Most notably there are wide structural differences in the legal requirements and legal possibilities for policy formation from one issue to the next and in the political strengths and capabilities of political actors involved in different issues. There are also differences in the nature of the issues over which policy must be formed. In particular, the divisibility, scope, and affect of any particular issue are central to the process by which that issue is resolved.

Before examining these five variables in detail, it is necessary to say a word about their interrelationship. Their interactions are not random or free-floating; instead, just the opposite seems to be the case. The central argument here is that the variables converge and reinforce one another in such a way as to provide two cases of policymaking at theoretically polar extremes, with another somewhat midway between these two. In short, they interact in relatively fixed ways so as to form three distinct patterns or ideal types of policymaking. This is borne out by an assessment of the variables as they emerge from general theoretical works on policymaking and from empirical studies of Japanese policy formation.

The divisibility of an issue concerns the degree
to which it can be subdivided for decision-making
purposes into a multitude of subissues or component
parts. Lowi[9] and Zimmerman[10] after him note the sus-
ceptibility certain issues have to such division, the
most familiar of which is the "pork barrel." There,
innumerable component projects can be isolated for
individual decisions, and "logrolling" or political
accommodation of many diverse interests is particularly feasible. By way of contrast, many other issues demand by their very nature a yes or no answer.
Practically speaking, they are indivisible. Some of
the foremost problems of business-labor relations,
for example, concern the presence or absence of the
right to unionize, strike, engage in secondary boy-
cotts, demand union shops, and so on, none of which
is inherently susceptible to "splitting the difference." A parallel situation exists in most issues of
religious or ideological difference, linguistic or
ethnic dominance, and of course open warfare between
two opposing sides. The difference between these two
types of issues is somewhat comparable to Riker's
differentiation between zero-sum situations, in which
one side's gain is the other side's loss, and non-
zero-sum situations, in which certain solutions may
be mutually profitable or both players may "win"
something.[11] And of course it is the zero-sum or
nondivisible situations in which the likelihood of
head-to-head political confrontation is the highest.

In the Japanese situation, several case studies
suggest the significance of such a distinction. Policies that approach zero-sum nondivisibility would
have to include the U.S.-Japan Security Treaty, most
attempts to revise the postwar constitution, and policy toward the right to strike, all of which clearly
required some either-or solution and all of which simultaneously represented some of the most controversial policymaking situations in postwar Japan.[12] In
contrast, governmental subsidization of big business,
administrative reform, the implicit support for main-
taining trade relations with both mainland China and
Taiwan, the generation of national-level macroeconomic plans, and the budget-making process have emerged
as both far less bipolar and more amenable to middle-
ground solutions.[13]

The second issue or functional variable concerns
the scope of any particular policy. Froman's distinction between issues that affect the entire community and those that affect only some small segment
of that community represents one important aspect of
political scope. It parallels Lowi's distinction

15

between policies that would affect specific interests
or single individuals and those that would be centralized or systemic in their impact.[14]  Regardless of
terminology, some policies are clearly more "total"
in their consequences, while others affect a much narrower subset of society.  Some policies of their very
nature will have highly diffuse impacts; others will
be much more specific.

The diffuseness or specificity of any issue exerts a major influence on the probability that any
specific political actor(s) will become involved, as
well as on the nature of that participation.  Other
things being equal, highly diffuse issues affecting
large segments of society should foster interest and
activity by a much broader spectrum of actors than
issues of much narrower and far more specific scope.
Simultaneously, however, it is not unlikely that the
quality of that participation might well be less intense when a broad number of actors is affected than
when the scope of the policy and the interests affected are more narrow and specific.

Intense and quite specific activities have been
the result of actions aimed at compensation for both
former landlords and those having lost property once
part of Japan's overseas empire at the end of World
War II.[15]  Similarly strong and specific reactions
can be seen to the attempts to regulate Japanese doctors[16] and to establish an organization for small and
medium-sized businessmen.[17]

At a potentially opposite extreme of diffuseness
one could point to macroeconomic measures such as efforts to control inflation or consumer prices, which,
at least until the rather recent organization of specific consumer groups, were generally so broad and
untraceable in their impact that virtually no tangible, organized reaction could be measured.  Similar
lack of reaction could be noted in a category of
problems generally not analyzed, namely policies with
specific impacts, but on groups that are politically
immobilizable, such as children, the physically hand-
icapped, those using public transportation or other
public services, and the like.

There is clearly an interaction between the diffuseness or specificity of an issue and the mobilization capabilities of the groups or sectors most likely to be directly affected, and this relationship
will be assessed subsequently.  At this point it is
sufficient to note that one can anticipate quite different patterns of policymaking depending on whom the
issue is most likely to influence.

The third important aspect of any political issue is its _affect_, or emotional content. In any society, certain kinds of issues have a much greater
ability to touch off passionate reactions than others.
In most cases these have been associated historically
with the struggle of particular groups, classes, or
organizations within the society to achieve certain
political goals, such as civil, religious, or political liberties, the rights of labor, social and economic equality, linguistic unity (or diversity), and so
on. At other times these issues touch on the broad
principles of society in its existing form: free market economy, political equality, states' rights, national liberation, and the like. Clearly, not all
issues are comparably capable of exciting high emo-
tion, either among specific groups or among the society at large. Important as such things as the postal
system, museum maintenance, highway construction, or
zoning may be, and despite the fact that slow mail
service, banking regulations, most occupational li-
censing, highways through a particular community, or
specific zoning variances may in specific cases engender rather specific controversy and high emotions,
from a broad societal perspective one can say that
they are normally perceived with large doses of dis-
passion.

There is of course nothing immutable about the
categorization of one issue as highly affective and
another as less so. Such matters will differ greatly
from one society to another and within specific societies over time. Religion, for example, while once a
highly volatile issue throughout most of Europe, no
longer engenders the same spirited political controversy. Changing patterns of immigration have made
race a salient issue today in nations that had not
experienced this problem in earlier decades.[18] The
emotional dimension of any issue is ordinarily a
function of its historical background. But perception is the critical point, for if men perceive an
issue as of vital concern, then surely it is likely
to engender passions.

This point is particularly noteworthy in the case
of Japan, where, as will be examined in Chapter 4, two
major political "camps," divided and highly antagonistic on a number of passionately perceived issues, confront one another. On economic matters, for example,
the conservative camp openly professes adherence to a
capitalistic economic system, while members of the
progressive camp conversely hold to varying degrees a
Marxist economic vision that condemns capitalism to

an inevitable death.  On foreign policy, the conservatives have strongly supported a policy of alignment
with the United States, including the retention of
U.S. bases in the country and ultimate reliance on
U.S. military power for external security.  The progressives, despite certain differences among themselves, have consistently stressed the need for either "positive neutralism" or an overt alliance with
the very countries against which the conservatives
have deemed it most necessary to defend Japan.  Mili-
tarily, the conservatives have supported the Self-
Defense Forces, many arguing the need for constitutional revision to strengthen their legal position,
others pressing for a strengthening of their military
hardware as well.  The bulk of the progressives have
contended, conversely, that the forces are unconsti-
tutional under Article 9 of the constitution and that
on this point the document must not be altered.  Others go further to argue that existing forces should
be abolished.

These positions have not been constant throughout the period, and many interesting developments and
changes have occurred since the end of World War II.
Bearing this in mind, however, these issues have still
been among the major ideological sticking points of
political organization in postwar Japan, and the bipolarity in Japan is deeply rooted in such fundamental
differences over a broad sweep of social, economic,
political, and philosophical points.

Robert Dahl makes a strong argument that few political regimes are bipolar in nature.  He contends
that "human and organizational preferences tend toward
diversity and multipolarity rather than toward bipolarity: to many groupings rather than merely two."[19]
Both the general truth and the distinct limitations
of this proposition must be recognized.  On the one
hand, political conflict almost always has more than
two dimensions, and rarely do opinions on any issue
cluster conveniently into two, and only two, antagonistic perspectives.  This is particularly so in the
earliest stages of issue germination, when it is
quite possible that every group and individual having
a "position" on an issue tend to have one at least
slightly at variance with all others.  At the same
time, in many cases of political conflict a dyadic
pattern of polarization does emerge, and useful analysis demands little more than assessment of these two
sides.  In the Japanese case, the point is not whether
the society is inherently bipolar or not.  But a number of issue areas touch on important ideological
fault lines, arousing the deepest emotions in both

18

camps, almost without regard for the specifics of the
policy involved. Such issues consequently are seen
in passionate bipolar terms. The shiboleths of the
past come to define the battlelines of the present.
Hence, on certain issues, regardless of the inherent
merits or demerits of specific proposals, bipolar conflict becomes the norm.

Such highly affective issues can be expected to
guarantee the mobilization and passionate interest of
the organizational members of both camps, and to make
correspondingly easier the mobilization of large segments of the attentive public. In contrast, issues
that cannot be linked concretely to such highly affective elements will not generate the same bipolar controversy. The lines of cleavage in such cases will
cut across camp lines or be intracamp in nature, and
political passions will be qualitatively different.

In addition to these issue-related variations
which influence the process of policymaking, there
are two major structural influences on differences in
policymaking. One central difference arises from the
fact that not all political actors are of equal organizational and mobilizational strength, either generally or on particular issues. Even if a specific segment of society may be strongly affected by a policy,
if that segment is totally unorganized, the subject of
repression, or the victim of false consciousness, it
is unlikely to be very intense, visible, or effective
in its political activities. Conversely, a well-
organized, politically astute organization with a sur-
plus of political resources should be expected to act
in a very different manner. This will be particularly true when it is likely to suffer or benefit greatly from a particular policy.

On this point there is a wide agreement among
political scientists, and even two schools of thought
as diverse as the so-called pluralists and so-called
elitists concur that not all groups, sectors, or interests are of equal political weight. The major
disagreement concerns the question of whether some
groups or sectors possess a preponderance of weight
on all issues, or whether different groups and sectors exercise different influences over different
types of issues.[20]

In studies of Japanese politics there is a similar agreement on the fact that not all are politically equal. Again, however, the question concerns the
extent to which influence is general or particular.[21]
A wide body of analysis has suggested that Japan is
governed by a triumvirate of big business, the Liberal Democratic Party, and the senior echelons of the

civil service. To some the influence and power of this triumvirate is translatable over the entire range of policy questions and is a policymaking constant. Far more persuasive is the evidence that such influence is a function of the particular item in question.[22] In addition, a substantial body of scholarship supports the proposition that a number of other organizations or groups can mobilize influence on particular questions of relevance to them. Repatriates, doctors, outcaste communities, trade associations, small and medium-sized businessmen, farmers, and many others have been shown to influence certain types of decisions.[23] Clearly, the structures of Japanese politics are not so fixed as to prevent variations in influence on different issues, and a sensitivity to these variations is essential to understanding Japanese policymaking.

One final structural variable demands attention: the differences in the legal requirements and possibilities of policymaking that affect different political questions. Under any political system certain matters demand by law that a specific formal political process be followed. In the United States, France, or West Germany, for example, numerous rights of citizens are formally guaranteed by the written constitution and subsequent court rulings. Any legitimate attempt to abridge such rights demands the passage of a constitutional amendment through explicitly designated procedures. At another extreme, many other issues can normally be decided by a single governmental or quasi-governmental official, largely through administrative procedures. To cite two extreme cases, a policy establishing the work schedules of individual sanitation crews rarely requires anything beyond the decision of a shop foreman, and many policies regarding old age or welfare benefits are simply an outgrowth of the particular interpretations given to laws by specific offices or officials. Among the many gradations between these extremes, two can be highlighted: 1) certain matters codified in law can be changed significantly only by the passage of a new law or an amendment to existing laws; 2) other functions specifically designated as within the exclusive purview of some governmental or quasi-governmental agency can be dealt with by the responsible official or his representative. In certain cases some specific legal formula exists for making decisions on these matters and must be followed; in other cases no such requirement exists, or the possibility is high that such provisions can at least be circumvented.

Usually there is a very close correlation between the structural requirements for dealing with an issue and that issue's scope. That is, constitutional issues most frequently are those presumed to have the most diffuse social scope, while legal or administrative issues tend generally to be far more specific. Still, a limited number of constitutional issues may in practice be quite narrow and specific, while many areas under the control of single administrators are of exceptionally broad social import. It is thus helpful to distinguish an issue's scope from the legal requirements surrounding it and to keep both dimensions and their more complex possibilities separately in mind, rather than simply to presume that one is a surrogate for the other. For, regardless of the actual scope (or divisibility or affect) of any issue, its very subject matter will at times require as a matter of legal and political course that some fixed, institutional set of policymaking channels be adhered to. It is within, or in conjunction with, such explicit requirements that the three policy variables exert their influence, not in contradiction to or totally independent of them. Similarly, there is a close relationship between the power, influence, legitimacy, and mobilization capabilities of groups and the scope of an issue. Thus, highly diffuse issues such as economic policy or pollution in Japan generated little response during the 1950s and 1960s but created quite a different response once consumer and antipollution groups were formed in the late 1960s and early 1970s.

It is therefore clear that the five variables are not totally independent of one another. From one perspective, all five can be considered elements closely tied to the nature of any specific political issue and varying dramatically from one individual issue to the next. Viewed slightly differently, the formal political process and the organizational strength and mobilization capabilities of actors affected could as well be seen as long-term political givens, different over time but relatively consistent on particular issues within any political system over the short run. It is helpful to keep both perspectives in mind, since one can simultaneously conceptualize a rather consistent process for, let us say, constitutional revision while at the same time recognizing that not all issues could even remotely be considered "constitutional" and hence subject to such a procedure. Similarly, Group A or B in any society may be generally powerful or weak, but its relative

21

strength or weakness might interface in very different ways with different issues. Even if business, the military, or peasants are widely recognized as strong in a particular society, such groups may still be unable or unwilling to bring that power equally to bear on all issues.

With these factors in mind, it becomes possible to turn to the types of policymaking process that emerge as composites of the interaction and collective influence of these five variables. The two delimiting or extreme types of policymaking could be labeled "policymaking through camp conflict" and "incremental policymaking." Between these two exist numerous possibilities and combinations, but one that is of particular salience will be examined as well, "pressure-group policymaking."

Most simply stated, "policymaking by camp conflict" involves the process surrounding issues that are nondivisible, broadly diffuse in scope, highly affective, and that most often require constitutional or legislative activity and affect highly mobilizable interests and groups. "Incremental policymaking," by way of contrast, arises over issues that are highly divisible or segmental, narrowly specific, nonaffective, and that affect few and generally less mobilizable sectors and can be dealt with primarily through administrative channels.

In policymaking by camp conflict, the issues involved are typically extremely broad in their probable impact. They touch on the interests of numerous sectors of society, including many if not all of the most politically organized and mobilizable segments of the Japanese polity. The matters at issue are perceived to be vital to most, if not all, of the affected sectors, with the result that their emotional impact is extremely high. Those who will be influenced see the issue in more than instrumental terms; involved, rather, are matters perceived to touch on major principles, over which they are willing to expend great political resources. And the indivisible, nonsegmental nature of the issue and principles involved makes a two-party, zero-sum confrontation most probable. Most frequently, resolution of the problem requires a constitutional or legislative process and, in theory, each side is willing to pull out all the stops to achieve its policy ends. For example, most studies of the U.S.-Japan Security Treaty controversy of 1960 come quite close to describing such a pattern. Similarly, the domestic political process involved in the Police Duties Bill of 1958, the Okinawan question, much of

the policymaking in the area of labor relations,
questions surrounding Article 9 and constitutional
revision, and a host of other issues show roughly
comparable patterns.[24] Chapter 5 will argue that the
policymaking process involved in matters of university administration is extremely similar.

In contrast to the process of policymaking by
camp conflict is what I have labeled incremental policymaking. The issues involved here are highly segmental and divisible, in contrast to the indivisible
issues involved in camp policymaking. Typically,
they revolve around an almost infinite aggregate of
numerous small and divisible items, over which compromise is relatively easy, such as money or project allocation. As a result, the zero-sum nature of camp
politics is not in evidence, and all key parties involved are capable of realizing some portion of their
aims. Correspondingly, the issues are more specific
and narrower in their probable impacts than the issues resulting in camp policymaking. Specific groups
are affected and in extreme form are among the least
mobilizable sectors of society. In part because of
their high divisibility and their rather specific
scope, such issues are also virtually nonaffective.
Any passion generated over them either is very limited or can be attributed to political posturing.
Procedurally, such problems can usually be resolved
through administrative channels, and public visibility and media coverage are at a minimum.

Presumably because of their less visible nature
(and possibly their presumed dullness), such matters
have occasioned far fewer studies in Japan than examples of camp policymaking. Nonetheless, a few
studies suggest strong parallels with the theoretical
construct. Available information suggests, for example, that the policies of import control and support
for certain critical domestic industries have evolved
largely through the comparatively quiet administrative
guidance of the Ministry of International Trade and
Industry.[25] Similarly, research and development policy has evolved through quiet and interrelated work
by a series of ministries.[26] Despite the paucity of
studies on this pattern of policymaking in Japan, a
number of case studies in other countries suggest its
broader applicability.[33] Moreover, as will be examined in greater detail in Chapter 4, the bureaucracy
plays, particularly through advisory committees and
the use of administrative directives, a major policymaking role, whereas in the Diet, presumed to be the
hub of controversy in Japanese politics (which of
course it frequently is), the great bulk of legislation

passes by unanimous or nearly unanimous votes. Thus, there are good prima facie arguments for the existence of an incremental pattern, even if examinations of its existence in Japan are sparse. Chapter 6 will examine the policymaking process involved in enrollment expansion within Japanese universities as a close empirical approximation of this pattern.

Thus, two patterns of policymaking can be conceptualized that involve composite extremes on all five variables. Realistically, concurrence of all five at some absolute extreme is infrequent, but, as will be examined subsequently, actual policymaking situations sufficiently approximate such hypothetical extremes as to warrant the formulation.

Between these two extremes lies "pressure group policymaking," defined here as the process occurring at the approximate midpoints of all five variables. That is, the issue is neither as indivisible, diffuse, affective, or constitutional as in policymaking through camp conflict, nor as divisible, specific, unimpassioned, or administrative as in incremental policymaking. And, as the label indicates, pressure group policymaking can be expected to involve more mobilizable actors than is usually the case with incremental policymaking, but without the same magnitude and impact on its actors as is the case with camp policymaking.

Here, too, examples based on empirical studies can be suggested. Pressure from and governmental response to groups representing former landowners, overseas businessmen, and property owners suffering losses as a result of World War II and U.S. Occupation policies might serve as the classic examples,[28] with Japanese-Soviet relations on fishing rights serving as a partial parallel.[29] Other somewhat different examples of pressure group policymaking include pressure group response to proposed governmental actions in relation to the Japanese Medical Association and to attempts to establish an organization of small and medium-sized businessmen.[30] The pattern suggested, one that is well known in political science, will be examined in Chapter 7 in conjunction with moves concerning the specialization of Japanese higher education.

Summarizing briefly then, three issue-specific variables--divisibility, scope, and affect--combined with two structural variables--different legal requirements on the one hand and organizational strengths and mobilizability on the other--interact to produce two extreme and one intermediary pattern of policymaking. The five variables when collectively

24

present lead in one extreme to what has been called policymaking by camp conflict, while in precisely the opposite guise they generate a pattern of incremental policymaking. Between these two, roughly at the mid-point convergences of the five variables, exists the pattern labeled pressure group policymaking. A summary of the interrelationships is presented in Table 2-1. While the three patterns can be conceptualized in pure form, in reality, of course, cases will only approximate one or another of the three; they will by no means replicate the theoretical constructs. But in chapters 5 through 7 specific policymaking situations in the area of higher education will be examined which closely parallel these three theoretical patterns. Before such an examination, however, it is essential to examine in greater detail the specific higher educational issues themselves to understand both their constant elements and how they vary on the three issue-specific variables suggested, and to look, too, at the postwar Japanese political situation with particular reference to questions of institutional and structural consistency and variance and problems of organizational strength. These problems are the subject of the next two chapters.

TABLE 2-1

Relation Among Key Variables

| | ISSUE | | | STRUCTURE | | | | PROCESS | |
|---|---|---|---|---|---|---|---|---|---|
| | Scope | Divisibility | Affect | Institutional Requirement | Power Resources | Actors Involved | Cleavage | Intensity of Conflict | Locus of Resolution |
| Camp Conflict | Broad and specific | Low | High | Constitutional-legal | Many powerful and well-organized participants | Many | By camp | High | Diet Cabinet Bureaucracy |
| Pressure Group | Narrow and specific | Medium | Medium | Legal-administrative | Few participants but usually well-organized | Few | Fluid groups vs. one another and/or govt. agencies | Medium | Central bureaucracy, often public-private agreements |
| Incrementalism | Narrow or diffuse | High | Low | Administrative | Disorganized if any | Fewest | Disorganized interests vs. usually one govt. agency | Low | Bureaucratic agency |

# 3. Nature of the Issues

Higher education has always been an important and frequently a political issue in modern Japan. Its importance and the context of its political implications have, however, varied significantly over the last century. To understand the nature of the policy issues in their contemporary context, it is important to highlight certain historical antecedents. This is particularly important in understanding the affective component of each of the issues under scrutiny. But the present scope and divisibility of these items as well as the limitations on the major political alternatives and the positions of the most significant political actors are also functions of this historical background.

For our purposes, two distinct periods of Japanese history must be considered: the period from the onset of the Meiji Restoration in 1868 through the end of World War II; and the period of the U.S. Occupation, which lasted from 1945 through 1952. During the prewar period the issues under analysis first emerged as objects of major policy consideration, while the Occupation period takes on significance because of attempts made then to alter radically the prewar higher educational system and to bring it more into conformity with American political and educational values. Some elements of the prewar system underwent drastic realteration; others continue to exert strong influence even to the present. The same can be said of the Occupation-induced changes: a good deal of the policymaking since the end of the Occupation has concerned concrete attempts at "correcting the excesses" of the Occupation and counterpressures to insure that the "democratic reforms" of the Occupation not be undermined. In still other areas, the changes introduced under the Occupation formed the basis for trends that have continued unabated. These pasts thus become important keys to the issues as they have subsequently developed.

In what are now the industrial nations of Western
Europe and North America, higher education developed
with a highly liberal cast independent of the particular regimes in power.  In contrast, early Meiji political leaders saw higher education as an integral component of their plans for the industrialization and
modernization of the country.  The earliest major pro-
nouncement of the new government, the so-called Charter Oath, issued in April 1868 in the name of the new
emperor, set forth five brief principles which were to
govern the new regime.  The fifth of these indicates
both the importance attached to education and the purpose for which education was to be encouraged:  "Knowledge shall be sought throughout the world so as to
strengthen the foundations of imperial rule."[1]

Fortunate by comparison with political leaders in
many other modernizing societies in having a relatively broad educational infrastructure and a comparatively high rate of literacy, the Meiji leaders quickly
saw that a literate populace with at least a rudimen-
tary knowledge of the three R's and a few other subjects such as history, geography, and ethics was an
integral component of a modern, civilized state.[2]
Thus, in 1872, only four years after the Restoration,
a bold plan was put forth to establish a compulsory
system of more than 50,000 locally financed primary
schools as well as a number of institutions at higher
levels.[3]  Although the vast plan was never realized
in full, it provided the rough guidelines for the
system that eventually developed and was quite successful in rapidly educating the populace.  Only eight
years later more than 41 percent of the six to thirteen year old population was enrolled in primary
schools, and by 1910 virtually this entire age group
was in attendance.[4]

Above this common base of primary school was a
series of isolated tracks or streams into which entry
was more limited.  Those who did not terminate their
education at the end of primary school had to choose
between entering a middle school, which would be the
first step toward the university, or entering one of
several types of vocational schools.  By 1940 nearly
20 percent of the appropriate age cohort was in attendance at some form of middle school.

At the apex of the educational pyramid were the
universities.  The first of these, Tokyo Imperial University, created in 1877, was initially developed as a
training ground for government bureaucrats.  Todai, as
the institute came to be called, has since then always

occupied a place of central prestige in the Japanese educational system. Six additional imperial universities (administered under government control) and some forty-odd other universities (both public and private) were created prior to World War II, all of which combined to provide Japan with a highly educated group of business, industrial, and political leaders, thereby aiding greatly in the industrialization of the country.[5]

Several facets of this prewar system deserve underlining. Perhaps the most significant concerns the relationship between the government and the university, in terms of both purpose and administrative control. Japan's industrialization and modernization was a far more conscious, governmentally directed effort than was that in Western Europe or the United States. Not surprisingly, the entire educational system was viewed by government modernizers as an important contributor to the entire process, and it therefore evolved under the tight supervision of the government.

State Dominance

From the perspective of the rest of the educational system, higher educational institutions were comparatively free from government supervision. At the lower educational levels, conscious and conscientious control over the schools was maintained through government control over teacher training, textbook supervision, and syllabus monitoring. Extensive effort also went into the instillation of patriotism and support for the imperial system through such items as ethics courses, the wearing of school uniforms and caps, military control over physical education, the periodic reading of the Imperial Rescript on Education, and the required daily bow of all pupils before each school's picture of the emperor. In accord with the overall perceptions of Mori Arinori,[6] architect of the prewar educational system, however, the universities were accorded far more intellectual and administrative leeway than the schools. Nevertheless, by comparison with other countries at similar points in time, and with most better universities today, the controls were quite significant. The first article of the Imperial University Ordinance establishing Tokyo University, for example, declared quite explicitly that "The purpose of the imperial university shall be to provide instruction in the arts and sciences and to inquire into the mysteries of learning in accordance with the needs of the

29

state" (italics added). A series of education ordinances in the mid-1880s asserted the supremacy of the state in all areas of education, and the 1890 Imperial Rescript on Education stressed service to the state as the national educational ideal.

Harmony between university and state was by no means insured through such simple legal exigencies, however, and university-state conflicts arose from two rather separate features of the higher educational structure throughout much of the prewar period. The first of these was the comparative autonomy and anti-establishment nature of the earliest private universities. While the imperial universities were created explicitly for "purposes of state" and were aimed primarily at training government bureaucrats, the private universities were founded by nongovernmental and often antigovernmental individuals, such as Fukuzawa Yukichi (Keio), Ōkuma Shigenobu (Waseda), and Niijima Jō (Doshisha). Waseda University in particular was heavily involved in the antigovernmental "People's Rights Movement" following the Meiji Restoration, and Ōkuma at one point declared his philosophy on ties between government and the university to be as follows:

> From the beginning we have held to one simple proposition: the will of the people is never identical with the opinion of the government. At times, popular will and government opinion run counter to one another. If education exists under the control of a single power, will not the state be misled in its purposes?[7]

With such a philosophical base, Waseda and other private universities became the early homes of antigovernmental activities. Government reaction involved simultaneous efforts to break down the independence of the private institutions and to insure even greater loyalty from government-administered institutions. The private universities, through a combination of financial pressures, lack of government recognition, and not infrequently overt government harassment, soon came to an accommodation with the government. In 1918, with the promulgation of the University Ordinance, the private universities were subsumed into the system they had originally been established to counter, and with few exceptions they mollified their high levels of independence from the government, becoming instead the occupationally centered training schools for white collar salarymen.

30

The best of the imperial universities were in fact most prominent in attempts to achieve independence from government control. Organized in accord with German principles, these universities were divided internally into faculties (gakubu), which were to be the ultimate decision-making bodies in the governance of the universities, the second factor in prewar government-university conflicts, and an aspect that has come to be of particular significance in administrative disputes in the postwar period.

During the prewar period several significant government attempts to intervene in university policy or to insure some form of ideological conformism were stoutly resisted by autonomy-minded university members. At Tokyo University, for example, seven faculty members were suspended in 1903 for criticizing government foreign policy, and nearly 200 faculty members united to oppose the government's demand.[8] At Tokyo Kōtō Shōgyō Gakkō, now Hitotsubashi University, faculty and student protests in 1908 forced an end to government attempts to turn the institution into a purely teaching institute for the training of businessmen, and in 1919-20 Tokyo University again became embroiled in a major conflict when government officials demanded the resignation of Professor Morito Tatsuo for the publication of an allegedly subversive article on the thoughts of Kropotkin.

At Kyoto Imperial University faculty opposition to covert cooperation between the Ministry of Education and University President Sawayanagi to force the resignation of several professors led to Sawayanagi's resignation in 1913, while in 1933 then-Education Minister Hatoyama Ichirō successfully demanded that an allegedly subversive criminal law reader not be used in the university, resulting in another major university-government clash. Even more serious disputes broke out during the 1930s involving the famous "organ theory of the emperor" postulated by law professor Minobe Tatsukichi and the theories of the state put forth by Yanaihara Tadao and others. In numerous less famous conflicts during the prewar period, the government forced many resignations or dismissals in the face of often strong faculty protest.

Although by no means always successful in their attempts, particularly as government conservatism and repression increased during the 1930s, faculty members did initiate a tradition of faculty autonomy vis-a-vis government that became important in the postwar period. There was also a converse heritage, however, of successful government intervention in the university to suppress allegedly dangerous or subversive thought. Hostility between the two sides occurred with sufficient frequency to establish many of the parameters for postwar administrative policy and policy attempts. The roots of postwar student protest can also be noted in this period as faculty attempts to withstand government demands were sometimes supported by small but ideologically committed knots of student radicals. Quiescence and apoliticality rather than conscious political activism tended, however, to be dominant in the student sector.[9]

## Institutional Differentiation

A second feature of the prewar educational system was its high degree of institutional and occupational specificity. In contrast to the American system of education in which, from grammar school through college, most students enroll in structurally comparable institutions and move in a single stream from grammar school to high school to college, Japanese students under the prewar system, in a pattern much more comparable to the systems of continental Europe, moved in highly differentiated channels after the six years of elementary school. As noted above, a key distinction was made between institutions in the purely academic channel and those which were occupationally specific.

Students who proceeded beyond the required primary level would enter either middle school, which was the first step in the academic channel, or higher elementary school, secondary vocational school, or part-time "youth schools," all of which were vocation-specific and aimed at providing the practical skills required by an industrializing Japan. At this level segregation according to sex also took place, with special tracks for female students, the best of whom could proceed only to women's colleges (not to be confused with the more prestigious "universities" open only to males).

Not all those who continued on to middle school, however, entered universities. Upon completion of the five-year middle school, students took rigid competitive examinations, on the basis of which even more radical streaming took place. For those who continued, the choice again was between purely academic and purely vocational training, with entry into the academic higher schools being a virtual guarantee of subsequent entry into and graduation from the university. Those who did not gain admittance to higher

32

school through the examinations could enter either the job market or schools designed to prepare them for careers in such fields as architecture, dentistry, engineering, forestry, medicine, or pharmacy.

The emphasis on practical and vocational training continued to the highest levels of the system. There were numerous single-faculty universities, both private and national, geared toward vocational training in medicine, commerce, and engineering. The specific character of many such institutions is captured in an excerpt from the statement of the committee responsible for the formation of Tokyo Institute of Technology.

> Scholars have a common weakness. They tend to indulge in the study of abstruse theories and to be ignorant of the present conditions of industry. Furthermore, while the scientific aura of their research is pronounced, their studies are far removed from the actualities of industry, which they despise. Nevertheless, the newly established [Tokyo Institute of Technology] . . . shall seek to maintain intimate contact with the realities of industry, to conduct practical research on industrial problems, and to develop a faculty and student body who will focus their attention on the problems of industrial operation.[10]

Clearly, functional specificity and preparation for future occupations was an integral part of the prewar system of education at all levels.

Such ever-narrowing channels meant that entry into universities was extremely difficult and highly competitive. At all stages in the educational process constant socialization sought to insure the successful adaptation of the individual to his increasingly determined and narrowed future role. Little leeway was provided for the "late bloomer" or for individuals with uncertainties or mind-changes about careers. Cultivation or encouragement of individuality was not a prominent feature of the prewar system; rather, a premium was placed on acceptance of outside direction and conformity to external determinants. Moreover, functional specificity among institutions and a high reliance among employers on an individual's background as a criterion for employment meant that one's job and future success depended to a large extent on one's education. These factors went a long way toward institutionalizing a third important

33

characteristic of the prewar educational system:
elitism.

## Elitism

Elitism in the prewar system took two forms:
that which arose as a function of the limited number
of individuals continuing on to the highest levels of
education, and that which resulted from the sharp
prestige gradations among higher educational institutions. At the unquestioned top of the pyramid was
Tokyo University, which occupied a national position
akin to the University of Paris in France, Bologna in
Italy, or Oxford and Cambridge in England. Among the
sources of its prestige were its having been the
first university created, the intellectual merits and
achievements of its faculty and students, and the
successes of its graduates. Below Todai were the
other national universities, the cream of which were
the other six imperial universities. Private universities were generally accorded lower prestige, although the best private universities, such as Waseda
and Keio, were sometimes more highly esteemed than
some of the lesser national institutions. Still
lower were the various "colleges" (semmongakkō) and
"higher colleges" (kōtō semmongakkō), and so on. In
the business world such gradations were consciously
attended to. The school one attended typically determined one's subsequent job, chances of promotion, and,
not infrequently, starting salary within individual
companies.[11]
Such differentiation among institutions put a
premium on entry into the best of these, and competition was intense. Only one out of thirteen middle
school graduates was admitted to the higher schools
that were the sine qua non for a university education.
Only one out of 100 students in a graduating elementary school class could be expected to enter any university, and only one out of 200 could expect to enter one of the seven imperial universities.[12] In
summing up this facet of prewar education, Henry
Smith aptly described the system as one that provided
"a little education for the many and a great deal of
education for the few."[13]
Although a very small number of universities
provided virtually the only channels to the most important positions within the society, and even though
only a very limited number of individuals could enter
these universities, the system was comparatively non-
elitist in that rigid status and class barriers were
never strong in Japan. The Japanese higher educa-

34

tional system was thus less instrumental in reinforcing inherited privilege and in preventing upward mobility by bright but impoverished children than that
in Western Europe. Such common informal barriers as
modest family financial status and geographical mobility, as well as more psychological pressures from
one's parents, peer group, and community, clearly
operated in prewar Japan. But at the same time the
open examination system combined with the low tuition
in national universities and with opportunities for
side jobs such as tutoring made the universities a
significant channel of social mobility and gave prewar higher education in Japan a comparatively non-
ascriptive character. In 1939, for example, 16.2
percent of the students at Tokyo University were farmers' sons.[14] The elitism of the prewar system was
institutional, rather than societal, and is perhaps
best characterized as "meritocratic elitism." It
never led to the class-based political conflicts that
occurred in some European countries.

In summary, what was most noteworthy about the
prewar system was the high degree of governmental
control, combined with examples of resistance by certain elements within the university, which thereby
laid the basis for the development of a notion of
faculty autonomy; the highly vocational orientation
of the entire educational system, reaching up into
many aspects of higher education; and the narrowness
of educational channels and the constraints thereby
exercised over social mobility. These dimensions
were of greatest concern to the Americans in charge
of restructuring the educational system under the
Occupation and were also the most salient aspects of
the prewar system in the post-Occupational development of higher educational issues.


HIGHER EDUCATION DURING THE OCCUPATION

Initial Occupation policy toward higher education represented a reaction to and an attempt to
eliminate most of the major tendencies of the prewar
period illuminated above. In keeping with its perception of Japan as a country whose social and economic structures were integral props for, if not
direct catalysts of, the politics that had led to
World War II, the American Occupation sought to
bring about major changes in the entire Japanese way
of life that perforce included higher education. The
core principles under which the Occupation initially
operated were "demilitarization" and "democratization."

35

## Demilitarization

Any and all promilitary vestiges were to be removed from educational institutions, while simultaneously prodemocratic sympathies were to be encouraged.
An October 22, 1945, directive by the Civil Information and Education Section (CIE) made this quite
clear:

> The content of all instruction will be
> critically examined, revised, and con-
> trolled in accordance with the following
> policies:
>     1) Dissemination of militaristic
> and ultranationalistic ideology will be
> prohibited and all military education
> will be discontinued.
>     2) Inculcation of concepts and es-
> tablishment of practices in harmony with
> representative government, international
> peace, the dignity of the individual, and
> such fundamental human rights as the
> freedom of assembly, speech, and reli-
> gion will be encouraged.[15]

"Demilitarization" was most specifically aimed
at the lower levels of education, where it had its
greatest impact, but it also had a definite influence
on higher education.  While courses and books escaped
the rigid ideological checks made at lower educational levels, all personnel were subjected to ideological strutiny so as to eliminate known exponents of
militarism and ultranationalism.  A number of such
individuals were purged from universities.  In addition, the military academies were ordered closed and
all military courses were eliminated in other institutions.  Moreover, in November 1945 the Americans
took quick action to counter a series of moves by the
Japanese Ministry of Education seen by the Japanese
Left as promilitary.  The minister of education had
established special schools for returning Japanese
soldiers and had allowed students from the disbanded
military academies to enter nonmilitary universities
during midyear, bypassing the entrance examinations
required of other students.[16]  These actions were
seen as an attempt to give special privileges to
military students not available to others in the
country, to perpetuate militarist thinking, and to
infiltrate liberal or progressive universities with a
core of military-oriented students.  The Americans
were quick to reverse them all.

The antimilitary posture of SCAP (Supreme Commander for the Allied Powers) and its CIE section set a clear psychological mood throughout higher educational institutions, many of which were particularly diligent in removing "tainted" faculty members and in welcoming back many previously imprisoned liberal and leftist scholars. In that much of this activity was concentrated on a few noteworthy campuses, the overall political impact of the demilitarization campaign was heightened. Clearly, in terms of the atmosphere created, the program was of positive benefit to progressively oriented members of the academic community, and on numerous campuses faculty and student groups came under progressive influence. This control was to become quite significant in subsequent government-university conflicts and was even to affect later aspects of SCAP's higher educational policy.

## Democratization

The demilitarization phase of SCAP's higher educational policy, while not to be minimized in significance, served primarily as a backdrop for a broader goal. Demilitarization of higher education meant primarily the removal of individuals and attitudes deemed pernicious, whereas democratization meant a far more total and integrated restructuring. In order to lay the groundwork for such a policy, SCAP invited twenty-seven American educators to Japan to meet with a comparable number of Japanese to examine the prewar educational system and to make broad recommendations for change.

The group's report focused on most of the characteristics of the prewar system noted above.[17] Strong opposition was registered to the stress on "needs of the state" as a precondition for virtually all higher educational activity and to the strong bureaucratic controls, primarily from the Ministry of Education, over finance, courses, student activities, the actions of faculty members, and so on. Further, strong emphasis was placed on eliminating the inequalities of educational opportunity in the form of sex discrimination, tracking, and the large gaps in quality between the old imperial universities and all others. Finally, there was great concern to eliminate the stress on vocational and specialized training and to inaugurate some form of general education in institutions of higher education.

In the report higher education was alleged to have three distinct aims: first, the protection and advancement of knowledge and the enlightenment of

society; second, the training of efficient and humane
individuals; third, the promotion of technical profi-
ciency in response to the changing needs of society.[18]
Of the three, the first and second recurred most often
in the report, while the third received scarcely any
subsequent attention. Indeed, the report cautioned
against the dangers posed to the university's freedom
by financial pressures and business demands. Using an
American analogy, the report stated that "the aims of
trade and higher learning are as distinct as those of
church and state, and they must be kept so."[19]

In the area of university autonomy and government
control, the report called for a "recovery of spirit"
regarding academic freedom and noted that "one sure
way to preserve academic freedom is to give authority
to the faculties themselves in academic matters,"[20] a
suggestion seen by many academics as a strong endorse-
ment of the position held by most academics that the
faculty conference should be the supreme governing
organ on individual university campuses.

Beyond this the report took a strong stand a-
gainst almost all forms of government supervision of
the universities.

> A highly centralized educational system, even
> if it is not caught in the net of ultrana-
> tionalism and militarism, is endangered by
> the evils that accompany an intrenched bu-
> reaucracy. Decentralization is necessary in
> order that teachers may be freed to develop
> professionally under guidance, without regi-
> mentation.[21]

To this end, the mission recommended that:

> Except for examining the qualifications of
> a proposed institution of higher education
> before it is permitted to open its doors,
> and assuring that these initial require-
> ments are met, the governmental agency
> should have practically no control over
> institutions of higher education.[22]

To improve educational opportunities, the report
noted that "Recognition of the right of access to
higher learning must be made clearer to the people
and to the administrative powers controlling higher
education, as the prerogative and special advantages
of the few are relaxed and redefined for the many."[23]
To accomplish this, more institutions of higher education were to be created and the distinctive position

of the old imperial universities was to be eliminated.
In the interest of equal opportunity the report also
recommended that "Freedom of access to higher institutions should be provided immediately for all women now
prepared for advanced study; steps should be taken
also to improve the earlier training of women."[24]

The overall quality level of facilities of higher
education, while quite good in prewar Japan, had suf-
fered severe physical damage as a result of the U.S.
saturation bombing campaign during the war. More than
one-fourth of the total building area of institutions
of higher education was so damaged. Further, most
private institutions lost virtually all their assets
as a result of the severe inflation in the immediate
postwar years.[25] The report thus proposed that university quality be equalized through measures aimed
at improving the financial situation of the private
universities, hitherto unsupported by the government.

Finally, the report showed concern for the content of higher education, noting that general education had in the prewar period usually terminated with
middle school; where it existed at higher levels, it
fell

> far short of meeting the real needs for
> general education. . . . For the most
> part there is too little opportunity for
> general education, too early and too
> narrow a specialization, and too great a
> vocational or professional emphasis. A
> broader humanistic attitude should be
> cultivated to provide more background
> for free thought and a better foundation
> on which professional training may be
> based.[26]

The report was received enthusiastically by General MacArthur and formed the basis for initial efforts by SCAP and CIE to initiate changes in higher
education. The major goals of the report and of in-
cidental CIE recommendations were quickly reflected
in Japanese law. Article 1 of the Fundamental Law of
Education, which was passed by the Diet on March 31,
1947, stated:

> Education shall aim at the full development
> of personality, striving for the develop-
> ment of a people, sound in mind and body,
> who shall love truth and justice, esteem
> the value of the individual, respect labor,
> and have a deep sense of responsibility,

and who shall be imbued with an independent
spirit as builders of a peaceful state and
society.[27]

Articles incorporated into the new constitution also
echoed these themes. Freedom of thought and con-
science (Article 19), academic freedom (Article 23),
and the right to an equal education correspondent with
ability (Article 26) were guaranteed. In the School
Education Law, passed on March 29, 1947, the university was declared to have as its aim "the in-depth
teaching and studying of specialized arts and sciences
as well as the provision of a broad general culture
and the development of the intellectual, moral, and
practical abilities [of the individual]" (Article
52).[28] On the basis of this cataloguing of legal
principles, the more difficult problem of making
structural changes in the higher educational system
was begun. To understand the constraints operating
within the three areas of higher educational policy
to be investigated, it is necessary to look beyond
these principles and to examine the structural changes
in higher education that were attempted or established.

The structural keystone of the new system was to
be the four-year liberal arts college, open in principle to all academically qualified high school graduates. Drawing heavily on the American system and its
underlying rationale, SCAP and CIE officials saw such
a change as one that would significantly democratize
the opportunities to receive a university education
and provide a broad and general rather than a particularistic and vocational education. Such a system
meant the complete realignment of the vast and complicated prewar system of more than 525 different institutions of eight main types.

The question of restructuring was delegated to
the Educational Reform Committee, the main advisory
group established under the Ministry of Education.
The committee first considered the American proposals
at its seventh general meeting on October 18, 1946.
On December 27 the committee recommended to the Japanese government that "Schools following high school
shall in principle be four-year universities,"[29] a
point subsequently written into the School Education
Law of March 31, 1947 (Article 55). On the same day,
in the Fundamental Law of Education the concept of
equality of opportunity was similarly adopted.

Insuring liberality in the curriculum was delegated to a nongovernmental group, the University Accreditation Association, set up at the direction and
encouragement of the Americans and relied on heavily

for higher educational policy during the Occupation
period.[30] The association set forth on July 8, 1947,
a set of minimum standards for university accreditation, which were accepted by the Ministry of Education as the official requirements for charters,[31] effectively negating the unwritten and often arbitrary
prewar standards of the ministry. The new standards
required at least a two-year general education program in all four-year institutions. Thus, with the
cooperation of both the Educational Reform Committee
and the University Accreditation Association, the
Americans began the creation in Japan of a higher
educational system based on institutional homogeneity
and universality of access and keyed to the transmis-
sion of broad liberal arts principles.

The new system came into effect in 1948, and by
1952 some 226 new-system universities had been established, the bulk of which represented various combinations of several prewar institutions of higher education.

The increased opportunities resulting from this
reorganization have long been touted by Americans as
one of the more significant accomplishments of the
Occupation. The 1944 enrollment in universities was
84,000;[32] by 1952 the figure had jumped to 502,000.[33]
Unquestionably the absolute increase in the number of
university students was tremendous. It is necessary
to qualify this in certain ways, however. For example, the total enrollment in all institutions of
higher education, rather than simply that in universities, was nearly 400,000 in 1944.[34] Furthermore,
4 percent of the higher educational cohort attended
higher educational institutions in 1940. In 1950 6.1
percent did so.[35] Although the ages counted are different and hence not absolutely comparable, some increase in the percentage of the age group attending
higher educational institutions unquestionably took
place. Nevertheless, the increase from 4.0 percent
to 6.1 percent over the ten-year period 1940-50 is
not at all disproportionate in light of the increase
from 2.9 percent to 4.0 percent in 1935-40 and the
substantial demobilization that freed many youths to
return to school.

What really happened under the American plan was
not so much that opportunities to attend institutions
of higher education were increased by the shift to a
four-year university system, although the psychological impact of the move in the direction of democratization of higher educational opportunities should not
be minimized. Instead, there was a standardization
of the differentiated prewar opportunities into a

41

more homogenous set of chances to attend one unified
type of higher educational institution. An examination of the reorganizational bases on which the new
four-year universities were formed, however, shows
that little real standardization took place and that
the institutional elitism that was an alleged target
of the reorganization emerged comparatively un-
scathed.[36] Prewar differences in prestige and power
continued to be reflected in the merged institutions
of the postwar period.[37] The national, and especially
the former imperial universities were most particularly favored.

Of the new four-year universities, some were organized around an existing university and others were
not. As tables 3-1 and 3-2 show, of 83 universities
formed around extant universities, 26 were national,
14 were local public, and 43 were private, while of
143 universities formed without such a basis, the
distribution was 46, 20, and 77 respectively. These
figures represent percentages almost identical with
the total distribution of national, local public, and
private universities at the time, so no discrimination seems involved here. A look at the actual combinations is more revealing, however.

TABLE 3-1

Universities Formed Around an Existing University

| No. of Components | Type of School Formed | | | |
|---|---|---|---|---|
| | National | Public | Private | Total |
| 1-3 | 3 | 13 | 38 | 54 |
| 4-5 | 11 | 1 | 4 | 16 |
| 6-8 | 12 | 0 | 1 | 13 |
| Total | 26 | 14 | 43 | 83 |

Source: Mombushō, Zenkoku daigaku ichiran (Japanese
Universities at a Glance), annual.

Of 54 schools reorganized from three or fewer
institutions, only 3 were national universities, while
of the 16 schools composed of 4 or 5 constituent organs, 11 were national and only 4 were private. All
but one of the schools composed of 6 or more units
were national. Thus, all but 3 national universities

42

formed around existing universities included 4 or
more units, while only one of 14 local public and 5
of 43 private schools had such diverse roots. Those
national universities formed by regrouping around existing institutions thus were far more institutionally complex than their private and local public
counterparts, adding immeasurably both to their existing prestige and to their physical assets.

Among the schools with no ongoing university as
a nucleus, the pattern was the same, as Table 3-2
shows. Again the bias is clearly in favor of the national universities, as 36 of 46 national universities were formed from mergers in contrast to 3 of 20
public and 5 of 77 private universities.

TABLE 3-2

Universities Formed Without an Existing University

| No. of Components | Type of School Formed | | | |
|:---:|:---:|:---:|:---:|:---:|
| | National | Public | Private | Total |
| 1 | 10[a] | 17 | 72[b] | 99 |
| 2-3 | 25 | 1 | 5 | 31 |
| 4+ | 11 | 2 | 0 | 13 |
| Total | 46 | 20 | 77 | 143 |

[a]Includes one university established de novo.
[b]Includes two universities established de novo.

Source: Mombushō, Zenkoku daigaku ichiran (Japanese
Universities at a Glance), annual.

This distinction between national universities
on the one hand and public and private universities
on the other must not obscure the fact that comparison within each group yields equally revealing distinctions. This can be seen in Table 3-3.

Of 38 national universities composed of 3 or
fewer subunits, 35 were not formed around existing
universities, while of 13 universities consisting of
6 or more components, all but one were formed around
existing universities. The 7 former imperial universities among them totaled 33 components, or an
average of 4.7 per university.

TABLE 3-3

National Universities Formed With or Without
an Existing University

| No. of Components | With University | Without University | Total |
|---|---|---|---|
| 1-3 | 3 | 35[a] | 38 |
| 4-5 | 11 | 10 | 21 |
| 6+ | 12 | 1 | 13 |
| Total | 26 | 46 | 72 |

[a]Includes one university established de novo.

Source: Mombushō, Zenkoku daigaku ichiran (Japanese
Universities at a Glance), annual.

A similar distinction can be found among the far
less well-endowed private universities, as Table 3-4
shows.

TABLE 3-4

Private Universities Formed With or Without
an Existing University

| No. of Components | With University | Without University | Total |
|---|---|---|---|
| 1 | 16 | 72 | 88 |
| 2+ | 27 | 5 | 32 |
| Total | 43 | 77 | 120 |

Source: Mombushō, Zenkoku daigaku ichiran (Japanese
Universities at a Glance), annual.

What all of this demonstrates is a dramatic re-
inforcement in higher education of the old adage that
the rich get richer and the poor get poorer--at least
in the absence of external controls. The most prestigious universities attracted the most complex and

desirable mergers; the less prestigious schools were far less attractive, both to the better schools and to one another, and for the most part simply upgraded their titles. But for the former imperial universities this somewhat natural law of attraction and repulsion was enhanced by a set of special provisions in the regulations establishing the four-year system ("Shinsei kokuritsu daigaku jisshi yōkō," July 1948). This Ministry of Education regulation provided that all national schools in a single geographical area would be amalgamated to become the single four-year university for the prefecture. The specific areas in which the former imperial universities existed, however, were exempted from this provision, thus giving them carte blanche to make the most advantageous mergers, trading on and enhancing their already high prestige rather than having it limited as had been an initial Occupation goal.

Efforts were also made to equalize higher educational opportunities for women, in an effort to advance their overall social and political emancipation. They were given the constitutional right to vote (Article 15) and hold public office (Article 44), and absolute equality between the sexes was written into the constitution (Article 14). Yet without a genuine elimination of existing educational barriers to allow women to take advantage of such social and political advantages, these others could have been relatively empty guarantees.[38]

As early as December 4, 1945, at the initiative of CIE, the Ministry of Education issued general outlines for a program to eliminate sexual discrimination. Entitled "The Women's Education Renovation Plan," it called for university and college courses to be opened to women and for the revision of all regulations that discriminated against them. More formally, Article 3 of the Fundamental Law of Education required the elimination of educational discrimination on the basis of sex.

The effects of this policy on female enrollment in universities were significant. In 1940 there were 97 women registered in university faculties. An additional 5 were in graduate facilities, and 109 were classified as "other." At most, therefore, approximately 200 women were enrolled in universities.[39] Table 3-5 shows the striking increases after the war.[40]

As with the figures on overall enrollment, those for women in universities can be somewhat misleading. During the period 1934-36 women made up 9.5 percent of those enrolled in institutions of higher education,

TABLE 3-5

Number of University Students by Sex

| Year | Total | Male Number | % | Female Number | % |
|------|-------|-------------|------|---------------|------|
| 1948 | 11,978 | 10,032 | 83.6 | 1,946 | 16.4 |
| 1949 | 126,868 | 118,732 | 93.9 | 8,136 | 6.1 |
| 1950 | 224,923 | 207,599 | 92.3 | 17,324 | 7.7 |
| 1951 | 313,158 | 283,975 | 90.7 | 29,183 | 9.3 |
| 1952 | 399,513 | 358,562 | 89.7 | 41,251 | 10.3 |

Source: Mombushō, Kyōiku tōkei shiryōshū (Collected
Statistical Source Materials on Education), pp. 9-14
(new-system universities only).

though few were in universities, so the figure of 10.3
percent at the end of the Occupation does not mark a
phenomenal educational liberation of Japanese women.
On the other hand, since the university is the final
stage in the educational system, previous discrimination at lower levels continued to be felt in the universities for several years. Thus, the entering
class for universities in 1951, rather than the entire student population of that year, was composed of
nearly 13 percent women, indicating a more significant
increase than appears in the total figures. Moreover,
in the junior college system nearly 46 percent of the
entering class in 1951 were women. Thus the actual
percentage of women entering institutions of higher
education by the end of the Occupation was more than
18 percent, a doubling of the prewar figures.[41]
Still, sexual equality remained far more of a goal
than a reality in that the sharp imbalance between
the percentage of women entering four-year colleges
and those entering junior colleges indicates the reemergence of a subtle form of the double standard in
higher education.

Consequently, higher educational democratization by the Occupation, in terms of increased opportunities to attend, sexual equality, and equal prestige among higher educational institutions, must be
judged only a partial success in light of the goals
set. Certain residues of prewar elitism remained.
Nonetheless, the psychological impact of the Occupation measures must be recognized, and by the end of

the Occupation there was a high degree of social and political consensus on issues of enrollment expansion and equality of opportunity. The huge number of institutions made possible an incremental approach to expansion, with each university making many of the key decisions about enrollment. The class component of the issue that activated debates on enrollment in Europe was also defused. Meanwhile, the principle of a common institutional and educational basis--the four-year liberal arts college oriented toward a broad general education--was widely established, in contrast to the more structurally and functionally specific prewar system.

By far the most politically contentious and complicated policies undertaken by the Occupation came in the field of administration, where Occupation policies left their most controversial impact. Two overlapping and reinforcing problems emerged in this area: the organizational problem of authority over the universities, and the larger problem of the Occupation's ideological direction. The former left the more explicit legacy for post-Occupation policymaking toward university administration; however, the latter, while less explicit, involved an important alteration in the climate of values surrounding policymaking generally, which in turn proved politically and affectively important in the area of university administration, as well as in Japanese politics more generally. By the end of the Occupation, political and intellectual positions on matters of university administration had become rigidly polarized: government vs. university, conservatives vs. progressives. This polarity continued to dominate policymaking in university administration throughout the period following the ending of the Occupation.

The earliest American proposals concerning university administration were aimed at decentralizing the vast authority exercised by the Ministry of Education during the prewar period. The report of the first U.S. Education Mission called for the ministry to exercise simply "functions of leadership, stimulation, and encouragement," not control.[42] The Fundamental Law of Education declared that "education should not be subject to improper control,"[43] with clear allusion to the Ministry of Education. And in line with this, an early CIE report noted that "ultimately, . . . the Ministry will be largely an advisory and reporting agency, not an administrative one. It will receive and summarize reports, carry on research studies, and publish many types of material. Its direct control over education, however, will be greatly reduced."[44]

The initial proposals of SCAP and CIE concerning decentralization took a singularly American form paralleling the shift to local U.S.-style school boards for primary and secondary education. CIE demanded the transfer of control over all but ten national universities from the Ministry of Education to that of local (generally prefectural) governments.[45] On the Japanese side, numerous quasi-governmental political and academic groups were quick to offer their own plans on how best to dissolve the Ministry of Education and transfer its powers. More than twenty such plans were forthcoming from various organizations.[46] While many Japanese groups supported the notion of a less powerful Ministry of Education, there was little agreement among them as to where the former powers of the ministry should devolve. Academic groups generally favored granting university faculties supreme powers, while others favored the creation of some intermediary administrative advisory organ, between the ministry and the faculty councils, to exercise overall supervision of the system.

The Ministry of Education, meanwhile, in accord with all known axioms of bureaucratic theory, stoutly resisted any proposal for its elimination. One member of the Educational Division of CIE described the reaction as follows:

> The Japanese are showing increasing signs
> of balking when it comes down to the dirty
> work of making any real changes. The fa-
> mous old phrase of having "the Mombushō
> emasculate itself" isn't working out so
> well. The boys over there, when the knife
> comes into actual view, show a singular
> reluctance toward the idea of emasculation.
> They've taken the phrase "freedom of educa-
> tion" to their bosoms, but figure it should
> mean that the Ministry of Education is free
> to run it as it sees fit.[47]

This early CIE plan to shift administrative control over universities to the prefectural level has often been criticized by Japanese leftists as the first indication of nascent conservative educational impulses in the Occupation and as the beginning of efforts to undercut the power of the Left on university campuses.[48] Such a judgment seems unfounded; American actions at this time make more sense in the context of a nonpartisan American orientation toward decentralization growing out of the U.S. experience. Regardless, opposition to the plan was fast in coming

as certain conservative implications of decentralization were realized.

The University Accreditation Association in its
"Opinion Paper on the Transfer of University Educational Administration to Local Control" declared that
the lack of a local financial base capable of supporting these universities would be more detrimental to
university autonomy than would be leaving the universities under the central control of the Ministry of
Education.  The proposal was also criticized as per-
mitting political and economic interests to manipu-
late universities for their own interests, thereby
negating any connection between decentralization and
autonomy.[49]  The Education Reform Committee opposed
the plan for similar reasons in a December 26, 1947,
report.[50]  Opposition came as well from a group of
national university officials meeting at Tokyo Institute of Technology on December 23, 1947,[51] from the
board of directors of the Association of National
University Professors at their January 17 meeting,
and from the Association of Technical School Presidents.  Additionally, a number of ad hoc faculty and
student groups held demonstrations against the
plan.[52]  And of course the Ministry of Education was
also opposed. In the face of such widespread opposition and with virtually no internal political support
from Japanese groups, this early SCAP-CIE plan quickly died.  But it died a bipartisan death.  Political
battlelines on matters of administration were still
quite fluid.

This was not the case with the second major proposal on university administration.  Then the lines
of major cleavage between university and government
and between progressive and conservative camps took
on the shape that has dominated policymaking in this
area ever since, as the concrete issue of university
structure became enmeshed with the broader ideological issue of the Occupation's "reverse course."  The
debate on these issues dominated much of the most
visible politics of higher education until the end
of the Occupation.

With the defeat of the proposal to shift administrative controls to local governmental units, CIE
at the beginning of 1948 began promoting an alternative (but equally American) notion of decentralization, namely boards of trustees.  Informal suggestions were made to a number of private and quasi-
governmental organizations that some board of outside
overseers should be created to control the overall
administration of each university in the country.
Numerous plans and long political arguments emerged

following the CIE proposals, with virtually every academic and political organization taking a well-developed position on the question. The debate continued until the end of the Occupation and left an enormous legacy for post-Occupation policymaking.

Each of the individual plans had its distinguishing characteristics, but the main lines of cleavage were between the progressive and conservative camps as they solidified in the face of the Occupation's reverse course, and between university and state as had been true in earlier struggles. The main focus of combined government-conservative planning was a joint proposal that emerged from CIE and the Ministry of Education,[53] according to which the Ministry of Education would create a National Advisory Board (Chūō Shingikai) composed of fifteen members, six elected by and from among the presidents of the national, local public, and private universities of the country (three private, three public), one member from the Education committees (Bunkyō Iinkai) of the upper and lower houses of the Diet, and seven members appointed by the minister of education and approved by the Diet. The new board would advise the Ministry of Education on a variety of subjects, including general policies for university education within the country, the revision of laws dealing with universities, the establishment and elimination of universities, and tuition raises and facilities.

On individual campuses "governing boards" (kanri iinkai) or boards of trustees would be established composed of thirteen members: the university president, three members appointed by the minister of education and confirmed by the Diet (at least one of whom was to be from the local area of the university), three appointed by the governor of the local area and ratified by the local assembly (all three were required to be from the local area of the university), three alumni chosen either by direct election or by some other means provided in law, and a final three selected by the faculty conference of the university. The board would have vast powers to set administrative and financial policy for the university; it would also choose the president and, with the recommendation of the faculty conference, the faculty chairmen and individual members of the faculties. Its powers would include the establishment of new departments, budgetary policy, new lands, the number of student entrants each year, and the awarding of diplomas. In short, the board was to have exceptionally broad powers of personnel and finance as well as overall supervisory powers.

Each university president meanwhile would be appointed for a period of six years by the university's board and would be responsible primarily for carrying out its policies. He could give advice to the faculty conference and would be responsible for reporting on all matters to the Ministry of Education.

The powers of the faculty conference were to be sharply curtailed. It would lose its power to select the university president and faculty members, its role being reduced to making nominations. Additionally, it would lose personnel, finance, and disciplinary powers.

SCAP and the Ministry of Education both argued that this plan represented university democratization in that it would decentralize higher education, taking control away from the Ministry of Education and giving it to representatives from local areas. The reactions of many academic and political groups were initially mixed. As the proposal advanced toward legislative action from 1948 through 1951, however, and the direction of SCAP's reverse course became clear, increasingly the two issues became entangled, and positions on each of the two overlapped.

## The "Reverse Course"

The phrase "reverse course" has occasioned great debate in Occupation history. Suffice to say that the term implies that early Occupation activities were aimed explicitly at Japanese democratization and by implication were favorable to Japan's progressive political forces, while activities after roughly the consolidation of Communist control in China seemed aimed explicitly at making Japan into an economically solid and ideologically stalwart ally of the United States. The political positions generated by this change left a strong impact on the field of higher education as well, particularly in the area of university administration and autonomy.

In 1945 the Occupation had taken the position that "discrimination against any student, teacher, or educational official on grounds of . . . political opinion . . . will be prohibited" and had held that "students, teachers, and educational officials . . . will be permitted to engage in free and unrestricted discussion of issues."[54] The organizational successes of the Left in the area of education and their willingness to resort to mass protest actions, however, combined with the increased American opposition to socialism and communism and led to sharp reversals in this rather broad encouragement of opinion.

51

The most striking indication of this change came with the speeches of Walter Crosby Eells, adviser on higher education to SCAP from 1947 to 1951. Eells first articulated the shift against the Left in a speech at the opening ceremonies of Niigata University on July 14, 1949, in which he stated that faculty members who were also members of the Communist Party would be subject to control from party headquarters and therefore could not be free. Thus, he argued, they should not be permitted to remain on campuses where it was essential to have "freedom."[55] Elsewhere he argued that professors should be deprived of their status for mere membership in a political party regardless of any commission of overt acts. As Eells describes his counterposition:

> The Civil Information and Education Section of SCAP . . . approved the . . . position . . . that Communists, by virtue of their membership in that party, are thereby unfitted [sic] to be teachers in the schools of the country. The situation admittedly had some elements of difficulty since the Communist Party is legalized in Japan and has elected many members to the Diet, and academic freedom is guaranteed in the constitution of the country. [Nevertheless,] a definite effort has been made to help Japanese educational leaders to distinguish clearly between political rights of all citizens in a democracy and fitness for the privilege of teaching in a university, and to show that Communist professors by joining the party have thereby surrendered their freedom to think independently.[56]

Eells and the other members of CIE spent the greater part of the six months between November 1949 and May 1950 defending this peculiar notion of academic freedom.

The shift to overt anticommunism was also tangibly revealed with the second U.S. Education Mission to Japan. This group, composed of a minority of the initial mission, submitted a "supplementary" report on education in the fall of 1950, which radically revised many earlier assessments. Included was a declaration that "one of the greatest weapons against Communism in the Far East is an enlightened electorate in Japan."[57] The sole purpose of this second mission seems to have been to weaken the progressive thrust of the initial report and to provide a legitimation for the increasingly conservative policies being advocated in higher education.

Between July and November 1950 the so-called red purge was carried out, affecting virtually all areas of Japanese society, including universities. Several thousand teachers, from all levels of education, were removed from their posts with rarely any need to prove overt antigovernment acts, subversion, intentions, or communist affiliation to insure that a person be removed.[58] In fact, Eells noted that it was rarely even necessary to raise the question of communism to insure the purge of particular individuals.[59] The effects were felt well beyond those who simply lost their positions, in the more subtle form of withdrawn manuscripts and academic resistance to participation in round-table discussions of even minimally political topics.[60]

During this time of acute hostility and suspicion the proposals to alter the power distribution affecting higher education emerged. The Ministry of Education and SCAP were concerned about the potential exploitation of the university as a base from which to advance what they saw as dangerously radical political ideas. They were particularly fearful of the retention, let alone the expansion, of the powers of the faculty conference on individual campuses, whereby each university could become a potential bastion of radicalism. Indeed, many faculty conferences had demonstrated open hostility to the conservative government and the Ministry of Education and to American opposition to the Left. Despite whatever may have been the original motivations of SCAP, CIE, and the Ministry of Education in the proposal to establish a system of boards of trustees, as anticommunism became an overt motivation of actions vis-a-vis the university, the proposal took on explicitly political implications.

The Japanese university community contended that the new arrangements would merely transfer the direct power of the Ministry of Education to a central board, the majority of whose members would in fact be appointed by the Ministry of Education and whose own powers vis-a-vis the ministry would be merely advisory. The board of trustees on each campus, meanwhile, was seen as a device to transfer power from the faculty conference to a group of men made up of only four academicians compared to nine "outsiders," raising fears that the proposed "decentralization" would guarantee not university autonomy but rather subservience to "bureaucrats, big business, and local bosses."[61]

Numerous proposals to counter the government's plan emerged from organs closely tied to the progressive camp and to the academic community more broadly. Although each had varying elements of individuality, one feature was common to all: in contrast to the Ministry of Education plan, they would give no decision-making powers on internal university administration to nonacademics--i.e., no outsiders or "local representatives." Several proposed giving strong powers to some national-level organ below the Ministry of Education. In all such cases, however, the members of such an organ would have been elected from national or functional constituencies rather than being governmentally appointed.

An interesting political situation was presented by the outpouring of concrete plans in the period preceding the height of the red purge. Since some bill was seemingly desired by a number of groups, the political situation was perfect for pluralistic compromise, the solution to which was obvious: bring the representatives of the differing viewpoints together in a common committee and allow them to work out their differences among themselves. This was the tactic chosen by the Ministry of Education, although the results proved to be unexpected.

As established by the Ministry of Education, the Committee to Draft a National University Administration Bill was beyond doubt the most broadly representative ever assembled in Japanese education. Its initial form, as announced on August 5, 1949, called for eight members: two each from the Educational Reform Committee, the Japan Science Council, the University Chartering Council, and the Assembly of National University Presidents.[62] By September 6, the time of the committee's formal inauguration, its membership had been broadened to twenty: the above eight plus representatives of the University Accreditation Association, the Association of University Professors, the League of Private University Associations, the Japan Teachers Union, business groups, and additional outsiders.[63] The group met twenty times from September until the following February, hearing the opinions of virtually all groups with an expressed interest in higher education, after which it published its first draft recommendation. A revised draft then became the basis for a national public relations effort culminating in large-scale public hearings in Tokyo and Osaka aimed at generating discussion of and support for the proposed bill. Thereafter, a slightly revised third proposal emerged.

Structurally, all three drafts resembled those of earlier plans.[64] At the national level under the Ministry of Education would be a National University Council composed of twenty-three members, all appointed by the minister of education. Six of these were to be representatives of university presidents, four were to be nominees of the Japan Science Council, three were to be nominees of the Association of University Professors, and ten were to be "men of learning and experience" approved by the Diet. The council was to have broad powers in the area of higher educational budgeting, legislation for national universities, and the establishment and elimination of universities.

At the university level a council (shōgikai) parallel to the earlier boards of trustees was to be composed of from ten to thirty members, no more than one-third of whom were to be faculty members. The university president was required to "listen" to the opinions of this body on a host of matters, including revision of major statutes, budget formulation, establishment of faculties, courses, graduate facilities, personnel standards, and student entry quotas. This council was also to select the president, who was required to act in conjunction with it on major matters concerning the university.

The proposals in the first draft would have distinctly curtailed the existing powers of the faculty conference and would have centralized controls under the council or board of trustees. At the national level, however, the National University Council was to be broadly representative of faculty and other potentially or actually Left-leaning groups. The powers of the council would be great, since the Ministry of Education would be required "to act in accord with its decisions." While the proposal was by no means favorable to opponents of the earliest Ministry of Education draft, it was not a uniformly conservative bill.

Several dramatic changes took place, however, from draft one to draft three, and from draft three to the final bill presented to the Diet in February 1951. The three most significant, all generated by the Ministry of Education, indicate its desire and power both to restrict encroachments on its own authority and to limit the prerogatives of faculty and student groups. Draft one would have required that three members of the National University Council be nominees of the Association of University Professors. This provision was dropped in subsequent drafts and the membership was set at twenty, eliminating any explicit provision for faculty representation at the national level. Drafts one and two would have required formal exchanges of views between faculty heads and university presidents on the one hand and student groups and their representatives on the other, a major advance in the recognition of students as an integral part of the university. Among other things, the faculty chairman was required to seek agreements with student representatives regarding student organizations, student life, and student activities for each of the individual faculties of the universities. He was explicitly required to take steps to improve student life and to determine through consultation with the faculty conference the best methods for selecting student representatives. Subsequent drafts eliminated such provisions as "unnecessary formalization."[65]

The third change went to the heart of government powers over the university. In all three of the council's drafts, the National University Council was given considerable powers over the minister of education. In all areas of legislation, budget planning, and establishment or elimination of universities and faculties, the minister was required to act in accord with the decisions of the council. That is, he could not act in these matters without the consent of the council. The final bill submitted to the Diet in February 1951, however, required that he merely "listen to their opinions" on such matters. This change, made unilaterally by the ministry after the council had agreed on its final third version, fundamentally undermined any chance that the bill would restrict the powers of the government.[66]

These changes, and particularly the final change by the ministry, destroyed any hope that the plan would engender broad support from concerned groups. Instead, it polarized political and academic groups over the question of administration. Coming as it did in the midst of a broad climate of hostility toward the progressive camp and university freedom, it fostered fear and suspicion, even from groups desirous of decentralizing the powers of the Ministry of Education, that many of the newly acquired freedoms on university campuses throughout the country were in danger of being lost once again to the central government and to conservative forces in society.

In that the issue took the form of an indivisible legislative proposal for the restructuring of all university administration and the broad redistribution of power within the entire university system, it is not surprising that open conflict and high visibility marked the debates surrounding its resolution. In the ideologically charged political atmosphere of the red purge, the issue reinforced mistrust and antagonism and in turn became a historical reference point for future policymaking in the area of administration and autonomy.

When the final bill was presented to the Diet, some of the strongest opposition came from two of the organizations that had participated in the drafting of the original version--the Japan Science Council and the Japan Teachers Union. They were joined by all parties of the progressive camp and numerous ad hoc academic groups. Once again, the progressive camp's opposition to the government proposal received widespread support from the mass media and public opinion.

A wide-ranging debate took place in Diet committees over the proposal; conservative groups lobbied for its passage and progressive groups sought both inside and outside the Diet to block its passage. While the government clearly had the Diet votes, no vote was ever taken on the legislation. Instead, once introduced in the Diet, the legislation lingered and died an unheralded death. But by the time the proposal was withdrawn, the lines of political and ideological cleavage were starkly fixed, and they heralded the positions taken in subsequent debates over administration. Further, the entire policymaking process served as a prototype for actions in several policymaking efforts during the ensuing decade and a half. Facing rather unified political, academic, and, perhaps even more significantly, public and media opposition to their proposal, the conservatives refused to push through the legislation, despite their Diet majority.

Before proceeding, it would be well to highlight certain aspects of the material presented on the nature of the three issues under question, not only to isolate some of the historical constraints thereby imposed on subsequent policymaking efforts, but also to extract in more clearcut form the issue-specific dimensions noted in Chapter 2.

Without a doubt, the most highly affective and emotionally charged issue area in the prewar and Occupation eras was that relating to university administration and the corollary issues of faculty autonomy and academic freedom. Issues in this area evoked the greatest concern and the deepest emotional commitments from the widest variety of political actors. Since this has been true in many other countries, it may emerge as no surprise.

What is more surprising perhaps, when seen in comparative perspective, is the fact that university

57

entrance and questions of enrollment opportunities
have been virtually nonemotional. Lacking the class-
based history of discriminatory admissions, the prewar Japanese university system was relatively meritocratic and open (with the notable exception of discrimination on the basis of sex, which of course
lacked the topicality it currently enjoys). With the
structural reorganization initiated by the Occupation
and the injection of new and publicly accepted values
of opportunity and democracy, such problems were even
further reduced in emotional content. A relatively
broad (though by no means universal) consensus that
all able students should have the opportunity for
higher education existed by the end of the Occupation.

Somewhat between these two extremes were matters
relating to the functional specificity of institutions. Opposition clearly existed to the statism and
vocational direction of prewar higher education, but
this appears to have been limited and these features
of higher education were attacked and largely removed
early in the Occupation. The structural elimination
of tracking undoubtedly played a large role in diminishing any emotionalism the issue might have evoked,
as did the requirement that all universities offer
programs of general education. The Occupation by no
means resolved the issue to everyone's satisfaction,
and its partial reversal of the issue at the time of
the second Educational Mission served to reignite
some sentiment on the issue, but the problem never
reached the same proportions as matters of university
administration.

Turning to questions of scope and divisibility,
a similar pattern emerges. Administration of higher
educational institutions always emerged as a rather
holistic issue. Broad and general regulations governing all, or at least very broad categories of institutions marked both the prewar and Occupation
periods; decisions were not ad hoc in nature.

Questions of alleged interference with university autonomy and academic freedom, particularly as
these emerged during the prewar period, are less
easy to categorize clearly. Taking most often the
form of government attempts to insure certain behavior, either by specific universities or individual
academics, these questions could be considered highly
divisible in nature. Academics might suggest the
relevance of the adage about dividing and conquering.
But precisely because of this perception, the issues
rarely remained confined to a single institution or
faculty member. The perception of a seemingly unfair

threat to broad principles of academic freedom, no matter how localized or specific, was almost always sufficient to insure a much broader response. Individual faculty members sought and often gained support from colleagues at their own and other universities; institutions did the same. Precisely because of the principled nature of the questions involved, the problems rarely remained highly divisible or subject to difference-splitting, for any decision adversely affecting an individual or a school could subsequently become the precedent for similar action against others. Thus a certain indivisibility, at least in the way the issues were perceived, must be accorded to such matters as well.

Finally, it should be noted that such breadth of perception frequently went beyond the confines of academe. During the prewar period, political parties of the Left were considerably weaker than they have been since the war. But at least by the Occupation most issues of university administration and autonomy were seen as explicitly political, and by no means exclusively educational. Thus, trade union federations and more explicitly the political parties (generally the Japan Socialist Party and the Japan Communist Party) were willing to take actions in support of what they saw as correct positions on issues. Since individual cases of academic freedom almost always involved faculty members or student groups explicitly supportive of these parties, and since administration proposals by the government were almost always perceived as attempting to curtail political activities beneficial to these parties, such behavior was logical enough. What emerges then is a picture of administrative issues as virtually nondivisible and almost always quite broad in at least perceived, if not actual, impact and scope.

From one perspective the issue of enrollment could be seen as equally broad and indivisible. Involved was potentially the entire cohort of university-aged youths. But more salient is the fact that no policy decision affecting this group, qua group, emerged. At no time was there a decision or set of decisions attempting to set forth a comprehensive policy toward enrollment.[67] Rather, universities in both the prewar and Occupation periods established their own standards for admission, and the closest thing to national supervision consisted of government standardization of entrance examinations into national universities and perfunctory ratification of the entrance quotas established by individual universities. Thus, while the cumulative effect of enrollment

59

policies was broad indeed, this was only as the result of numerous specific and divisible component decisions. It is as though the enrollment policy affected each applicant as an individual, with the aggregate impact on the totality of the university-aged cohort emerging only as a by-product. Furthermore, the issue was never perceived by political organizations as broad enough for battle. Indeed, as well as can be determined, none even saw fit during the prewar and Occupation periods to adopt anything more than the most cursory statements of general support for sweeping and unobjectionable principles of equality of opportunity. Thus, the breadth of the enrollment issue remained considerably less than that surrounding the administration and autonomy issue, while being far more subject to divisibility for its solution.

Again occupying something of a middle position between these two extremes is the issue of specialization and functional differentiation. During the prewar period, for example, a multiplicity of higher educational institutions existed and regulations concerning them were collectively broad and general but distinct from one another. The greatest commonality was the statist orientation to which all were expected to adhere; within this framework considerable specificity existed as to the structure, course requirements, and so on expected of the different institutional types. Furthermore, within these general constraints there was leeway concerning course and degree requirements, with individual institutions, particularly universities, having extremely heterogeneous internal compositions. It would seem, therefore, that divisibility was far greater than in matters of administration but by no means as great as in matters of enrollment.

Under the Occupation both the replacement of institutional diversity with the single four-year university and the requirements concerning general education within the university represented policies of considerable breadth and indivisibility: common standards of national scope were required. But beyond this, considerable flexibility remained for institutions in terms of courses of study made available beyond the general education requirement and of the types of faculties and the field of concentration to be established within each university.

Furthermore, during both the prewar and Occupation periods the perceived political scope of such matters never reached the same proportions as university administration matters. They were of concern to universities and academics, to be sure, but they did not take on the significance for nonacademic groups that administrative matters did.

Thus, in summary, the issue dimensions of university administration emerge as congregated on one extreme, while those involving enrollment approximate an opposite extreme. By no means precisely midway between these two, but clearly in no way as extreme as either, lay issues of specificity and differentiation.

Before examining how these factors have interacted in post-Occupation policymaking, however, it is necessary to examine explicitly the political context within which they have emerged, devoting particular attention to the key variables of organizational strength and mobilizability and to certain formal political requirements, legalisms, and broad trends in formal decision-making. This is the subject of Chapter 4.

# 4. Nature of Political Structures

All states exercise some degree of control over
the societies they govern; all societies in turn exercise certain influences over state actions.  What
differentiates the absolute totalitarian political
system from the liberal-pluralist is the relative
weight of these two competing influences.  While
there are legitimate disagreements over the exact
degree to which social influence is reflected in
state behavior in Japan, it is clear that, when compared with most other countries, Japan emerges on the
liberal and democratic ends of the spectrum; most
analysts readily categorize Japan as a democracy.
Obviously, policymaking in Japan is therefore characterized by a general openness not found in totalitarian systems.  Newspapers, radio, and television report actively on important aspects of public policymaking; interest groups seek actively to influence
decision-makers in various party and governmental offices; opposition groups are relatively free to petition and to protest actions with which they disagree;
parliamentarians are openly elected, and to a greater
or lesser extent they are expected to represent certain of their constituents' needs; if they fail to do
so, Japan's relatively free elections can serve as a
device for removing them.  All policymaking takes
place within a comparatively democratic political
culture.  Even though Japan, as is true of any country, has areas where improvements are possible, by
most instrumental definitions of the term, Japan is
democratic.  So too is policymaking within the country.
Beyond this, most policymaking in Japan takes
place according to various legally or traditionally
prescribed procedures.  The mechanics of policymaking
are neither personalistic nor arbitrary.  Law and
custom make clear which state and which nonstate organs are responsible for the initiation, formulation,
and implementation of policy alternatives under a

63

variety of different circumstances. Certain rights
are clearly guaranteed by the constitution, and their
abrogation demands an amendment, through established
procedures, of the constitution. Other matters are
set by law and can be altered only through changes
carried out through prescribed Diet proceedings.
Still other matters are delegated to a particular
government agency, while others still are removed
from governmental auspices completely and are delegated to some specific quasi-public or social organization, whether a public corporation, an advisory
committee, or some totally private group such as the
Japan Medical Association or the trade association of
textiles, steel, or shipbuilding.

This is particularly significant for the cases
under examination here since, for example, most matters of university administration involve Diet-
directed changes in law; so too do many of the matters concerned with functional differentiation among
higher educational institutions. Other items connected with differentiation, as well as most matters
concerned with increasing specialized education, are
exclusively within the province of the Ministry of
Education. A few items are left exclusively to the
affected institutions of higher education. Finally,
some aspects of chartering that affect enrollment expansion are under the control of specific advisory
committees within the Ministry of Education, while
others are under the control of the private University Accreditation Association, and still others are
left entirely to individual universities or to the
"free market." Such formal requirements quite obviously make for very different structural constraints
on policymaking. These constraints, in turn, make
it easier or harder for specific social sectors or
political groups to exert an impact on policymaking
and the policies decided, while guaranteeing an impact to others.

In addition to such formal procedural elements,
political structures shape policy formation in a
second critical way. While Japanese policymaking is
obviously more "open" than that in most other countries, it would be a mistake to presume, as is all
too frequently done, that this general openness in-
sures some element of egalitarianism among all social sectors. There is a distinct bias to Japan's
openness, a distinct list to the balance of forces
within the country favoring political conservatism
and state power that is perhaps among the most pronounced in all states generally conceded to be democratic. The nature of Japan's overall political

orientation is bipolar, with the more conservative of the two poles in a position of hegemony. This in turn has made possible a widespread increase in the power of state agencies.

## BIPOLARITY AND HEGEMONIC PLURALISM

The previous chapter noted that the Occupation's "reverse course" shifted political aims from democratization and demilitarization to economic recovery, and political support from the emerging progressives to the refurbished conservatives. At least by this time, if not before, Japan's most significant political forces had become divided into two mutually antagonistic "camps," the progressives and the conservatives.

The term "camp" is used by those who consider themselves members, as well as by outside observers, to convey at least two notions: first, the comparative agreement and unity among the members of each camp, and second, the mutual hostility of the two camps and their readiness for political battle with one another. In the immediate postwar period the Japanese conservative camp was represented politically by several parties, most notably the Liberals and the Progressives (later known as the Democrats). From 1955 until the mid-1970s there has been a single conservative political party, the Liberal Democratic Party (LDP), formed from a merger of the existing conservative parties. Throughout this period the key support for the party and the key social components of the conservative camp have been big business and agriculture.

The progressive camp, meanwhile, has lacked the structural unity of the conservatives. There have always been at least two, and often three, political parties claiming to be "progressives": the Japan Communist Party (JCP), the Japan Socialist Party (JSP), which was split during the early 1950s into the Left Socialists and the Right Socialists, and finally the Democratic Socialist Party (DSP), formed in 1960 from remnants of the earlier Right Socialists. In addition, the Clean Government Party (CGP), which first emerged in national elections in 1956, has on various occasions counted itself as a member of the progressive camp. In contrast to the conservatives, the progressives have garnered the bulk of their support from organized labor, intellectuals, and, to a less specific extent, the urban dweller.

The major members of each of these two camps share a variety of fundamental assumptions about socio-political problems and solutions that serve to minimize the intracamp differences that frequently arise, while maximizing differences from one camp to the next. The proper level of military expenditure, the country's alliance and defense framework, the basic economic structure and the relative shares allotted to different social sectors, the degree of social welfare to be sustained by the state, the legitimacy of extraparliamentary and extraelectoral political participation, and a host of other basic questions find the members of each camp relatively close to one another and far distant from those in the opposing camp. On such issues there is little free-floating political exchange or transference of partisan affiliation between the leaders of the different political organizations; political exchange takes place almost exclusively within the grounds of one's own camp.

In this sense, Japanese political forces line up in a manner more akin to that of postwar France or Italy or of Weimar Germany than to that of postwar Britain, the United States, Canada, Austria, or West Germany. Political forces in the former manifest what Duverger has called "philosophical dualism"[1] and what Kirchheimer has labeled "opposition in principle,"[2] the opposing sides seeking radically different solutions to existing political problems. In the latter, most politically significant groups have arrived at a fundamental consensus on the nature of the political game and the boundary between "legitimate" and "illegitimate" solutions to problems. Despite the fact that all are "open" and "pluralist," there is a world of difference between the relatively moderate politics of accommodation that characterize the one group and the far more extreme and ideologically antagonistic politics of the other.[3]

Although post-Occupation Japan has been marked by political and ideological bipolarity, the two poles have by no means been equally successful in securing control of the governmental apparatus of the country. Control was monopolized for over two decades following the ending of the Occupation by the conservative camp, or, more accurately, by its electoral standard-bearer, the LDP and its predecessors. Under Japan's parliamentary system the government is chosen by the Diet, with the Lower House having the major powers; and the conservatives

have enjoyed very comfortable, though declining, majorities there since 1952. Only in the elections of
the late 1960s did they begin to fall below the 60
percent mark. The progressives during this same period generally gained a combined total of only one-
third of the seats.[4] The result has been that for at
least two decades during the post-Occupation period,
the conservative camp enjoyed a position of unchallenged dominance in the parliament and total control
over the cabinet and the offices of government. This
in turn meant a monopoly over the formal processes of
governmental policymaking. The progressive camp
meanwhile remained a rather isolated, semipermanent
minority. In this regard, postwar Japanese politics
could be called the politics of hegemonic pluralism.
     The conservatives' hegemonic position has meant
that the linkages between the LDP and the organs of
government have become sufficiently institutionalized to make the LDP the party of government, while
the close ties between the senior ranks of the civil
service and LDP parliamentarians have become highly
institutionalized.
     With a single party dominating the Japanese gov-
ernment, the basic  tendency toward strong government
control, evidenced in Japan since the Meiji era, has
become increasingly pronounced.[5]


BUREAUCRATIC CONTROL

     A number of factors point to the close ties be-
tween the LDP and the civil service. LDP Diet members, and particularly cabinet ministers, are increasingly drawn from the ranks of retired bureaucrats.[6]
In addition, the top posts in the bureaucracy, while
theoretically nonpolitical and meritocratic, are
awarded only after candidates have been screened by
the LDP. Candidates unacceptable to the party are
in effect unable to rise above the level of bureau
chief (kyokuchō).[7] For the formulation and implementation of policy the LDP has increasingly depended on
the bureaucracy. The outline of the party's electoral strategies, for example, ends with a list of policies proposed by the individual ministries. Within
the LDP the committees of the Policy Affairs Research
Council, which sets party policy, are organized in
functional parallel to the committees of the Diet,
which in turn are parallel to the ministries of the
government. Close formal and informal ties easily
emerge between LDP members and senior bureaucrats

working on similar areas of public policy.  Frequently, the same LDP members generate party proposals in conjunction with their opposite numbers in the ministry affected and then argue for these proposals within the Diet, drawing, where necessary, on the technical expertise of the senior civil servants most closely involved.

This closeness between the LDP and the civil service has obviated the need for elected officials to monitor the bureaucracy.  In Japan, insuring that government policy is not stymied by antagonistic bureaucratic independence is not the problem that it is in countries where changes in government and in basic policy direction are frequent.  The comparative homogeneity of policy orientation within the LDP, combined with the party's hegemonic position, has insured a high degree of consistency in government policy, while the close relationship between the party and the bureaucracy has enabled the latter to operate with increased independence in policymaking without concern that its actions will be antagonistic to elected officials.  Cabinet ministers, for example, are rotated almost annually with no apparent worry about the resulting power of and ministers' dependence on the senior bureaucrats.

This broad picture of cooperation between party and bureaucracy has resulted in a marked increase in the autonomy of the latter.  Indications in at least four specific areas point in the same direction of increased powers to the Japanese bureaucracy.

Advisory Committees

One of the most significant bureaucratic influences on Japanese policymaking is almost invisible. The bureaucracy exerts tremendous influence over the multitude of advisory committees that winnow multiple possible approaches to a problem down to manageable proportions and tangible proposals.

Most modern bureaucracies rely heavily on advisory committees for indispensable technical and specialized information as well as public input into bureaucratic policymaking.[8]  In addition, where specific groups affected by bureaucracies are formally represented, advisory committees help to consolidate differing opinions and forewarn of probable conflict over government proposals.  From a purely political perspective, such organs benefit a bureaucratic agency by inducing nongovernmental interests to run political interference for the agency both in the legislature and before the general public.[9]  They have certainly been important devices in higher educational policy.

In Japan at least four different types of advisory committees are identifiable. The largest of these deliberates and makes policy recommendations to governmental agencies;[10] the others act as administrative courts and adjudicate differences among governmental ministries, assess standards for accreditation purposes, and hear public complaints.

Advisory councils established under governmental ministries have proliferated since 1952, when 165 advisory councils were functioning under ministerial laws. By 1975 this figure had increased to 246.[11] Further, these figures represent only advisory councils formally established under law; an even more significant increase occurred in the number of lower-level study commissions established by ordinances. The scope of activities investigated has broadened correspondingly, and virtually all aspects of policymaking have become potentially scrutinizable by one or more of these bodies.

Numerical analysis alone does not fully indicate the important policymaking role of these groups. Originally allocated rather perfunctory roles, they have become major organizational tools in overall policy formulation. The Central Education Council, for example, the most important of the groups affiliated with the Ministry of Education, initially had the areas of its inquiry determined through consultation among representatives of the several bureaus within the ministry. The directors of the various bureaus met with the educational vice-minister, presenting short papers on subjects deemed of possible importance. Based on these meetings and subsequent consultations with the minister of education, a decision was made on what area(s) should be investigated by the council.[12] Council investigations were brief, often of two to four months, and reports rarely were longer than three or four pages.[13] Lacking serious investigation and study, the reports were almost devoid of policy influence. Thus, in its early phase the Central Education Council was of limited political significance. Similar situations prevailed in other ministries.

This has changed. In 1965 planning divisions were established within the ministries to determine areas of investigation. Decisions regarding areas to investigate alone entail as much as a year's planning, and the advisory body's anticipated role is usually substantial. One 1971 report, for example, required four years of investigation, and the interim report alone was a 465-page compendium of essential data on the basis of which major policy proposals were formulated.[14] This work was no anomaly, and councils have come to have major impacts on such diverse areas as foreign trade, tax structure, education, industrial restructuring, the legal system, the postal system, and local finance, among others.

As the significance of these advisory bodies has increased, so has their dependence on the bureaucracies they allegedly advise. They are far more the tools of bureaucratic control than independent policy-generating organs. At least four specific points support such a conclusion: 1) the controls over the areas of investigation; 2) the manner in which research is done; 3) the writing of reports; and 4) selection procedures for committee members and the resultant membership composition.

Areas of investigation are determined exclusively by the bureaucracy, i.e., by the ministry or agency under whose aegis the committee serves. Even the most broadly mandated committees must confine themselves to the topics chosen for them. In almost all instances these topics are rather narrowly defined, and in many cases the manner in which the investigative questions are formulated strongly determines the direction the recommendation is expected to take. Several cases in point include the terms of reference for the 1963 report of the Central Education Council, the 1967 directions to the Science and Technology Council, the 1968 instructions to the Subcommittee on University Disturbances, and the 1970 directions concerning hijacking made to the Advisory Committee on the Legal System. All had long prefatory comments outlining the problems as perceived by the upper echelons of bureaucratic agencies, followed by specific instructions as to the direction investigation should take. Not surprisingly, the major thrust of subsequent reports was to prove what were effectively prestated conclusions.[15]

In addition to sharply delineating the scope and direction of investigations, bureaucratic agencies exercise control over investigations in a second way. Most advisory committees do not have independent budgets or research staffs, and all research and investigation is carried out by staff members of the controlling government agency. The committees may request that certain data be included or that specific points be examined, but the ministerial personnel who do the work exert tremendous power over the committee's eventual report. This is even more so since the staff members who work in conjunction with a committee attend all of its meetings and discussions.

The fact that most committee reports are written, not by the committee itself or by a subcommittee, but by bureaucrats constitutes a third form of control.[16] The power of synthesizing discussion and preparing final reports accorded to top bureaucrats gives considerable control over the committees' eventual products. This power has become increasingly significant as the topics for research become more and more comprehensive. Even independent committees with neutral staffs find it almost impossible not to be heavily reflective of official thinking within the bureaucracy.

A fourth area of bureaucratic influence is on the membership of advisory committees. To analyze this dimension extensive background data were collected on all 676 members who have served on seven different education advisory committees.[17] Committee members are appointed by the agency they are to serve, normally by the permanent vice-minister, the highest ranking career bureaucrat, and in the analysis of background data the most significant feature for our purposes is the preponderance of bureaucrats and ex-bureaucrats. At the time of appointment to the various committees, members from the field of education made up 78.7 percent of the total, with members of government-related agencies totaling only 10.9 percent. (Businessmen constituted 6.3 percent, with 4.1 percent from other categories.) Such figures initially do not suggest the preponderance of bureaucrats, but titles at the time of appointment to a committee barely scratch the surface of committee members' backgrounds. Further examination reveals that at least one-third of all members of the seven committees investigated were at one time or another government bureaucrats. A high percentage of advisory committee members, while not bureaucrats at the time of appointment, served as bureaucrats and retired to some other form of work--often university teaching or administration--only after which were they appointed to advisory committees.

Furthermore, bureaucratic background is far more common among those holding top committee positions, those with greatest seniority, those serving on other government advisory bodies, and those on committees dealing with broad policy questions as opposed to more technically oriented committees. Looking at these four categories, the importance of the bureaucrats and ex-bureaucrats becomes even more evident. While constituting only one-third of the total membership, bureaucrats and ex-bureaucrats make up 40

percent of the chairmen and vice-chairmen, 42.5
percent of those on broad policy committees, 66.7
percent of those having served ten or more years
on individual committees, and 74.3 percent of those
who have served on three or more government advisory
committees.[18]

The picture that emerges from such figures is
of an advisory committee system in which bureaucrats
and ex-bureaucrats are disproportionately represented: longer tenure, positions of both general and policy responsibility, and greater interaction through
overlapping membership on other committees give them
far greater potential influence over committee proceedings than is possible for other members. Though
it is difficult to predict behavior patterns precisely from background variables such as previous
employment, it is likely that those possessing per-
sonal ties to the bureaucracy will be more disposed
toward bureaucratic desires than those lacking them.[19]

Some additional statistics further clarify the
character of the 78.7 percent of the advisory committee members who could be classified as school or university educators. More than one-half were presidents
of higher educational institutions and an additional
16.8 percent were administrators (faculty chairmen or
above) at such institutions. Administrators at research institutes or other educational institutions
made up an additional 7.4 percent of the total. Only
24.1 percent of the "educator" group were active
teachers or researchers. Therefore few of the "uni-
versity-affiliated" members in fact represent university faculty members. Although university administrators have hardly been sycophants of the government bureaucracy, they have, nevertheless, the most
direct contact with government agencies and would
be, of all academics, the most sympathetic to bureaucratic and governmental perspectives.

What can be said of such factors over time? Is
the bureaucratic presence on advisory committees increasing, decreasing, or remaining constant? In
Table 4-1 the data have been aggregated into five-
year periods to allow for an assessment of trends.
The actual percentage of bureaucrats and ex-bureaucrats on committees has gone through two phases: an
increase in the fifteen years from 1945 to 1960 and
then a decline in the following ten years. In contrast, all four of the other indicators of bureaucratic influence remain consistently higher than the
percentage of actual bureaucrats and in all cases
either have remained relatively constant or have increased. Thus, these four indicators belie the

TABLE 4-1

Percentage of Advisory Committee Members
with Bureaucratic Backgrounds

| Category | 1945-50 | 1951-55 | 1956-60 | 1961-65 | 1966-70 |
|---|---|---|---|---|---|
| Total members | 41.2% | 43.2% | 43.7% | 36.0% | 27.6% |
| Committee or sub-committee chairmen or vice-chairmen | 40.0 | 45.5 | 36.4 | 43.8 | 37.5 |
| Broad policy committee | 44.4 | 50.0 | 47.4 | 51.2 | 42.0 |
| Members serving ten or more years | -- | 64.3 | 66.7 | 66.7 | 64.7 |
| Members serving on three or more additional committees | 66.7 | 75.0 | 100.0 | 66.7 | 81.3 |

initial impression given simply by the recently declining percentage of bureaucrats and ex-bureaucrats
and suggest at least the continuous, if not rising,
influence of bureaucrats and ex-bureaucrats.

Not every policy proposal in Japan emerges after
investigation by an advisory committee; however, increasingly, most important decisions are reached only
after at least partial inquiry by one or more such
committees. Japanese newsmen and popular critics are
fond of describing the advisory committee system as a
cloak to hide the actions of the bureaucracy.[20] Even
if this is an overstatement, the analysis of the
structure, modes of action, and membership backgrounds
of the committees suggests that extremely close ties
exist between the committees and the bureaucratic
agencies they advise. The analysis also implies that
the lines of influence between the two groups are far
stronger from bureaucracy to committee than vice versa.
Clearly, the committees have not served as channels of
broad and open public input. Rather, they have contributed to the increased powers of the bureaucracy
and to the hegemonic closure of certain aspects of
Japanese policymaking, particularly during the initial
phases. The advisory committee system provides those
outside conservative camp organizations with no formal

input into these important early stages of policymaking and eliminates most of them from the important
pulling and hauling in the initial identification of
problems and definition of solutions. It is a major
tool in the hands of a strong Japanese state.

## Decline in Private Sector Autonomy

Closely related to the situation of advisory
committees and the closed nature of the initial policymaking process has been the comparative decline in
the formal delegation of policymaking responsibilities to nongovernmental groups. The practice of del-
egating primary responsibilities to such groups,
while subject to wide debate on its normative merits
and demerits, is prevalent in many countries.[21]
Under the Occupation numerous groups were encouraged to organize as a counterbalance to the powerful and independent bureaucracy that had dominated
Japanese policymaking before the war. Under the
heavy influence of the American pattern of directly
involving major interest groups in legislative and
administrative policymaking, many of these came to
occupy formal and significant roles in the formulation of higher educational policies. With the end
of the Occupation there began a significant reversal
of this pattern. The educational bureaucracy rejected the concept of formal reliance on concerned
interest groups, and most groups that acquired important roles during the Occupation have been systematically shunted to the periphery of the political processes.
The earliest and most explicit rejection in the
area of higher education came with the establishment
of the Central Education Council. The council's
predecessor, the Educational Reform Council, when it
completed its original mission of recommending reforms in the educational system during the Occupation, suggested the creation of a replacement committee that would represent various organized groups.
The council proposed that its replacement be made
up of eighteen or twenty members elected by the other
advisory committees established under the Ministry of
Education. Explicit representation was to be assured
for the Japan Science Council, local boards of education, the outgoing Educational Reform Council, and
several other groups. A specific numerical ratio was
also to be established for the inclusion of representatives from the fields of science, culture, and education on the one hand and from the areas of politics, industry, and society on the other.[22] This

plan was rejected by the ministry; instead, all
rights of appointment and dismissal were given to
the minister of education, and no provision was made
for the formal inclusion of any group or sector.

Explicit inclusion of outside groups on educationally related advisory committees is now limited
to two of the earliest committees established under
the Occupation. Two-thirds of the members of the
Private Universities Council must be representatives
of the private universities, and they are appointed
in accord with the joint recommendations of the private university federations.[23] The University Accreditation Association, meanwhile, holds twenty-
two of forty-five seats on the University Chartering
Subcommittee of the University Chartering Council.[24]
But in both cases the roles of the committees have
been sharply circumscribed.

Originally established to "make recommendations
to the minister of education on important matters of
relevance to private universities,"[25] the Private
Universities Council in reality has been restricted
to approving changes in the composition of legal
bodies governing private institutions of higher education. It serves merely as a screening committee
for the ministry over the membership, and occasionally over the legality, of certain actions taken by
the administrative organs of private universities.[26]

The case of the University Chartering Council is
more complex. Its history is intimately tied to that
of the University Accreditation Association. The
Accreditation Association began meeting in the fall
of 1946 and was formally established in July 1947 to
accredit and evaluate universities. Originally relying on the staff and headquarters of the Ministry
of Education, the association established its own
headquarters and staff during 1946-47 and in its
subsequent actions gained gradual independence from
the government bureaucracy and virtually total control over these functions, which previously had been
the exclusive purview of the ministry.[27]

In 1948 the University Chartering Committee
(later Council) was created by and under the jurisdiction of the ministry in an effort to regain control over these functions. Nevertheless, the association continued to maintain considerable influence
due to the support of SCAP and CIE. The standards
it established were maintained by the Chartering Committee as its own, and half of the latter's members
were by law chosen by the former.[28] With time, further steps were taken to reduce the association's
effectiveness, such as exempting premedical and

dental programs from the association's standards in 1954, and more notably the passage of university chartering standards in October 1956.[29] These sharply affected the association in that its standards, which had hitherto been used by the Chartering Council in evaluating charter applications, lost all government sanction and became merely the requirements for universities seeking to acquire membership in the association as a private group. The regulations of the Chartering Council were subsequently further revised, resulting in, among other things, a diluting of the numerical importance of association members on the Chartering Council, so that where formerly it had twenty-two of forty-five members, it then had twenty-two of ninety-five.[30]

The role of the association was further weakened by the government's failure to encourage national universities under its control to seek accreditation. Thus, although twenty-one of seventy-five national universities are accredited by the association, a percentage comparable to public and private universities, eighteen of these have merely kept up their charter membership. Only three national universities have been accredited in the eighteen years since then. Of thirty-eight universities joining the Accreditation Association after 1952, only three were national universities;[31] fifty-four national universities could have joined the association but chose not to do so. The overall impact of government action regarding the association has therefore been to limit sharply that group's formal and informal impact on government policymaking.

Two other cases exemplify the government's efforts to reduce the formal participation and effectiveness of such outside groups. The first group, the Japan Science Council (JSC), was initially established at the encouragement of the U.S. Occupation to serve in a capacity similar to that of the American National Academy of Sciences. Its relations with the government are by law quite close.[32] Its administrative personnel are government employees, and it is established as "the legal and official body of the scientists of Japan."[33] Despite the original proposal for close ties between the JSC and the government, as Long has noted, the American model on which these ties were formulated "did not survive the cultural transplant."[34] In fact, the government began actively undermining what little formal powers the JSC has had when Prime Minister Yoshida publicly accused it of manifesting too many left-wing tendencies.[35] In 1956 the Science and Technology Agency was established at

76

cabinet level, taking over many functions of the JSC, and in 1959, over the strong opposition of the JSC, the Science and Technology Council was created as a special appointive consultative organ to the prime minister.[36] This new group became responsible for advice on all matters of science policy, effectively bypassing the elective JSC. Subsequently, the JSC's powers to make the preliminary decisions on the allocation of government scholarship monies to advanced scholars was curtailed, and although it still has the power to "recommend" government action, former Education Minister Sakata stated that these powers "produce no substantial effects."[37]

The second case is that of the Japan Teachers Union.[38] The union is known as the representative of the vast majority of Japan's lower school teachers; however, it has been a rather constant spokesman on all educational issues, including those related to higher education. Members of the union were included in the committee to design a university administrative bill in 1951, but this appears to have been about its only formal inclusion in governmental policymaking processes. Almost from its origin the union was at odds with the government because of the former's strong Marxian tradition and its tactics of almost constant opposition to government proposals. A policy of formal isolation of the union, including an unwillingness on the part of several ministers of education to meet with the president of the union, lasted from the early 1960s to the early 1970s.[39] The Ministry of Education has not sought so much to weaken its ties with the union and to minimize the role of the union as to avoid according this significant group any formal role at all.

The exclusion of outside groups is related to Japan's ideological bipolarity. Many of the groups noted have been openly identified with the progressive camp, and their inclusion would have given added power and legitimacy to government opponents. Not all of them are so obviously identified with the progressive camp, however, and the exclusion of some involves nothing more than the general reluctance of the conservative camp and, in particular, the Ministry of Education, to grant legal representative roles to any outside group in an attempt to keep tight constraints on as many policymaking arenas as possible. When the government wants the opinions of some particular group, it solicits them on an ad hoc basis, either privately or in the form of public testimony or written proposals. Such opinions may then be taken into consideration, but at almost no time

are outside educational groups given either autonomous powers or the important role of meeting together,
arguing out differences, and making broad policy recommendations to the government. If they were, experience in the United States and most European countries
suggests that their policymaking influence could be
strengthened immeasurably.[40]

## Legislation and the Diet

When one turns to the most visible, and perhaps
most well studied, arena of policymaking in Japan,
the obviousness of conservative control based on
heavy reliance on the bureaucracy is again evident.
The Diet, Japan's parliament, is the focal point of
all policymaking activities involving legal or constitutional matters. The very close ties between
the various bureaucratic agencies and the policymaking organs of the Liberal Democratic Party and the
tight constraints over formal participation in the
earliest stages of policy deliberation bear particular importance in the legislative process. Most legislative proposals are generated by a bureaucratic
agency and then submitted to the appropriate section
in the LDP's Policy Affairs Research Council (Seimu
Chōsakai). Upon approval, the bill is passed on to
the Policy Deliberations Council (Seisaku Shingikai),
to the Executive Council (Sōmukai) of the party, to
the party's Diet Policy Committee (Kokkai Taisaku
Iinkai), and finally to the cabinet Bureau of Legislation (Hōseikyoku) and the cabinet for refinement
and final preparation. At all of these stages there
is close interaction between party functionaries and
agents of the concerned bureaucratic organs. In almost all cases, only after cabinet approval of a
proposal does the Diet as a body become meaningfully
involved.[41]
This gives tremendously important powers of policy initiation to the conservative camp and to government agencies and means that by the time bills
materialize in the Diet, a general agreement has usually already been reached, both within the bureaucracy and between it and the LDP. Opposition and/or the
generation of successful alternatives from within the
Diet is thus extremely difficult in the face of such
basic consensus.[42]
Within the Diet this bias is further evidenced.
Constitutionally "the highest organ of state power,"
the Diet has probably never fulfilled the expectations
of those American drafters of the Japanese constitution who seemingly anticipated the development of a

rather autonomous institution comparable to the U.S. Congress. Indeed, as an integral component of a parliamentary rather than a presidential system, the Diet should by no means be expected to act in competition with the executive branch; cooperative relations between the two would appear to be far more the norm than under a presidential system, particularly when the cabinet and the legislature are dominated for long periods of time by a single party.

Still, a parliament can be a source of policymaking independence in at least two ways. Individual members and opposition parties can introduce their own legislative proposals, and both can serve as opponents of government-proposed legislation. Not all legislation passed need be that proposed by the cabinet, and not all legislation need pass unopposed. The evidence suggests, however, that Japanese legislative independence, by both measurements, is declining in the face of a growth in the combined legislative power of the bureaucracy and the ruling conservative party. Particularly since 1955, when the two conservative parties, the Liberals and the Democrats, merged to form the since-dominant LDP, there has been a clear shift.

At least three indicators point to this: success rates of governmental and individual member bills; the declining rate of amendments added; and the singular lack of success for opposition-sponsored bills. In looking at the passage rates for bills, two caveats should be kept in mind. First, the role of the individual parliamentarian as the main bulwark in the fortress of democracy has been overly romanticized in Japan as elsewhere. Ozaki Yukio, perhaps Japan's most famous speechmaking parliamentarian, was an anomaly in his own time, mythologized as an ideal so removed from general reality as to parallel that of the "independent backbencher" in Britain.[43] In an era of administrative complexity and strong party discipline, the role of the single parliamentarian is perforce diminished.

Second, even the mere submission of nongovernmentally sponsored measures is extremely difficult. In the lower house at least twenty representatives must support a "member" bill before it can be introduced, while in the upper house ten supporters are required. Should the bill require the expenditure of state funds, fifty and twenty supporters respectively are necessary. This procedure alone works against the submission of such proposals. Nonetheless, during the bulk of the postwar period approximately 40 percent of all bills submitted have rather

consistently been member bills. Somewhat ironically, only during the Occupation period was this
figure significantly lower (22.6 percent).[44]

It is axiomatic, however, that introduction of
legislation is far less significant than its passage,
and there the Japanese situation is of far more interest. While the ratio of government-sponsored to
member-sponsored legislation has remained roughly the
same, a marked decline has taken place in the chances
of the latter eventually to become law.

As Table 4-2 indicates, government-sponsored
legislation was extremely successful under the Occupation, with more than nine of every ten proposals
becoming law. From the end of the Occupation, however, until 1955 the rate dropped to 75 percent.
Since then such legislation has shown a slow but
increasingly steady success.

Individually sponsored legislation, on the other
hand, shows a drastic decline in success. From a high
of 70.4 percent under the Occupation, the passage rate
for such bills dropped to just under 35 percent in the
1952-55 period and remained in the 10-14 percent range
until 1970-75. From a somewhat different perspective,
18 percent of the successful legislation during the
Occupation involved member bills. From 1952 to 1955
this rose to more than one-quarter. In the next five
years the success rate was halved, and during the
1960s it remained below 10 percent. Thus, while government bills were only 1.3 times more likely to succeed than individual bills during the Occupation and
about twice as likely to do so from 1952 to 1955, by
1970 they were seven times more likely to pass.
Moreover, since 1955 approximately 90 percent of all
successful legislation has been cabinet sponsored.[45]
Only since 1970, with the waning of LDP dominance,
has there been a slight increase in the success of
private member bills.

In addition, even those member bills that are
enacted are usually introduced by Diet standing committee chairmen (of the eighteen such bills passed in
the 63rd Diet, for example, sixteen were introduced
by chairmen). Most frequently these deal with local
or specialized benefits and hence pose no serious
challenge to the bureaucratic-LDP monopoly of broad
policy.[46]

Beyond this, available evidence suggests that as
a "potential" amender the Diet has not been notably
active. Two devices are legally open to it: it can
"amend" (shūsei) or it can "add a supplementary resolution of clarification" (futai ketsugi). While insufficient data make full trend analysis impossible,

TABLE 4-2

Successful Cabinet-Sponsored and Individually Sponsored Legislation

| Diet | | Cabinet Bills Passed | | | Individual Member Bills Passed | | |
|------|------|--------|-----------------------------------------|------------------------------|--------|----------------------------------------|------------------------------|
| Number | Date | Number | As % of total cabinet bills submitted | As % of total bills passed | Number | As % of total member bills submitted | As % of total bills passed |
| 1-13 | 5/47-7/52 | 1352 | 91.1 | 81.6 | 305 | 70.4 | 18.4 |
| 14-23 | 8/52-12/55 | 567 | 74.9 | 74.7 | 192 | 34.8 | 25.3 |
| 24-37 | 12/55-12/60 | 822 | 75.3 | 88.5 | 107 | 14.1 | 11.5 |
| 38-50 | 12/60-12/65 | 845 | 77.9 | 92.2 | 71 | 10.7 | 7.8 |
| 51-64 | 12/65-12/70 | 609 | 76.8 | 90.4 | 65 | 12.5 | 9.6 |
| 65-76 | 12/70-12/75 | 480 | 81.7 | 84.8 | 86 | 22.2 | 15.2 |

Source: Kokkai Shugiin kaihō (Report of the House of Representatives) (Tokyo: Shugiin Hakkankō, annual).

81

from 1955 to 1960 just over one-third of all successful government legislation went through one or another of these processes. Since supplementary resolutions that have no force in law, however, constituted
nearly one-half of these, only 19 percent of the successful legislation was amended.[47] In the 48th Diet
(1964-65) this rate was 17 percent; in the 63rd Diet
(1970) it was 15 percent; and if one is to believe
the contentual analysis of Takagi, most of these
amendments were more procedural and definitional
"sops" than they were substantive alterations.[48]

Finally, opposition bills (also individually
sponsored bills) have no chance of success. The
bulk of these seek merely to counter government-
sponsored bills deemed to be strong in ideological
content. Throughout there is little real expectation
of passage; instead, these counterplans serve as
rallying points for a public relations campaign
against government-initiated legislation. Thus, of
317 opposition bills introduced from the 37th (1960)
through the 46th (1963-64) Diets, not one became
law.[49]

The picture that emerges of the Diet, therefore,
is of an institution dominated by the government and
the party of government, in which success has become
more and more difficult for bills they have not generated and supported. Individually sponsored measures
have become increasingly unlikely to succeed, and such
success as they have managed has tended to be in very
limited areas. Amendments have become infrequent and
of narrow consequence, and there is no chance that proposals by opposition parties will be enacted. Success
for these latter must come through informal amendments
or additions to government-backed bills, which have a
declining chance of being adopted. The main alternative thus becomes to delay or completely block such
bills.

This is not to suggest that the Diet is but a
functionless appendage. Both in its committees and
in its full sessions, the Diet is often a significant
organ of investigation and public communication. As
far as policymaking is concerned, however, it is less
the independent conceptualizer and structurer of legislation and much more the reactive amender and legit-
imator of proposals generated by government agencies
and consolidated through bureaucratic-LDP cooperation.

Administrative Directives and Bureaucratic
Communications

The independent legislative power of the Diet is
on the wane, but the legislative process by no means

82

defines the policymaking universe in Japan. An important and frequently overlooked power of Japanese government agencies is the issuance of ordinances and ministerial communications.

Technically, there are two types of ordinances in Japan: cabinet (seirei) and ministerial (shōrei). In contrast to laws, which are to be enacted by elected public representatives through an explicitly political process in the Diet, ordinances are clearly intended to be directives dealing with "nonpolitical," technical matters under the jurisdiction of the cabinet or some group of ministries, or, in the case of ministerial ordinances, under the jurisdiction of a single ministry.[50] "Communications" (tsūtatsu) are supposedly simple directives issued from an official to groups or organizations under his jurisdiction concerning similarly nonpolitical matters of even less moment than those dealt with by ordinances.

The power of technical interpretation of a law can be tantamount to complete revision of the original intentions of that law, in contrast to the implications of a rigidly hierarchical Weberian model of a bureaucracy in which "policy" is made "above" and is meticulously "administered" by those "below." Interpretation and administration are clearly powers; they are not politically neutral techniques that will be performed in precisely the same way by any appropriately trained bureaucratic technician. From such a perspective alone, the policymaking powers of the Japanese bureaucracy must be recognized as substantial.

Related though they are to such a general power, ordinances and communications deserve special attention for several reasons: they are highly authoritative devices for overtly or covertly bypassing the more public policymaking forum that is the Diet; they have in many cases been explicitly political in their content; and finally, ordinances have come to carry increasing weight in the totality of Japan's public policymaking.

Reliance on the Diet involves a certain investment of the government's time, effort, prestige, and other political resources. Opposition forces, the media, occasionally dissident LDP factions, and eventually the public can and often do discover through the open and combative nature of the legislative process numerous negative and/or embarrassing elements in government proposals. Every snippet of possibly embarrassing detail in a proposal is quickly seized upon and subjected to minute scrutiny by such groups, and corrections are occasionally forced before final passage can be accomplished. Even when such corrections are not made, the public nature of the process carries a threat of electoral revenge in cases of sufficient public moment. None of these democratic controls is insured for ordinances or communications. In the absence of a detailed content analysis of all ordinances and communications, one cannot draw absolute conclusions about the balance between "nonpolitical" and purely "political" ones. Examples suggest, however, the large political role they have played.

A clear illustration of how these powers can be used to circumvent the Diet occurred in April 1953. With major legislation aimed at bringing about radical changes in the university system facing serious Diet scrutiny and the likelihood of nonpassage, the Ministry of Education issued an ordinance, and subsequently a communication, to effect most of the desired changes. Coming as they did during the four days between lower house and upper house elections, the two occasioned little public attention despite their significance. In fact, it was not until nearly two months after their issuance that they were first reported in the media, and then only in a student newspaper. Although public disclosure eventually resulted in heated Diet debate, the policy had been effected regardless.

A number of other clearly political matters have been dealt with through communications or ordinances. The Ministry of International Trade and Industry has been at the forefront in using such powers to aid or encourage specific developments in various sectors of Japanese industry. Checks on student protests, a complete revision of the general educational system, and numerous alterations in the university system have been but a few of the educational areas affected. And Steiner notes that communications from the Autonomy Ministry are "the main means of exercising ministerial controls under Article 15 of the Government Organization Law and Article 150 of the Local Autonomy Law."[51] A high degree of authority is attached to such communications and ordinances, and questions of their legality are rarely posed by the recipient, despite possible violations of the law they are to "interpret" or the disregard they may show for established rights. In short, they often represent major policymaking devices and are a substantial political weapon in the hands of the bureaucracy.

Such powers, it must also be noted, are on the rise. Complete figures for the number of communications are not presently available, to the best of my knowledge, but as Figure 4-1 makes clear, ordinances

84

FIGURE 4-1

Ordinances and Laws as a Percent of Sum Total of Both

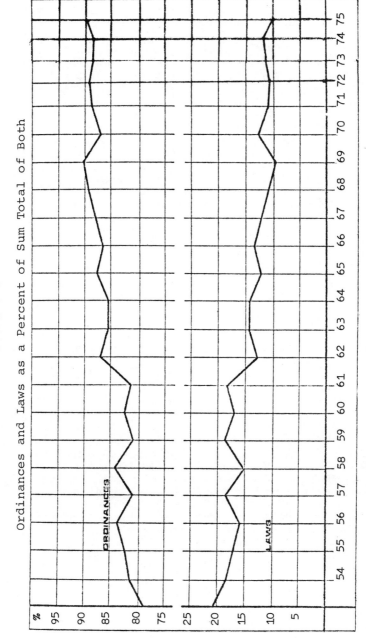

Source: Ministry of Finance, ed., Hōrei zenshō (Collected Laws and Ordinances)
(Tokyo: Ministry of Finance, annual).

are clearly growing in importance as policymaking devices as compared to laws. In the period 1953-76 ordinances, which were four times as numerous as laws, grew to be nine times as numerous. This general situation is in no way different within the field of education. Indeed, the trend is at least as clear as within the government generally. In 1953 laws accounted for 40 percent of the total, but by 1969 they had dropped to 19 percent. Cabinet ordinances and ministerial ordinances related to education combined to form a total of more than 80 percent, with ordinances issued by the Ministry of Education jumping most appreciably from 24 percent of the total during 1953-59 to 42 percent during 1964-69. The emerging picture is of an increasing proportion of the serious political policymaking in Japan taking place outside the public arena of the Diet and under the increasing control of a democratically unresponsible and conservatively oriented bureaucracy.

In various ways, therefore, many of the fundamental structural features of policymaking in Japan suggest a tightly controlled process in which the conservative camp relies heavily on the internal mechanisms of the LDP and, increasingly, on the variety of devices open to the civil bureaucracy to limit access to the formal channels of public policymaking and to insure a tight control over the policy agenda. Furthermore, public, open, and visible channels seem to be losing significance to state-dominated, closed, and invisible channels. Even though different processes and arenas of policymaking make this more true in some cases than in others, the overall control provides inherent limitations on policymaking patterns generally, but more especially on the capabilities of nonconservative camp interests and pressure groups to enter formally and frequently into all stages of policymaking.[52] Furthermore, when the legally prescribed arena of policymaking is the bureaucracy or the bureaucracy and the LDP, this is clearly more likely to be the case than when the dominant arena is the university or the Diet. Where the primary arena of decision-making is formally open to direct influence by nongovernment and/or explicitly progressive groups, there is no major problem. For example, when policies in higher education are determined primarily by the universities, particularly by the faculty conference, there is ample opportunity for progressive academics to exert powerful influence. Thus, in some public policy areas formal channels are readily open to the articulation of nonconservative interests. Most of the evidence, however,

suggests sharp limitations on such representation in
the legislative area generally, and in the bureaucratic area particularly, in educationally related
matters. How then, if at all, do nonconservative interests seek representation on matters likely to be
heavily decided in the bureaucracy or the legislature?


## THE DILEMMA OF NONCONSERVATIVE INTERESTS

It is fruitful to conceptualize such influence
possibilities as rather dichotomous in nature.[53] On
the one hand, there is quiet compromise and indirect
conciliatory appeal; in contrast, there is direct and
antagonistic confrontation. Which of these two possible paths is followed in any specific case (assuming that some attempt is made to exert influence) is
largely a function of the specific issue involved.
The more affective the issue, the more specifically
it concerns a nonconservative group, and the closer
its relationship to the broader ideological struggle
between Japan's two political camps, the greater is
the likelihood that dialectical conflict will result.
On the other hand, when the relevance of a particular
issue to such broad values or to the specific demands
and needs of an organization is limited, the likelihood of compromise is increased. Thus, the choice
between compromise and conflict depends largely on
the nature of the issue, or more exactly, on a particular group's or individual's perception of the
nature of the issue.
In the Diet, for example, there are several ways
in which progressives can exert informal influence.
At what might be called the prelegislative stage, an
opposition member may raise a teian shitsumon, a legislative proposal in the form of a question to a top-
level bureaucrat making general testimony. "Would it
not be a good idea for your agency to consider the
following form of legislation . . . ?" This is a
step that is often taken during budgetary hearings.
If the idea proposed is deemed meritorious, the
bureaucracy, in conjunction with the LDP, frequently
responds with a formal legislative proposal on the
subject in the form of government-introduced legislation. The proposal for a United Nations University
in Japan was initially formulated in such a manner by
Socialist Party member Yamanaka Gorō in a question to
Foreign Minister Miki Takeo.[54] Similarly, informal
suggestions or formal proposals by nonconservative
groups or individuals may be submitted to a Diet

committee, where the progressives have, of course, an informed entrée, or to a bureaucratic agency or an investigative council. Such suggestions subsequently appear, usually in somewhat modified version, as government legislation or as an administrative directive.

At later stages too compromises are worked out. From 1955 to 1964, for example, about one-third of all successful government legislation had been "amended" or "clarified," the bulk of this as a result of informal negotiations with the progressive parties. Nearly 70 percent of these then went on to receive unanimous approval in the Diet, and most differences were of a nonideological, somewhat easily compromised nature. Indeed, only 10 percent of the successful government bills were both amended and then passed on a split vote, in most cases with only the Japan Communist Party in opposition.[55]

Such a strategy of compromise is largely limited, however, to proposals by recognized individual experts in their particular areas of expertise, to groups with some informal access, and to proposals that fall within the limits of ideological acceptability. Moreover, compromise with the conservative camp almost by definition implies a recognition of the latter's legitimacy and an acceptance of the definitional and problematic parameters it establishes. Therefore compromise is possible only on rather noncontroversial, technical matters, matters on which any ideological divergence is nonexistent or papered over, and on which the possible political payoff for either side is rather low. Nonetheless, within these limits compromise is a highly effective technique for insuring that proposals of widely recognized merit are implemented. Because in most cases such influence is so indirect as to be virtually invisible to the media and the general public, however, it is terribly ineffective as a device for gaining electoral or even emotional support for the original influencer or his organization. Most public credit accorded usually redounds to the benefit of the government, which appears as the prime, if not the sole, architect of any eventual legislation, and only a limited number of insiders are aware of the true geneology of many fine proposals. The ideological limitations and the lack of political payoffs therefore make such techniques anathema to many.[56]

The major alternative to compromise lies at the other end of the tactical spectrum involving rather unrelenting opposition. When a conservative proposal, for example, raises an ideological red flag, the result most frequently is the generation of an equal and opposite reaction. In the Diet this usually means the introduction, as noted above, of a counterproposal to serve as the formulation and focal point of basic disagreements.

With or without such a bill, the tactic of opposition must aim at blocking passage of the government bill, setting high costs on its passage, and minimizing the degree of "damage" by forcing various marginal changes. This may involve the revelation of any unsavory aspects of the government proposal, the generation of media opposition, and/or a public campaign against the legislation. At times the response also includes a variety of tactics from petition campaigns and public meetings of protest to street demonstrations and, in some cases, antigovernmental violence. Should opposition to some single specific proposal be effectively joined to opposition to other conservative activities or proposals, there is also the threat of a major drive to topple the entire government.

Such a dialectical pattern of political confrontation therefore makes great demands on all sides for talent, time, and political resources in general. For progressive groups and parties there is the additional danger posed by what may appear to be "unreasonable" opposition or opposition for its own sake. Although such activities may appeal to purists on the left, they are hardly likely to attract the sympathies of the less-committed. Rather, they potentially reinforce the stereotypical image of the progressive camp as rather unconcerned with "genuine" political problems, rather unpredisposed toward compromise, and inclined to call for blind, ideologically motivated opposition to any efforts made by the government at change. Thus, there is the ever-present danger that direct opposition used too frequently will create for the leftist political parties a situation comparable to that of the boy who cried "wolf."

Consequently, attempts by nonconservative or openly progressive groups to influence by total opposition are rather unappealing. Only on a few crucial issues has the progressive camp been willing and able to sustain a collective campaign of blatant and total opposition. As will be seen, in the area of higher education the primary area in which such total opposition is most readily forthcoming concerns university administration, while institutional differentiation, specialization, and enrollment problems have been more the objects of compromise tactics.

Thus, nonconservative groups are presented with

something of an undesirable choice--they must either
compromise and negotiate over matters primarily of
technique, thereby conceding much by way of legitimacy and problem parametric powers to the conservatives, or, alternatively, maintain a rigid posture of
ideological purity, insuring a near-total lack of
bargaining influence on specific issues and creating
a near-zero-sum situation. On different higher educational issues they have usually found themselves
impaled on one horn or the other of this cruel dilemma.

Japan is clearly openly pluralist by most definitions; it is apparent, however, that the structure of
its politics is hegemonic, with conservative camp influence and government power far outweighing that of
any opposition. Members of the progressive camp have
been permanently and systematically isolated from
most key organs of policymaking, leaving the formally
most important aspects of policymaking to the tight
control of the conservatives. The power of the bureaucracy is used to dominate policy initiation and
discussion in advisory committees and in legislative
proposals. The ability of the bureaucracy to issue
administrative directives further bolsters this control. Nonconservative groups have consistently lost
direct influence over many channels of policymaking
influence. Areas of direct influence remain open to
nonconservatives, of course. Particularly significant are the universities themselves, where the faculty conference is a key factor in most on-campus
policy formulation, and the Diet, where a legitimate
and tangible role is guaranteed to the progressive
parties and, through them, to their adherents. The
impact that these groups can exert, however, particularly in the legislature, is limited to two not particularly appealing extremes: compromise and conflict.
Thus, specific processes must be followed for
different political issues; different arenas of policymaking are more or less relevant to these different processes, which in turn mean greater or lesser
influence for different sectors and groups. Overall,
the presence or absence of links to the conservative
camp, however, is most significant.
These political features are especially important when combined with the nature of the specific
issues involved, as examined in Chapter 3. That is
to say, when an issue is highly divisible and non-
specific and at the same time is determined through a
bureaucratic rather than a legislative process, one
can reasonably expect a process that limits external

group input, minimizes overt conflict, and results
in a distinctly conservative policy outcome. By way
of contrast, a highly affective issue of high specificity requiring largely legislative action should
result in a process of intense camp conflict in which
there is a chance that the conservative coloration of
the final product will be tempered by progressive input and alteration. This is especially true when the
nation's political climate in the broadest sense is
charged with high affect of a bipolar conflictual
nature. Alternatively, if the government is willing
to risk a component of popularity and total opposition hostility, it may push its own version of a program through the Diet with no quarter asked or given.
When many such issues arise simultaneously, the significance and conflict surrounding any single one becomes that much greater. The combination and interaction of these various political and issue-related
factors in several discrete policy situations provide
the basis for the next three chapters.

# 5. Policymaking Through Camp Conflict: University Administration

During the politically heated summer of 1969 the Japanese government succeeded in pushing through the Diet the Law of Provisional Measures Concerning University Administration. Despite its somewhat innocuous title, the bill and the events surrounding it represented the culmination of a tumultuous controversy between Japan's conservative and progressive camps that was clearly the major political and media event of the year, and possibly of several years. The entire process surrounding its passage was a prototype of policymaking through camp conflict, following the pattern of earlier controversies in the same area. When the bill passed, it marked a significant shift in the relative balance of power between government and university, giving the government new and significant controls over university administration.

Controversy between universities and government was by no means new to Japan, a long history of antagonism having gone before this particular dispute. Nor is such hostility between the two peculiar to Japan. A university system worthy of the name is bound to perceive its interests as not totally harmonious with those of any government. By its very nature, a university is dedicated to principles and values transcending the quite justifiably more parochial concerns and interests of governments. Relations between university and government need not always be antagonistic; throughout Europe and North America, however, harmony has historically been more of an exception than the rule, and the predominant pattern of government-university interaction has at least until very recently involved more conflict than compromise.

In the fourteenth or sixteenth centuries universities and political rulers and ruling groups might well have ignored one another as mutually irrelevant. With the industrial revolution and the increasingly technological basis of economic growth, with the

93

expansion of the relationship between education and subsequent occupations and careers, and with relatively rapid expansion in the capacity of academics to disseminate their ideas on political, social, and economic questions as well as on scientific and technical problems, all ruling groups have sought to insure greater conformity between actions in universities and their own needs and interests. Conversely, universities have become increasingly dependent on government funding and tolerance.

In certain areas it has been possible for the state to exert virtually complete control over actions within the universities. In other instances the universities or groups within them have resisted such pressures. The abstract merits of conflict vs. compromise between state and university can be and have been debated endlessly in different societies. Certainly, from the standpoint of insuring a wide range of autonomous opinion within society and at the same time insuring the university's freedom from the constraints of isolated "ivory towerism," conflict between it and the state is essential. In other areas, such as manpower policy, it is difficult to see how university and state can interact without some mutual compromise and a balance between university autonomy and accommodation to the needs of an economically changing society.

In any event, controversies over university administration have a long and politically salient history in Japan. As noted in Chapter 3, the prewar record of university-state relations was marred by numerous controversies stemming from government efforts to minimize the opportunities for antigovernmental activity on campus and individual or group reactions to such attempts. The comparative weakness of the academic community and the political Left in prewar Japan made for great imbalance in the struggles, usually resulting in government success. As a result, the postwar academic community feared that such actions might recur and were convinced that constant diligence and resistance to government control was the best way to insure university autonomy. Thus, by the time of the Occupation there was already a firm basis for great hostility between government and university over questions of administration. This hostility was furthered by the Occupation-induced efforts before and during the reverse course to undercut some of the powers that were gained by universities and their faculties immediately after the war. This tradition of animosity continued through the post-Occupation period.

94

At base, virtually all problems of university administration since the Occupation have revolved around problems related to the justifiable degree of government supervision and control over the universities and to the types of acceptable political activities on campus. In broad outline, the conservative camp has maintained that the university should be politically "neutral," that its educational and research activities should be "responsible" to the broader society,[1] and that to insure these ends various forms of governmental and societal supervision of university governance are essential. To achieve these objectives the government has advocated a centralization of power in the system of university administration: more power to the Ministry of Education at the expense of university officials, and more control by university administrators vis-a-vis faculty and students. In addition, the government has sought to check outright the formal powers of the faculty conference and the student self-governing associations.

The progressives and academics generally have contended, in contrast, that the university must remain totally free from all "outside interference," either governmental or societal. All decisions affecting research and education, they argue, must be made exclusively by members of the university community. Decentralization of rights and powers have simultaneously been advocated on campus, with many to devolve upon junior faculty and students. Most explicitly, however, they have favored a strong and autonomous faculty conference, with university administrators acting as little more than surrogates for the conference. The proposed scope of power for the faculty conference has generally been quite wide, often encompassing the right, if not the moral duty, to take stands on political matters not immediately identifiable as directly relevant to the university.[2] Political resolutions, petitions, mass demonstrations, and on occasion unremitting violence have thus been defended as the essential weapons of a vigilant university community.

Embryonic formulations of such positions can be found in the prewar period, but they came to intellectual fruition during the battles over university administration under the Occupation. And each successive struggle over administration hardened even more the opposing positions. Chronologically speaking, three major struggles over university administration have taken place since the Occupation: in 1952-54, 1960-63, and finally 1968-69. All three,

which culminated in the events noted at the beginning
of this chapter, raised individual problems and had
certain distinguishable features but were quite similar in relation to the  issue-specific variables discussed in Chapter 2: all were highly affective, generating intense political emotions that followed the
camp positions outlined.  Furthermore, virtually all
proposals took forms calculated to produce effects
in all Japanese universities, giving the issue simultaneously great scope and specificity.  As a result,
intense interest and reaction was generated among the
university community.  Politically, the proposals all
required legislative action, entailing a far more
visible and potentially conflict-laden process than
would have been plausible if the matters had been re-
solvable through administrative measures.  Moreover,
they arose in the context of much broader controversies between the progressives and conservatives.
Such major similarities implicitly suggest the likelihood of comparable policymaking processes among all
three, which was actually the case.  All three represent almost prototypical examples of policymaking
through camp conflict.

At the same time, within these broad commonalities there were important differences among the three
struggles.  The specifics of each legislative proposal were different and the political strengths of the
two camps changed somewhat over time, with absolute
conservative control in the Diet declining but their
general organizational control over the organs of
state growing even stronger.  The Left, meanwhile,
lost, with time, some of the unity that marked the
earliest struggles.  Finally, a certain cumulative
quality has adhered to the political affect involved
in this, as any other issue: each successive struggle
has combined to make even greater the commitment to
previously held positions and to intensify the emotional stakes of victory or defeat.  Hence, the political resources each side was willing to commit to
the 1968-69 struggle far exceeded those of earlier
struggles.  The most significant difference among
the three, however, is that the battles in 1952-54
and 1960-63 resulted in the defeat of government-
initiated legislative efforts to alter the administrative processes of the university system, while
the third saw the successful passage of a 1969 law
introducing major changes in the balance of power between university and government.

In analyzing the three policymaking processes,
the search will be simultaneously for the commonalities defining the pattern of camp conflict and for

the differences that explain their respective paths
within that broad pattern.


THE CONFLICT OF 1952-54

    The problem from 1952 to 1954 emerged as very
much a continuation of the 1951 efforts to pass legislation altering the administration and management
of the national and local public universities.  As
noted in Chapter 3, the government submitted two bills
on these subjects to the Diet in February 1951, only
to abandon them in June in the face of strong opposition from the political Left and the academic community.  The period was, however, one of much broader
hostilities between Japan's two political camps.
    In November 1951 two incidents involving radical
student protest in Kyoto rekindled the government's
desire to increase university controls.  The first,
on November 7, followed a rally under labor union
auspices to celebrate the anniversary of the Bolshe-
vik Revolution.  Student protesters demonstrated
through the streets and stoned the home of Mizutani
Chōzaburō, a right-wing Socialist Diet member who was
supporting the U.S.-Japan Security Treaty.  This and
subsequent clashes with the police led to several
student arrests.[3]
    The second, and by far the more famous, incident
was the so-called Kyoto Emperor Incident.  The emperor,
on tour through the Kansai area in November, was met
at Kyoto University by about 1,000 student demonstrators shouting slogans, demands, and catcalls, including the frequent use of the familiar word for "you,"
kimi--an act that during the prewar period would have
been tantamount to lese majesty.  Such actions out-
raged conservatives; police were sent onto campuses
throughout Japan to investigate left-wing activities
and numerous clashes broke out between police and
students.  Eight Kyoto students, allegedly leaders of
the demonstration, were expelled,[4] and immediately
following these incidents Education Minister Amano
went before the Diet publicly to reprimand faculty
members for failing to exert sufficient leadership
over students.  He called too for the enactment of a
bill authorizing more stringent administrative controls over the university.[5]  In August the Ministry
of Education issued a white paper on student activities which attempted to demonstrate the narrowness of
the protesters' support and to link their actions to
a broad pattern of allegedly subversive activities by
the Left.  At the same time business groups began

issuing formal statements to the effect that radical students would not be hired.

The Popolo Theater Incident (February 20, 1952) served to heighten tensions even more.[6] An undercover policeman was found taking notes on attendance at a dramatic performance by the leftist Popolo Dramatic Troupe at Tokyo University. The policeman's confiscated notebook revealed that undercover monitoring of students was a normal part of police activities, reviving for many on campus the memory of prewar police surveillance of academics. Fears were further heightened by the government's efforts to pass an antisubversives bill in March of that same year and by the passage of the U.S.-Japan Security Treaty and Administrative Agreement, both of which the Left viewed as a return to militarism. Numerous leftist groups mobilized on May Day 1952, and a violent confrontation with police left two dead, 1,200 arrested, and scores seriously wounded.

Two additional events, the so-called Suita and Hirakata incidents, indicate still further the high level of confrontation. The first involved the attempted sabotage of American war equipment in the Suita area near Osaka by about 1,000 demonstrators on June 25, 1952. A violent clash with police guards left one student shot and many others injured. On the same day Osaka students marched to the suburbs of Hirakata and burned several homes belonging to those accused of cooperation with the American military.

It is within this context of mutual distrust, hostility, and confrontation between the progressives and the conservatives that one must view the government's attempts to tighten administrative control and the contrary reaction to such efforts. To the government, unremitting protest and demonstrations conducted by members of the progressive camp and many academics, particularly student organizations, against government ties to the United States, the government's military program, and many of its other broad policies represented a direct challenge to government authority and could not be allowed to continue. From the standpoint of the progressive camp, the actions of the government in these and other fields were seen as a consequence of the U.S. Occupation's reverse course and the return to power of the spiritual heirs of those who had led Japan through the tragedies of the 1930s and 1940s. Many intellectuals saw it as their moral obligation to protest against what they viewed as renascent militarism, especially in the light of the rather quiescent posture they and their predecessors

had taken prior to and during World War II.  Attempts
to tighten administrative control over the universities and counterattempts to block such moves were
hence part of a much broader struggle between the two
camps.

At the same time, a more immediate impulse for
the government action must be noted.  A key element
of the government's proposal of February 1952 would
have given the minister of education the power to
appoint the presidents of all national universities.
When the new system universities were organized in
1949, most national university presidents were appointed to four-year terms by the Ministry of Education.  By 1951-52 many universities had begun making
plans to elect their own presidents totally outside
the purview of the government.  Part of the government's plan was explicitly designed to prevent any
such unilateral selection.  Within the ministry there
was worry about the political consequences of such
elections, many bureaucrats fearing left-wing "take-
overs" on individual campuses.  Others were concerned
about the more educationally detrimental possibility
of infighting among academic factions during such
elections.[7]  In either event, many conservatives were
motivated by concern over this specific problem as
well as the broader issues of university governance.

The government proposal, known as the Ministry
of Education Secretariat Plan, sought to establish
the means for "appropriate governance" of the universities.  In contrast to the 1951 Board of Trustees
Plan, this new plan would have created no Board of
Trustees nor any Central Educational Advisory Board.
Its concerns were not with national supervision but
exclusively with changes in the distribution of powers
on campus.  The main structural change it proposed
involved the creation of a university council (hyōgikai) as the main administrative and policymaking
organ on campus.  Its responsibilities would include
personnel and disciplinary measures, with far fewer
guarantees of due process than then existed.  The
minister of education, meanwhile, would gain formal
power to appoint university presidents,who were to be
"subject to [his] supervision," an expansion of hitherto pro forma responsibilities and an indication to
many that the ministry planned to exercise strong
controls over the presidents' behavior once in office.
Strong protests from the academic Left, including
most notably Zengakuren, the Japan Teachers Union,
and the Japan Science Council, were delivered to the
minister of education.  Facing such strong protest
before the conservative camp had fully discussed the

problem and consolidated around a single position, the government denied that the exposed plan was in any way final and forwarded the entire matter to the newly established Central Education Council for further examination.

The secretariat plan was submitted to the council in March 1953. Between then and August the council's Special Committee on the University Problem held four general meetings. Its final recommendations, issued in February 1954, were virtual carbon copies of the Ministry of Education's earlier proposal concerning the powers of the university council and the subservience of the president to the minister of education. In addition, they suggested the establishment of a university advisory board (sangikai) to be composed of the president, "appropriate" faculty members, and "men of learning and experience" (i.e., nonacademics), which would make major policy for the university. Thus, as Kaigo and Terasaki have noted, "The proposed law was something which combined both the characteristics of bureaucratic control contained in the Ministry of Education Secretariat Plan and the system of governance based on outsiders in the plans that had preceded it."[8]

While the council was in the midst of its deliberations, however, the Ministry of Education took two significant bureaucratic steps that increased its overall powers in the area of university administration and management, thereby giving it some control over radical activities on campuses. The first of these was the issuance of a ministerial ordinance on April 22, 1953,[9] establishing a university council in all national universities having more than one faculty and such other national universities as were deemed desirable. The council was to be composed of the university president, individual faculty heads, from two to five professors from each faculty, and the heads of attached research institutes. Members were to be appointed by the minister of education, acting on the suggestion of the university president, and the council was to be given major deliberative powers over the budget, the establishment and dissolution of faculties or courses, personnel standards, student entry quotas, status and well-being of students, coordination of individual faculties, and many other areas. More importantly for the question of political autonomy, the council was to consider all matters of campus discipline, thereby removing such controls from the faculty conference.

The second measure, a day later, involved a communication (tsūtatsu) to the national university presidents, offering two plans for selecting subsequent presidents, both of which concentrated the bulk of the selection process within the university councils that had been the subject of the previous day's directive, thus further diminishing the role of the faculty conference.[10]

By these two measures the government was able to accomplish much of what was subsequently intended to be the subject of legislative debate. Taking place as they did between the lower house elections on April 20 and the upper house elections on April 24, they initially received little public or political attention. In fact, only three newspapers covered them as news items: the Mainichi (June 28), the Tōdai gakusei shimbun (June 11), and the Shakai taimusu (May 21). Of these, only the Mainichi was of national significance, and its coverage came two months after the events.[11]

As the directives became known and the realization spread that they effected bureaucratically items contained in proposed but unpassed legislation, they caused great progressive-conservative debate in the Diet.[12] The Ministry of Education, however, maintained that these were proper ministerial procedures and that they were, moreover, merely provisional measures intended to be operative only until the matters were resolved legislatively, which in fact they never were.

These two measures, taken while the Central Education Council was deliberating proposed legislation on the same matters, had a twofold effect on the policymaking process. On the one hand, they gave the Ministry of Education a great deal more influence over campus governance than at any time since the prewar period and hence minimized the need for legislation on the proposal of the Central Education Council. Simultaneously, however, they sharpened the opposition of the political Left and the academic community to the full legislative proposal, the political intentions and potentials of which were seen as even greater than when first proposed. Strong debate ensued in the Diet over the Central Education Council's proposal once it was presented legislatively, with the progressives united in their opposition. Outside the Diet public protests against the bill took place; additional opposition came from many of the major news media. The result was that the government finally tabled its proposal, secure in the knowledge of a partial victory through its administrative actions. The progressive camp, meanwhile, took heart from the fact that not everything the government had sought had been accomp-

lished.  Under the aegis of mutual "victory," the two
camps temporarily retreated from the issue of university administration, and from 1954 until the end of
the decade no substantive changes were sought and
none took place in the new balance struck on matters
of university governance.

Not at all coincidentally, this was a period of
serious decline in campus protest activities.  The
student movement in particular was exceptionally in-
active.  By 1955 only about 20 percent of the Japanese universities remained affiliated with Zengakuren[13] and the leadership of this student federation
was engulfed in serious internal dispute and self-
criticism.  This necessitated a period of reorienta-
tion and moderation for the entire organization which
lasted several years.


## THE EFFORTS OF 1960-63

In 1959-60 there was a dramatic upsurge in protest activities revolving around the renegotiated
U.S.-Japan Security Treaty, a nearly two-year coal
mine strike at Miike in Kyushu, the U-2 incident, and
a host of related issues that allowed the sparks of
left-right hostilities in Japan to blaze forth in
full.[14]  Once again on- and off-campus protests by
large numbers of students gave rise to governmental
efforts to tighten the formal controls over universities.  A series of speeches, communications, and directives from December 1959 through the major demonstrations of May-June 1960 indicates the Ministry of
Education's deep concern over the renewed protest
activities and the apparent inability or unwillingness of university officials to keep it in check.  In
January 1960 the minister of education called on university presidents to take "all appropriate actions"
including the expulsion of "those who are exerting a
significantly bad influence over the general student
body."[15]

This and other statements of concern sought to
jar university officials into taking action against
protesters.  Yet, coupled with the velvet glove of
indirection was the mailed fist: threats to alter the
administrative structure of the university system so
as to strengthen government control.  In a January
19, 1960, press conference LDP Vice-President Ōno
declared his intention "to eliminate government-sup-
ported humanities programs which simply serve to
support Zengakuren."[16]  Later that month Education
Minister Matsuda detailed a plan to concentrate

science and engineering departments in the national universities and to shift humanities and social science departments into the private universities. Implicit was the belief that such a change would reduce protest opportunities. Such a separation, however, was rapidly opposed by virtually all sectors of academia and was soon dropped, though it clearly impressed on academics the government's concern over the rising tide of protests and indicated the consequences if the protests continued.

In May 1960 a formal inquiry was submitted to the Central Education Council by Matsuda, calling for a comprehensive investigation of the problems in the university system established under the Occupation, "including a fundamental investigation of its aims, character, establishment, organizational arrangements, and administrative management."[17] Student protest itself was not explicitly mentioned as the basis for the request, although concern was expressed for ways to improve "the welfare and guidance of students." More explicitly, the minister declared: ". . . we believe there is a problem regarding the political activities of university personnel and the limits to university self-government."[18] The government in its formal directions to the council suggested quite openly the direction it believed should be taken to insure greater control:

> The minister of education under the Ministry of Education Establishment Law (Article 5, clause 18) does not have supervisory powers in regard to the general management of national universities. These in fact are entrusted to the self-government of the universities. As a result, we believe that the supervisory powers of the minister of education should be more explicitly acknowledged vis-a-vis national universities, which after all are established by means of public funds.[19]

In short, the Ministry of Education sought to increase its formal powers over the university, much as it had in the earlier policymaking efforts.

Following the June 15 protest concerning the security treaty in which one student was killed, Matsuda denounced university educators for having abandoned their responsibilities to keep students under greater control. On June 18, following continued student protests, he called for an investigation into concrete methods of prohibiting or mediating

in demonstrations at private universities.  In October
a lengthy report by the Investigative Council on the
Administration of School Corporations detailed lengthy
suggestions for such arbitrary proceedings.[20]  Then,
in December 1960 a twelve-member special advisory committee was established on the reform of university
administration.  This committee, separate from the
Central Education Council, which was at the time
studying the same question under a far broader man-
date, was given the primary responsibility of defining the powers of the university president and the
faculty conference and investigating ways to maintain
campus order in the face of antigovernmental activities by students and faculty members.[21]
    In January 1961 the committee submitted a six-
point report.  Participation in the selection of the
university president would be limited to permanent
lecturers and above.  Presidential powers would be
strengthened to include, among other things, the
selection of faculty chairmen.  The scope of powers
of the faculty conference and the university council
were to be reduced, especially in personnel matters.
Finally, membership in the faculty conference was to
be limited to full professors.[22]
    The plan would have centralized many powers on
campus and would have curtailed the ability of junior
faculty members, generally the more prominent left-
wing activists, to use the faculty conference as a
means to advance their causes or protect their jobs.
Also, by centralizing powers in the office of the
university president and the faculty chairmen and by
making them responsible to fewer university groups,
it was anticipated that these officials would be able
to deal more stringently with campus protest.  This
report became only one of many inputs into the calculations of the Central Education Council in its deal-
ings with the overall problems of the university, but
it signified the direction eventually taken.
    A major strengthening of measures to forestall
the Left from using the university to its political
advantage came in a May 1962 speech by Prime Minister
Ikeda, just prior to the issuance of the interim report by the Central Education Council.  Said Ikeda:

    When we consider the present condition of
    Japan, should we not be strongly disturbed
    by the fact that education is being used
    as a stepping stone to revolution . . . ?
    We must devise satisfactory measures to
    cope with this, and . . . accordingly I
    have directed Education Minister Araki to

reassess the present system of university administration.[23]

The reassessment of the university system proposed in the Central Education Council's report dealt with a wide range of issues, such as the role of the university in industrial society and the need for increased emphasis on science and technology. Its assessment of the administrative structure of the university and of the distribution of powers between university and state, however, are of paramount concern.

The 16th Subcommittee of the Central Education Council submitted its interim report ("Daigaku no kanri unei ni tsuite") on June 16, 1962.[24] It was greeted by widespread protest as its contents leaked out. Following the pattern of 1952-54 and the directions implied in the request for the investigations, the changes proposed were all in the direction of increased centralization of decision-making powers. Powers of individual faculty members and the faculty conference were diminished while the university council, faculty chairmen, the university president, and, most importantly, the minister of education would all gain substantial new powers.

The minister of education was given an explicit veto right over the selection of university presidents. As the logical continuation of the 1953 ministerial directives increasing the power of the university council in presidential selection, this new plan would have required the council to nominate more than one candidate for university president who would then be elected by the university faculty members. The incumbent president would notify the minister of education of the results of the election, and the latter could either accept its results or explicitly veto the choice of the faculty conference and call for another election.

In the area of faculty selection, similar concentration of administrative power was proposed. In contrast to the ongoing procedure in which the faculty conference made all choices for appointment and promotions, the council report proposed a system whereby the faculty chairman (gakubuchō) would compile a list of proposed appointees from which the faculty conference would merely make recommendations to the chairman of the faculty who in turn would notify the university president. The latter would then have the power, should he find the nominee unsuitable, to call for a new choice. Should he and the chairman be in accord, they would notify the minister of edu-

105

cation, who would make the final appointment. Thus, both the university president and the minister of education would have veto power over the selection of faculty members.

In addition, the university president and the minister of education would have veto power over the selection of faculty chairmen, who up until then were chosen by the faculty members. In short, virtually all personnel matters would involve a prescreening for suitability by some higher-level authority. Any subsequent choices would be made from among such approved candidates; these choices would in turn be subject to veto from higher administrative levels.

The powers of the university president and the faculty chairmen were to be expanded and strengthened in other areas as well. The president, who was then in charge of "administering school duties and having ultimate supervision over its personnel,"[25] was to become "the highest administrative and managerial official in the university." The faculty chairman, who had no formally defined duties other than being the department's representative on the university council, was to become "the executive in charge of the faculty and the chairman of the faculty conference."

Another centralizing element in the plan concerned participation in the faculty conference. At the time of the report, each university had its own system, with many universities allowing assistant professors, permanent lecturers, and in some cases even lower-level instructors and assistants to participate in the conference. The report included an absolute prohibition against such flexibility, limiting participation to full professors, except "in cases deemed necessary through consultation with the university council."

Finally, a "central organ" (chūo no kikan) was to be created on each campus. Its composition and formal powers were blurred in the initial report, but non-academic members would clearly be included as in plans of the early 1950s. This central organ was to be consulted in cases of "basic policies relating to education and research within the university" and was to be consulted by the minister of education in cases where he exercised his proposed veto rights over personnel.

Finally, these administrative changes were to be applicable not only in the national universities, as the introduction to the report makes clear:

> These means have been investigated with regard to national universities; however, it is hoped that the administration and management practices of the local public and

106

private universities will be examined in
light of these suggestions, since both
have elements in common with national
universities insofar as all are educational institutions.

Hence, the report implicitly would effect changes in
all universities in the country.
   If implemented, these changes would have meant a
significant increase in the powers of the Ministry of
Education vis-a-vis the university, as well as a centralization of authority on the campuses, and would
have given the government a strong weapon in insuring
that university presidents, faculty chairmen, and
faculty members would be at least minimally acceptable to the education bureaucracy, if not actually
close allies thereof.  Over the long run, the opportunities for these individuals to demonstrate open
hostility to the government or to challenge its policies would have been sharply diminished.  Clearly,
implementation of the Central Education Council's
plan would have moved universities far closer to the
conservative camp than they stood at the time.
   Japanese progressives were virtually unanimous
in denouncing the entire plan as inherently conservative and detrimental to university autonomy.  One
fear, as earlier with the Board of Trustees Plan presented during the Occupation, was that the inclusion
of those outside the university would not mean greater representativeness to the public but would simply
insure a distinctly conservative hue in the universities.  The expectation of most academicians was that
the minister of education would make appointments to
the "central organ" primarily from business and industry and that all selections made by the university
president would actually be under the indirect control of the ministry, since the president himself
would be subject to ministry approval.
   One critic complained as follows:

      Setting up within the universities advisory
      bodies that include outsiders will not
      necessarily reflect popular opinion in uni-
      versity adminsitration.  It may do nothing
      more than provide a way for capitalists and
      those in positions of authority to express
      opinions and exert pressure.[26]

   Other critics went further, declaring that any
legislation on the question of university administration could automatically be presumed to violate
the principle of university autonomy, since the

107

government had traditionally treated all education
as a tool of state policy. The Socialist Party, for
example, citing its version of government interference in the prewar period, stressed the dangers of
any government control over higher education, condemn-
ing any legislation, even that aimed explicitly at
student violence on campus. To the JSP, student violence was purely reactive, aimed at nothing short of
reducing government militarism. From this perspective, the party declared itself unalterably opposed
to any government intervention in university activities.[27]

The Japan Teachers Union, Zengakuren, and a number of ad hoc groups such as the Association to Protect University Autonomy engaged in various forms of
public protest to demonstrate opposition to all legislation on the question of university administration.[28]

In retort, the proposals were defended by the
conservative camp on the basis of the internal efficiency they would purportedly create. It was necessary, they contended, "to clarify matters that could
be considered by various university organs" and to
"eliminate internal factionalism in which status is
more important than ability."[29] Although few de-
fenses were made on ideological grounds, one notable
exception was offered by a member of the council:

> We need a system which acknowledges the
> powers of the minister of education to
> veto and demand the university's recon-
> sideration when a president is elected
> who is too much the representative of
> one faction's interests.[30]

Opposition from the established Left was to be
expected, given the bipolarity of earlier struggles
over university administration, the scope and specificity of the proposal advanced, and the highly
charged bipolarity of the general political climate.
Presumably the government and the Central Education
Council expected no less. More surprising was the
degree to which groups typically seen as moderate
were opposed. The University Accreditation Association and the Japan Science Council raised sharp criticisms, and university presidents, rarely the bearers
of radical guidons, joined in protesting the proposed
changes. Many contended that some reform of administrative and managerial procedures might be in order
but that the universities should be in charge of
their own housecleaning.[31] Support for these positions came as well from major newspaper editorials.[32]

The political anomaly of the strong opposition of university presidents to strengthening their own powers should be noted. Unquestionably, much of their opposition stemmed not so much from opposition to their own aggrandizement as to fear of the increased government powers they saw behind the increase in their formal powers. In the words of President Akabori Shirō of Osaka University:

> I am afraid that by giving a veto power to the minister of education, we shall be greatly adding to the political interference in the personnel matters of the university. This we cannot allow. The faculty conference must elect the president of the university and individual department heads. There is a danger of authoritative interference should the Ministry of Education and the so-called central-level organ come meddling in these matters, and they must therefore be restrained.[33]

Professor Ogawa of Tokyo University declared that he was afraid that the president would be given inappropriately large powers in the selection of personnel. "What is necessary," he declared, "is a system in which we rely on specialists to choose candidates from their specialized fields."[34]

As the political battlelines formed, a counterproposal put forward by the Association of National University Presidents (Kokuritsu Daigaku Kyōkai) finally became the rallying point for those opposed to the government's plans.[35] The informal protests of this influential group began almost as soon as the report of the Central Council was made public. Following informal complaints to him, on June 23 the minister of education addressed a meeting of the group and his first point was to stress that "there is absolutely no consideration being given to an unreasonable limitation of university autonomy."[36]

The first official action the presidents took came in an interim response to the proposals of the Central Education Council, which called on the government to respect the existing traditions of the various universities. It specifically opposed any standardization of administrative procedures through new laws, most notably the broad veto power over the university's elective organs, and it called for the admission of faculty members as low as lecturers to membership in the faculty conference and to participation in the selection of the university president.[37]

109

A more formal response came in the form of an explicit counterproposal issued on July 31, 1962.[38] This proposal of the university presidents differed substantially from that of the council. It proposed that the selection of university presidents be left to the prevailing customs within individual universities and that assistant professors and permanent lecturers be permitted to participate in elections. The university council would be more an independent board of inquiry responsible to the faculty than an organ of the office of the president, and the president was to be subservient to its decisions. Faculty chairmen would remain the elected representatives of the faculty and would be responsible to the faculty conference, which would continue to include assistant professors and permanent lecturers and to make all personnel decisions. As for the participation of non-academics, however, the report was somewhat closer to the council's proposal. It declared that "in cases where it is necessary to hear such opinions within the university, and to the extent that it does not interfere with the independence of the university, there should be no impediment to the establishment of organs in which suitable outsiders participate." Any outside organs set up, however, "would have to be limited to assisting in the functioning of the various [academic] organs . . . ," most notably the faculty conference.[39]

In short, the position taken by the Association of National University Presidents made few compromises of extant practices, supporting a far less centralized structure, subject to far less external influence than that in the original Central Education Council proposal. Moreover, it represented an explicitly political rather than an administrative model of the university in that it rested on no assumption of converging interests between government and university nor among university administration, university faculty, and students. Differences of opinion were seen as natural, and the administrative structure proposed was to be one in which the faculty conferences and the university councils retained power as political, quasi-legislative organs representing and attempting to reconcile this plurality of interests. Differences would have to be resolved more through politics from below than through administration from above.

In an effort to resolve the differences between the plans of the Central Education Council and the Association of National University Presidents, the prime minister and the cabinet secretary entered the picture. A consultation involving them, the education minister, and eight presidents of major national universities took place on September 18, 1962, only a few days after the formal issuance of the counterplan.[40] As a result primarily of this discussion, the Central Education Council revised its proposal, the most fundamental changes being the elimination of any references to a central organ, to a veto power for the minister of education, or to control over the selection of university personnel. References to the university president as "the highest administrative and managerial official in the university" were also deleted. Instead, he was labeled the official with "overall responsibility for the administration and management of the university." Moreover, the president was given no power to veto the selection of faculty chairmen or individual faculty members, while his own election was left open to lower ranking faculty members.[41]

These revisions mollified some of the more moderate opposition, but the committed Left and many academic groups remained strongly antagonistic. Numerous student demonstrations took place,[42] including a boycott of exams at Kyoto University.[43] The Japan Science Council, at its general meeting in December, declared its continued opposition to the government plan and called for the faculty conference to remain the focal point of university autonomy and for the president to be elected with no government interference.[44] Prefectural delegations also met with the minister of education to express their opposition.[45]

Most significantly, however, the presidents of the national universities and their association still refused to support the government plan, even though the revised plan included many of the changes they demanded. A number of questions still remained. The university president was still expected "to make a prudent evaluation" of those elected as faculty chairmen or chosen to join the faculty, and on the basis of such evaluations the minister of education would still make the final appointment.[46] Further, while many references to the centralization of powers were eliminated, government officials and Central Education Council members continued to talk as though elimination of formal references would not exclude their actual exercise. Kaya Seiji, a member of the Central Council, noted, for example, that the council had made no decision within its subsequent deliberations concerning a veto power for the minister of education; it simply decided not to touch on the question in its report.[47] Far more significantly, the minister of education, in testimony before upper house Budget Committee hearings, declared that since the minister of education already had the (pro forma) power to appoint university presidents, it was safe to interpret this to mean that he had veto powers as well.[48] Formal declaration in law, he said, was therefore unnecessary. At this same time he declared that he had every intention of submitting the revised plan to the next Diet for rapid legislative action,[49] the precipitate quality of which engendered further suspicion.

These fears were not relieved by further meetings between the minister of education and influential university presidents.[50] The presidents association, in an apparent effort to convince the government that the universities themselves were willing to consider administrative changes, established its own Advisory Council on University Administration to make recommendations on internal changes. In the meantime the association continued its strong opposition to the Ministry of Education's plans.

Such widespread opposition to the original plans of the Central Education Council and the Ministry of Education, most particularly the opposition of the Association of National University Presidents, was disturbing to the government. Virtually the entire academic community plus the organized political Left and most communications media were explicitly opposed to the plan. Although by no means strong enough to insure legislative defeat, this coalition had great potential to influence public opinion and had successfully stymied the government a decade before. The memories of government interference in universities during the prewar period, while waning, had by no means been erased from the minds of many Japanese, while the public demonstrations of 1960 that had brought down the Kishi government were at least as fresh in the minds of Japanese conservatives. To have pushed through the plan in such an atmosphere of tension would also have meant a sharp deviation from the Ikeda government's "low posture" politics and surely would have necessitated great efforts on its part.[51]

New legislative proposals were prepared in December 1962, based on the recommendation of the Central Education Council,[52] but as they emerged, a split developed within the government as to procedure regarding changes in university administration. At a cabinet meeting on January 11, 1963, the minister of education stressed his desire to have the broad-scale bill submitted to the Diet for rapid consideration. Cabinet officials, from the Legal Systems Division in particular, opposed this course of action, arguing instead for a program of incremental revision of existing laws.[53] Within the LDP, too, opposition to the Ministry of Education bill emerged, with Secretary-General Maeo insisting on no submission, his resistance based on the fear that if the bill were submitted to the Diet at that particular time, the opposition parties would be able to merge their opposition to it with that to the Japan-Korea treaty coming up at the same time. Opposition to the latter was certain to be strong, and Maeo argued that it was necessary to deprive the Left of any opportunity to fuse the two separate issues, making for a stronger opposition campaign. Postponing the Ministry of Education bill, he argued, would make it possible to keep the two activites separate and thereby defuse both.[54]

As the split within the LDP and the government grew, the conflict over the bill shifted to within the conservative camp. A joint delegation from the LDP's Education Committee (Bunkyō Bukai) and the Educational Investigation Campaign (Bunkyō Chōsakai) met with Education Minister Araki to protest any delay in submitting the bill, and another delegation met with Cabinet Secretary Kurogane to register opposition.[55] On January 25, 1963, the cabinet decided to postpone legislative consideration of the bill.[56] The minister of education and others supporting the bill expressed their hope that the bill would be submitted in the near future, and publicly the government claimed that the purpose of the delay was to allow "constructive public opinion in hopes of getting a better bill in a year or so."[57] In fact, the issue faded at this point, just as it had a decade earlier.

Parallels pervade the two cases investigated. Both concerned a basically nondisaggregable issue of high ideological salience, broad in scope, and quite specific in probable impact. Both were marked by a policymaking process characterized by a high level of confrontation between Japan's two political camps. Protests and demonstrations by progressive camp members over on- and off-campus issues stimulated efforts by the conservative camp to tighten controls over university activities and personnel through administrative measures, which in turn stimulated even greater opposition activity by progressives, usually with the strong support of most elements of the academic community. Bureaucratic activity in the drafting of proposed change, in the articulation of political positions, and occasionally in the implementation of specific changes was high, but the arena of ultimate decision-making was the Diet, where, despite clear conservative majorities, the proposals were stopped in the face of widespread intra- and extraparliamentary opposition.

This last point is of particular interest. When direct confrontation between progressives and conservatives took place, the progressives won. The Left's successful blockage of government legislative attempts through massive and coordinated efforts showed its tremendous ability to exercise a veto over the actions of a government having numerical superiority in the parliament. This ability rested heavily on a unified coalition of all forces in the progressive camp and on support from major newspapers, university officials, and their organizations, and some component of that ephemera, public opinion. Faced with such opposition, the conservative camp, itself not fully united, was forced to recognize practical limits on what even a legislative majority could insure.

## THE POLITICAL CONFLICT OF 1968-69

Most of these same phenomena surrounded the policymaking process involved in the final case in university administration, that of 1968-69. One notable exception, however, is that for the first time in the postwar period the government succeeded in its efforts to alter radically administrative powers in the university system. Whereas in the two earlier cases the Left had been united and strongly backed by a number of allies, in 1968-69 it was internally divided, had lost most of its earlier allies outside the hard-core members of the progressive camp, and faced a far more united and committed conservative camp, changes that altered completely the legislative outcome of government efforts to centralize control.

For most Japanese progressives the year 1970 was exceptionally important. It was then that Japan could legitimately demand a renegotiation of its military treaty with the United States, including the treaty's termination. While the progressive camp was openly hostile to the conservatives on many issues and sought constantly to confront the government on many of them, the issue of the military relationship with the United States was the keystone of much of this opposition. Hence, 1970 took on major significance as a target year for camp confrontation.

Student groups in particular became increasingly active as the target date drew near. Moreover, a shift in tactics occurred as student activities became increasingly centered on campuses, in contrast to earlier periods when the bulk of student protest took place off-campus and involved primarily noncampus issues. A survey of major "incidents" on university campuses for the period 1950-64 shows an average of fewer than one per year. In 1965 there were 25, a dramatic rise that turned out to represent nothing more than the first minor breeze before an onrushing tornado. The number of campus protests increased during 1966 and 1967 and climaxed in 1968 and 1969. In 1968, for example, 116 universities experienced significant conflicts, and a month-by-month analysis of conflicts in 1969 shows even further escalation. In January 18 schools experienced conflicts; in March, 43; in June, 57; in July, 75; and in October a high of 77 schools underwent major protest activities.[58]

Police figures for this period indicate their heavy activity on university campuses. There were 31 campus actions in 1968 involving more than 10,000 police and resulting in 425 arrests. For 1969 the figures were up to 938 campus actions, involving 243,000 police and resulting in more than 3,500 arrests.[59]

Moreover, these figures represent only on-campus disputes. Off campus, student activists began engaging police in numerous confrontations starting in late 1967 with the so-called First Haneda Incident. There, students wearing helmets and armed with staves and rocks sought to prevent by force Prime Minister Satō's departure for South Vietnam. The results were one dead, 58 arrested, and more than 600 injured. Similar confrontations followed, highlighted by the Second Haneda Incident (an attempt in November 1967 to prevent Satō from visiting the United States); the efforts in January 1968 to prevent the U.S. aircraft carrier Enterprise from docking at Sasebo; efforts to close Shinjuku station in October 1968 to prevent trains from carrying U.S. fuel allegedly used in the war in Vietnam; and dozens of lesser ventures.

Both on- and off-campus, student protesters focused their opposition on a number of explicitly political targets: U.S. military occupation of Okinawa, the war in Indochina, U.S. military financing of university projects, the attendance at university courses of members of Japan's Self-Defense Forces, the crash of a U.S. military jet on one campus, and, behind them all, the ultimate target of the U.S.-Japan Security Treaty.[60] This situation was similar to those of 1952-54 and 1960-63, when broader political questions formed the backdrop to the problem of university administration.

115

Nonetheless, a number of explicitly administrative problems arose at the same time, as student groups made fundamental criticisms of the ongoing university system. They attacked proposed tuition raises, demanded student control over dormitories and student unions, complained about inadequate teaching, equipment, and curricula, opposed various punishments meted out to students, insisted on limiting the number of entering students, and called for an expanded student role in the selection of university officials. All of these generated protest at one university or another.[61]

In several universities students had long been granted some significant role in such matters as selection of the university president, governance of student unions and dormitories, and the like. But underlying the protests of the late 1960s was the demand for acknowledgment of students as a legitimate political force on campus, as more than the passive purchasers of educational services.[62]

The explicit and widespread student demands for increased participation and powers within the university posed a direct challenge to the system and complicated university-government relations. In earlier times the balance of power between university administrators, faculty, and the government would decide the issue of university administration. To these debates were added the pressures for explicit powers for students and student organizations.

From 1965 until early or mid-1968, the problem of government policy and U.S.-Japan relations remained in the background and university issues predominated. Consequently, the problem of university administration remained rather isolated from broader national political currents. The government and members of the university were primarily involved, while other explicitly political actors, such as the parties or nonacademic pressure groups, showed little overt interest in the "university problem," as it came to be called.

The Ministry of Education was mainly concerned with the continuance of the "normal functioning of the universities." University administrators were explicitly concerned with students' substantive requests for internal changes in administration, seeking on an ad hoc basis to delimit these as much as possible. Neither the government nor the university administrators at this time gave signs of being anxious to reconsider the recently buried problem of overall administrative relations between government and university, and neither proposed any major structural changes in the governance of universities.

The government's light-handed approach in contrast to 1952-54 and 1960-63, when it sought so explicitly to strengthen its controls, reflected the fact that it had "more important" matters on its collective mind in the area of foreign policy.[63] But it also reflected a change in power within the Ministry of Education. During most of the 1950s and 1960s the ministry was dominated by what came to be called the "moralist" faction--a group of hard-liners committed to rectifying what they felt to be the improper balance between government and university powers and committed to eliminating left-wing influences in universities. The result had been a constant push for increased government control of universities achieved even at the expense of a high degree of conflict with the academic community and the political progressives. Gradually, however, a group known generally as the "modernists" emerged, individuals convinced that controversy between the ministry and the universities was neither necessary nor desirable. Instead they supported a more cooperative and cooptive posture,[64] particularly as regards university administrators. Mutual needs and interests were to be encouraged, and more subtle forms of influence were to be employed. The influence of the modernists came to be felt by the mid-1960s, and there was a juggling for power between the two groups until 1968, when the power of the modernists was consolidated with the appointment of Sakata Michita as minister of education. Sakata undertook a series of personnel shifts that put the modernists in the key positions in higher education, and for the most part the moralists were isolated from positions of influence. As a result of the modernists' increased role, however, the Ministry of Education became less likely to respond to every campus protest with cries for greater control by the ministry and increased its efforts to ally with university administrators and senior faculty.

Thus, when a one-month strike broke out at Waseda University over a proposed tuition raise, the education minister stressed that the universities and not the government should act to contain student protest.[65] This approach was taken, too, in a speech by the minister of education before the June 1966 meeting of the Association of National University Presidents. Citing the need for high quality administration to meet the threat posed by the student groups, he suggested that the presidents themselves should act on reforms from within their own campuses.[66]

As campus actions escalated, the Ministry of Education continued to press university administrators to initiate preventive measures by themselves. It

117

was not until June 1967, as the protests expanded, that the slightest hint came that the government might alter the existing administrative relations if university administrators did not deal with the protests autonomously.  Education Minister Kennoki stated that "despite the labors and efforts of university presidents, campus unrest has not been brought to a halt."  Consequently, he went on, "it is regrettable that new and improved devices will have to be added to the mechanics of university administration and management, starting with the organization and management of student guidance, in contrast to former times when you were more protective of students."[67]

National university administrators, while not unresponsive to the pleas for a cooperative approach, continued to focus more on a different dimension of the problem.  A November 1966 report by a committee of national university presidents dealt largely with the problem of preserving their own authority in the face of demands for increased power for student self-government associations, rather than with the problem of primary concern to the government: curtailing protest actions.[68]

Arguing that it was desirable to respond to legitimate demands for student participation,[69] the administrators then contended that "self-government by students is not an inherent right which exists in isolation from the university, which is essentially a teaching and research institution. . . . Students who stress unlimited self-government," it warned, "simply do not understand the true nature of the university."[70] Elsewhere the report suggested that student participation be limited to the areas of sports and extracurricular activities and noted that, in whatever areas students were allowed to govern themselves on campus, administration officials would be acting as overseers to insure that no administrative powers be allowed to devolve into the hands of students who were "administratively irresponsible."[71]  But the report also declared that academic freedom demanded that no police be allowed on campus without the explicit consent of administrators, regardless of the scope of campus protests.

Furthermore, no tangible changes in the administrative structure of the universities were proposed to curtail protest activities.  The report merely suggested that order was a precondition for the fulfillment of the university's teaching and research functions.[72]  Thus, from the standpoint of the Ministry of Education, the report was most unsatisfactory and suggested to the moralists that the modernists' strategy of compromise was unfeasible.

118

The off-campus student violence of the First and
Second Haneda incidents (October 8 and November 12,
1967) and at Sasebo (January 17-23, 1968) brought
strong protests from the Ministry of Education directed at university presidents,[73] who were urged to
exert increased control over student activities and
to provide sufficient "guidance" to prevent such activities. The government, however, still leaned more
toward cooperation than confrontation. In a September 29, 1967, communication (tsūchi naikan) the ministry, in an effort to limit campus protest activities on International Antiwar Day (October 21), re-
minded university presidents that "it is essential
that political neutrality be maintained within the
universities" and urged strong measures of campus
control so that "violent or political actions . . .
will be prevented." Where such actions took place,
severe discipline by university officials was urged.
"All prudent measures must be taken in regard to
[baneful] influences that could be exerted on [stu-
dents]."[74]

Increasingly, however, the government began to
raise the possibility that it would consider altering
the administrative structures of universities if university officials could not contain protest activities. On November 17, 1967, for example, Minister of
Education Kennoki called a meeting of all Japanese
university presidents to discuss the situation. While
cooperation between university and government officials remained the dominant theme, he also hinted at
what might happen should student actions persist:
"Widespread debate," he declared, "is taking place
throughout Japan over the need to strengthen administrative authority so as to improve student guidance
and administrative efficiency. . . . There are rumors
concerning [the need to take] stern measures for the
maintenance of public peace and order."[75]

A month later the suggestions from the minister
became more blunt: "I hope that the universities
themselves will carry out investigations aimed at
establishing responsible procedures . . . before I am
forced to take legal measures on the matter of university administration."[76]

As if further to stiffen the collective backbone
of university administrators, the Executive Council
of the LDP demanded a cut in the national universities' budget, one of the first official party statements on the problem during this period. Ōkōchi
Kazuo, president of Tokyo University and of the Association of National University Presidents, quickly declared his opposition to such a step, stating that
university presidents were making constructive efforts

to end protest activities. The Education Committee of
the LDP, apparently with the support of the Ministry
of Education, agreed, suggesting explicitly that the
university problem not be tied to budgetary considerations, and the budgetary threat was dropped.[77]    But
the proposed budgetary cut evidently served as an
appropriate political warning, for the formal position
of the university administrators began stiffening appreciably.

A second interim report on the student problem
was presented by the Association of National University Presidents in late 1967, the tone of which was
far stronger than that of the 1966 report.  Three
major points were stressed: 1) students cannot be
allowed to disregard existing regulations; 2) limits
on campus activities must be maintained; and 3) all
activities that "pamper" students must be corrected.[78]
The final report of the committee on the student movement was totally silent on the questions of student
self-government and student participation which had
earlier been of prime concern.[79]    Rather, it stressed
that administrators and faculty had strong responsibilities for guiding student behavior; they were directed to instill within students an overall respect
for learning and scholarship rather than protest and
violence.  In order to curb protests and presumably
to ward off direct governmental action, the report
also suggested that police be called when university
officials were unable to handle violations of university regulations.

The fear of government action became increasingly
obvious.  In a statement parallel to that made earlier
by Education Minister Kennoki, the Association of
National University Presidents declared, "We must explain to students that university regulations are
self-imposed rules aimed at allowing the university
to protect its own autonomy and that therefore respect
for them is essential to the existence of the university.  They must be made to realize that to ignore
the internal regulations of the university and to disregard its rules is to follow a course of action
whereby they themselves will destroy the autonomy of
the university."[80]

Despite the university administration's efforts
to placate the Ministry of Education, relations between the two cooled as increasing threats emerged
from the government.  Two incidents in April and May
1968 dimmed drastically any earlier chances for cooperation between the two sides.

On April 15 a meeting between Ministry of Education officials and national university officials

similar to that of the previous November was scheduled to take place the next month, and the minister of education called on the presidents of thirty-four universities to meet with him and other ministry officials for a discussion of "the student problem and university autonomy." President Ōkōchi of Tokyo University refused to attend, declaring testily that "on basic university problems we will follow the usual procedure of determining opinions within Tokyo University and then having the president make these known to the minister of education."[81] Following Ōkōchi's lead, several other presidents refused to attend the meeting; those who attended were sharply critical of its having been called, and an explanation was demanded from Vice-Minister Saitō. On balance, little more than a cooling of relations between government and university administrators was accomplished.[82]

The second incident took place in May, when the minister of education called for a similar conference of all faculty chairmen of national universities. The plan was to deliver a formal opinion on the student movement, and this time the meeting was canceled when the academics registered strong opposition on the grounds that the conference "could damage the independent character of the universities."[83]

In late June 1968 the Ministry of Education made it clear that it would no longer rely on simple cooperation with university administrators but would take steps of its own to curtail student protest activities. Solving the student problem, asserted Minister of Education Nadao, "is not the responsibility of a single university official [i.e., the university president]; moreover, no one can assert that it is a problem that can be solved by the universities themselves. . . . Great limits must inevitably be recognized on the autonomy of universities and . . . emphasis on university autonomy must be kept in tune with contemporary realities in order to insure the understanding and support of society in general."[84]

Tensions continued to grow, and in November 1968 the Ministry of Education called on the Central Education Council, which was then in the process of an overall reexamination of the university system, to establish a special subcommittee to consider explicit governmental measures to meet the growing tide of protest. Submission of the problem to the Central Council in itself signaled a significant increase in government action and a decrease in reliance on university administrators, but the terms of the Ministry of Education's reference were even clearer: ". . . we consider it necessary to reach a conclusion as soon as possible on the organizational and managerial measures which should be taken to secure the normal operation of Japan's university education."[85] The council was ordered to consider "measures to terminate disturbances which are difficult for the universities themselves to resolve."[86]

From November 1968, when the Central Education Council was first brought into the picture, until April 30, 1969, when it issued its report, the Ministry of Education moved increasingly closer to a position of generating and supporting legislation that would bring about major changes in university-state relations. During the period the problem of protest escalated drastically. First, at a number of individual universities student power victories were won. At Chuo University, student protest, combined with faculty opposition, led to the resignation of the university president and to a lowering and then a complete cancellation of a proposed tuition raise.[87]

At Nihon University, Japan's most factory-like "mass production university" with an enrollment of more than 100,000, an administrative embezzlement of $5.5 million (some of which allegedly found its way into the political coffers of the LDP) led to campus protests from leftist student groups. These were met with attacks by physical education club members and later a 400-man "private army," and the initially small protest grew into a major confrontation. Protesting students eventually forced President Furuta to attend several mass bargaining sessions, after one of which he "confessed" to several major errors and agreed to work for the accomplishment of various student demands, including the resignation of the trustees. On October 9 it was decided that the trustees would resign, and although Furuta subsequently reneged on these promises, the initial reaction of students and outsiders was to consider this a clear-cut student victory.[88]

A third victory took place at Nagoya University in late November 1968, when, after prolonged protest, students were granted the right to participate formally in a committee that would screen and nominate new faculty.[89]

These student victories and many others like them served to refocus attention in a dramatic way on the question of student participation, particularly on the part of the minister of education and the Central Education Council's inquiry. Moreover, the issue began to arouse broader interest and participation by previously quiescent groups. Particular

122

concern was expressed over the danger that such victories would feed the fires of protest throughout the country's campuses. President Nagasawa Kunio of the Japan Federation of Private Universities said at the time the Chuo tuition increase was voided:

> Chuo University seems to have acted rashly. If such a step sets a precedent, the private universities will no longer be able to raise tuition and fees. While it would be nice if we could go without increasing tuition, in fact if tuition is not increased, the private universities will run into greater financial difficulties only to accelerate the qualitative deterioration of private educational institutions.[90]

The increased concern over this problem of student power led also to a sharp rebuke by Ministry of Education officials when Nagoya University decided to give students a larger role in the hiring process. "Direct participation by students in personnel decisions is not permitted by existing law. . . . For Nagoya University to give students such rights is both excessive and illegal."[91]

The new Chuo University president specifically sought to halt any student momentum. "Any student participation in the management of the university is out of the question," he declared, and in a comic anachronism he advised faculty members to step up homework assignments to keep students otherwise occupied.[92]

Prime Minister Satō himself was reported to have been visibly infuriated during a cabinet meeting following the mass bargaining session involving his friend, President Furuta. Such actions, he declared, had to be viewed in political rather than educational terms.[93]

Furthermore, a number of LDP members agreed to cooperate with university administrators at Nihon University, and their support was instrumental in enabling Furuta to refuse to implement the administration-student agreement. This action also represented a substantial movement within the conservative party to take formal action against protesting students.[94]

Such student victories broadened the scope of involved political actors and put further pressures on the government to resolve the entire university problem. But even more significant in increasing the scope of the issue and the pressures on the Ministry of Education was the extension of student strikes to Tokyo University.

The Tokyo action began in January 1968, escalated throughout the year, and culminated in a nationally televised two-day battle between students and police that resembled the siege of a medieval castle (in this case, Tokyo University's Yasuda Hall). Coming as it did in the midst of a host of other struggles, the strike at Todai focused attention on the university problem as could no other individual strike. The first modern university in Japan, Todai remained unquestionably the best university in the country in the minds of most Japanese--both political actors and average citizens--and was the alma mater of the prime minister, the bulk of the cabinet, and scores of leaders throughout the country.[95] Any expectations that the problem could be quietly resolved by the cooperative efforts of university administrators and the Ministry of Education were totally shattered by the experiences of Todai.[96]

The general political shock presented by an immobilized Tokyo University was further compounded on January 10, 1969, when students there won a major victory in the form of a "Note of Confirmation" whereby Acting President Katō agreed in principle to ten major categories of student demands, including the dismissal of two faculty members, an apology for "arbitrary" administrative actions, virtual amnesty for students, and an overall expansion of student powers.[97]

The reaction within the LDP was particularly strong to what was viewed as an unwarranted capitulation by university officials to student violence. A joint meeting of members of the LDP's Research Council on the Educational System and the party's Education Committee on January 12 declared that the Note of Confirmation went too far on several points, and urged top party leaders to take official action.[98] The note was debated at the cabinet meeting of January 20[99] and was referred to the Jurisprudential Section of the Cabinet Legislative Bureau for an official legal opinion. The Ministry of Education on February 8 strongly denounced the move, decrying, among other things, the fact that "'self-reflection' seems to be required only of university officials, while students are made to appear blameless for the disputes, and their acts of violence and disruptions of order go unpunished, even though the Japanese people are far more concerned about the latter."[100]

The ministry was particularly critical of the possible influence this note would have on other

universities:[101] "If the university authorities do
not punish the occupation of buildings, blockades,
bombings, confinements, violence, and injury on the
grounds that 'there were serious mistakes made by
university officials' . . . this will adversely affect the settlement of future campus disputes and it
is a very regrettable attitude for the university to
take."[102] Stress was laid on the need to curtail,
not expand, the rights of student self-government
associations,[103] and finally the ministry noted that
"to grant the right of collective bargaining to student self-government associations . . . is to recognize their position as participants in the administration and management of the university. . . . This is
a serious problem that will result in radical revisions in the present concepts of the university, the
university system, and university autonomy."[104]

The increase in general attention to the university problem at this time was remarkable. Jour-
nalist Fukashiro Junrō noted somewhat plaintively how
he sought in vain for policy statements by the major
political parties and major political groups during
the summer and fall of 1968.[105] The issue had some-
how remained "nonpolitical" to the extent that most
of the normally involved political bodies had made no
formal comments on the subject. By late fall, however,
the situation had changed dramatically.

In November the police began to issue monthly
statistics on the number of university conflicts
that had occurred or were still in progress. In
November and December all five major political parties put forth tentative plans, proposals, or recommendations on the university problem. So too did the
Japan Science Council, the Japan Teachers Union,
the Japan Federation of Employers Associations, and
dozens of other organizations with more or less political relevance to universities.[106]

In addition, literature on the subject proliferated. Table 5-1 summarizes one bibliographer's figures on books and articles published about the university and the student problems in the period 1965-69.
Allowing for some time lag in publication, the tremendous jump in general interest in 1968-69 is clear.

As the interests of these many actors began to
focus on the university problem, the entire political complexion of the problem expanded well beyond
the original student protesters on the one hand and,
on the other, the Ministry of Education and university administrators, who were groping for some kind
of cooperative arrangement. And as more actors entered the picture, the problem took on the more

TABLE 5-1

Publications on the University
and Student Problem

| Year | Books | Articles, etc. | Total |
|------|-------|----------------|-------|
| 1965 | 27    | 229            | 256   |
| 1966 | 41    | 494            | 535   |
| 1967 | 25    | 401            | 426   |
| 1968 | 89    | 928            | 1017  |
| 1969 | 275   | 1746           | 2021  |

Source: Kitamura Kazuyuki, Daigaku, gakusei
mondai bummoku mokuroku (Bibliography on
the Problems of Universities and Students)
(Tokyo: IDE, 1971).

classic dimensions of a full-fledged camp struggle.
However, while in the earlier confrontations
over problems of university administration most members of the academic community joined a reasonably
united progressive camp in opposition to government
efforts to alter the structures of university governance, in 1968-69 this unity dissolved in the face of
incompatible positions on various component issues.
No longer was the problem defined solely in terms of
government intervention or nonintervention in university governance.  Rather, the issues of student
participation and the tactics of student protest were
interwoven with the broader concern in ways that reduced the sharpness found in earlier bipolar patterns.
During late 1968 and until the promulgation of the
Law of Provisional Measures Concerning University
Administration in August 1969, these three questions
continued to be interlocked in ways that prevented
the reemergence of the progressive-academic coalition
that with media support had been successful in blocking past government efforts to legislate changes in
the university system.
    Table 5-2 outlines the positions of the major
political actors at this time on the three issues.
Although there was rather widespread agreement that
students should have some voice in the running of
the university, the scope of this voice and the means
whereby it would be heard were subject to widespread
disagreement.  Only a few of the most left-wing
groups took the position that students, as integral
members of the university community, should have

126

something approaching an equal voice on all university matters. Slightly more moderate were suggestions that decisions be established democratically within the framework of the individual universities, generally, however, with the stress on increased formal participation.

University administrators, the LDP, and the business community, on the other hand, explicitly rejected any such changes. Although rarely asserting that students should be merely the docile recipients of education, they continued to maintain that broad student opinion should be heard but that formal participation should be minimal and/or limited to areas exclusive of personnel, finance, and curriculum.

On student tactics the division was also rather clear-cut. Even some groups generally regarded as progressive were sharply opposed to violence, with the Minsei student groups and the Communist Party explicitly denouncing those who engaged in such activities as counterrevolutionary Trotskyites.

Thus, on these two issues which were so intimately related to the overall question of the entire problem of university-government relations, the position of the main members of the conservative camp were, despite some shadings of hue, essentially unified, while in contrast the progressive camp and the academic community were split. Significantly, organizations of university administrators, whose earlier positions had been quite close to those of the progressive camp, now agreed with the conservatives on two major issues: student participation and student tactics. In this respect, the modernists within the Ministry of Education proved to be correct; there was indeed a good deal of common interest between the conservatives and many university administrators.

On the principle of governmental intervention, the split was different. There the progressives were uniformly opposed to any legislative actions that would increase governmental powers to intervene in university disputes. Moreover, national university administrators collectively adhered to this position.[107] The organizations of private university officials, meanwhile, remained officially uncommitted, although many individual members privately favored intervention. The split between progressives and university administrators on other issues, however, left the advocates of intervention in a comparatively strong position. What other alternatives, they could ask, could end violence and retain limits that were otherwise favored on the political power of students?

Moreover, the position of the conservatives was

127

TABLE 5-2

Positions of Major Actors on the University Problem, 1969

| | Participation | Strikes, Barricades, | Government Intervention |
|---|---|---|---|
| Zenkyōtō New Left | Maximize (varying demands on different campuses) | Justified in face of reactionary government and university system | Opposed |
| Japan Socialist Party | Must plan student participation in the management and administration of university with a focus on election of president and other personnel matters, curriculum, budget, self-government of student unions, dormitories, and discipline problems. | Must recognize fundamental rights of students, including collective actions and bargaining | Opposed |
| Japan Teachers Union | Maximize participation within framework suitable to each university; preserve the freedom of democratic actions of university self-government associations | Violence is only the result of undemocratic nature of the university and society | Opposed |
| Japan Science Council | Must be able to participate in fixed ways with each university deciding its own system | Strikes abuse right of students to receive an education, but must see violence in the context of government intervention | Opposed |
| Minsei Students and Communist Party | Establish an all-university conference, including students, to govern the university | Present violence is antirevolutionary action of Trotskyites; encourages repression | Opposed |

128

TABLE 5-2 (continued)

| | | | |
|---|---|---|---|
| Association of National University Presidents | Self-government not an unlimited student right; participation in limited, unspecified areas | Violence cannot be permitted under any circumstances | Opposed |
| Japan Federation of Private Universities | Essential to have student participation but not in personnel, finance, or educational matters | Students who engage in politically motivated group violence must be strongly criticized | (No public statement; many members privately favored) |
| Japan Association of Private Colleges | Hear student opinion but not in finance, education, or personnel | Cannot permit group violence or mass bargaining | (No public statement but membership favored) |
| LDP | True opinion of students should be reflected; no accession to demands of minority students; no rights regarding personnel, finance, exams, or curriculum | Violent acts disregard law and destroy order; must prohibit antisocial acts that would overthrow democracy and subvert academic freedom and university autonomy | Favored |
| Business: | | | |
| Japan Committee for Economic Development | Cannot deny student opinion if reflected within context of each university but would cut power of student self-government associations | Cannot support violence regardless of motives | Favored |
| Japan Federation of Employers Associations | Students are members of community, not laborers; opinions should be heard, but no bargaining | No mass bargaining; student violence is general problem of law and order beyond the university | Favored |

129

bolstered by an increasingly restive public opinion which, while not actively supportive of government intervention, could also see no alternative. A poll taken by Asahi shimbun in May 1969 showed that even though only 25 percent favored a law granting the government intervention power, an additional 28 percent, while in principle not approving this expansion of power, felt that there was no alternative under the circumstances.[108]

The report of the Central Education Council's 24th Subcommittee managed to blend the component issues to suggest that there could be no alternative to granting the government the power to intervene in university disturbances. On the specific matter of student participation, the report made an explicit distinction between "hearing student views" and allowing for student "representation"; only the former was advocated. University officials were called upon to pay due regard to student attitudes, but the student was seen as a "learner" who should "trust the scholarly attainments of his teachers and follow the educational program and guidance of the university."[109] The report also declared that "it is not appropriate, in view of the status of students, to recognize any system that would enable them to participate in any final decision-making bodies or to reject the decisions of such bodies."

From this perspective student self-governing associations, which had often been the organizational mainstay of campus political activities, came in for strong criticism. Of particular concern was the system of automatic student membership. Membership should be made voluntary, advised the report, and where it was not, "there should be severe restrictions on the areas of [their] activities so as not to infringe on the fundamental freedom of their individual members."

On the question of protests and violence, too, the report took a position advocated by most conservative groups and by university administrators. "At the center of the present university disturbances there are groups of politically motivated students more interested in the destruction of the existing [social and political] order than in the reform of conditions within the universities. To counter them, measures must be considered that will eliminate violence completely and will protect the order of the university."

With such positions on students, student participation, and violence so clearly marked out, the concluding section delineating the "responsibilities of

the universities and the government in terminating
present university disturbances" was something of an
anticlimax.  Upon the eruption of serious disturbances, universities were urged "to concentrate decision-making and executive powers in the hands of
suitable university administrators."  The government
was urged to do two things: 1) "to advise university
officials of the steps they must take . . . when disturbances occur" and 2) "to take steps to enable the
universities' founders to carry out the temporary
closing of the school for a period of up to six
months."

This section of the report was easy to anticipate in view of the fact that, throughout the deliberations of the subcommittee of the Central Council,
the conservative camp in general had been recommending,
and the government had in fact been taking, a number of
steps to do precisely what the committee report was
recommending.  In February the Japan Federation of Employers Associations had made precisely the same proposal to close schools affected by prolonged violence.
And numerous groups within the LDP were pushing for
strong government powers to act in such cases.  In
particular, the LDP's Research Council on the Educational System in early March[110] and Nishioka Takeo
and Kono Yōhei of the party's Specialists Committee
on the Educational System in early April[111] called for
a variety of measures to strengthen university administration and the government, as well as to cut back
the powers of the student  self-governing associations.

This growing pressure was bolstered by a number of
concrete government steps.  On November 16 the Ministry
of Education took the unusual step of issuing a direct
communication to the administrators of four national
universities undergoing student strikes, ordering them
to take measures to resume normal operations.  On December 23 the government canceled the spring entrance
examinations for Tokyo University, and three weeks
later Todai administrators and government officials
called in the police to end the student strike.  Then,
on April 21, one week before the final report of the
Central Council, the Ministry of Education issued a
communication entitled, "On the Maintenance of Normal
Order within the Universities,"[112] in which administrators were ordered among other things to "cooperate
positively with police authorities in taking rapid and
appropriate measures to maintain order on campus" when
violence appeared likely.  A number of specific student activities conducive to violence were expressly
banned, and prosecution was ordered for faculty engaging in illegal activities.

Thus, the general approach of strengthening the powers of university administrators and the Ministry of Education became clearly delineated, and the government was determined to introduce legislation to curtail the protest activities during that session of the legislature. The only delay was the wait for the final report of the Central Council, which would provide additional legitimation and some legislative specifics. By the end of April the questions remaining concerned only the specific form of the legislation and whether or not the proposed actions could be successfully legislated. The first problem revolved primarily around arrangements within the conservative camp. The concern and confidence of the conservatives on this matter are particularly noteworthy in that, contrary to normal practice, the government proposed its legislation with virtually no attempt to insure a conservative consensus on specifics. In fact, as a number of political journalists have noted, the Ministry of Education draft of the bill was made available to Diet members only two days before it was submitted.[113] Furthermore, the bill was introduced in an extended session of the legislature, during which two other major bills (on defense and health) were to be considered, whereas in previous situations of this sort the government had always sought to keep controversial legislative bills chronologically separate.[114]

The final law passed on August 7, 1969, was surprisingly mild in view of some of the demands made by the more "hawkish" conservatives inside and outside the government. Nevertheless, even though it was in principle a temporary bill granting powers that were to last only five years, those powers were substantial. The university president was declared "the person chiefly responsible for his institution," and he was required to "seek the normal functioning of his university." In the event of any disturbance he was to "demonstrate leadership and unite the entire staff of the university in seeking a settlement and to determine the principles and measures for its resolution."[115] He was also given powers to initiate changes in administrative structures, including the power to suspend all or part of the university's functions for up to nine months.

The more fundamental concentration of powers went not to university presidents or administrators, however, but to the minister of education. All disputes were to be reported to him, and he in turn was "to give to the president . . . the necessary advice on measures that shall be adopted to deal with the

dispute." In making these administrative changes, the
president was required to consult with the minister of
education, who would make all personnel appointments
involved. Most fundamentally, however, the minister
was given the power to suspend all education and research functions in universities engaged in disputes
of more than nine months' duration or in institutions
where a dispute of six months' duration recurred within one year of an earlier settlement.

The passage and promulgation of this law thus
marked the first time since the earliest reforms of
the Occupation that major legislation affecting the
overall governance of the university system had been
successfully enacted. In one sense it was the culmination of a long government drive significantly to
centralize powers within the university and to alter
sharply the balance of power between the universities
and the government. Stalled under the late Occupation,
in 1954, and in 1963, the government finally succeeded
with the passage of this law in accomplishing much of
what it had earlier set out to do. Certainly many of
Japan's progressive scholars have offered such an interpretation.[116]

The question naturally arises as to why the government succeeded in 1969 when it was unsuccessful in
earlier tries. One factor unquestionably was that
the university protests in the late 1960s far outstripped previous demonstrations in scope, violence,
and duration, taking on far more significance for the
overall conservative-progressive struggle than any
other postwar issue involving higher education, and
second only in overall significance perhaps to the
struggle over the U.S.-Japan Security Treaty in 1960.
Thus, the government was willing to risk even greater
political capital to end these protests than it had
in earlier cases, particularly since those early protest actions seemed to be withering partially of their
own accord. This factor also had its effect on nongovernmental actors.

The ability of the catch phrase "university autonomy" to mobilize the entire academic community and
the more liberal segments of public opinion was similarly far more restricted given these actions of violence under the auspices of autonomy. It was also a
less successful slogan than it had been earlier because the issue of student power was injected into
the autonomy matrix so that even academic liberals no
longer blindly defended the principle.[117]

The most important factor in the government's
legislative success, however, would appear to envelop
and transcend many of these points. This was the

133

breakdown in the earlier unity of opposition forces. The cohesive opposition to government action shown during the 1950s and the early 1960s had ruptured by the latter part of the decade. The electoral success of the Clean Government Party, which fit into neither the conservative nor the progressive camp, seemed to presage a popular concern for some new voice in electoral politics. The New Left, as epitomized primarily by Zenkyōtō and other student groups, rejected the leadership of the existing progressive organs, while the Old Left was sharply divided not only over that problem but over its own internal ideology. The Socialist Party, for example, was sharply divided over whether it should move "right" or "left," and the Democratic Socialist Party showed increasing signs of becoming more conservative than some elements in the LDP. All of this left little grounds for a repetition of earlier unified actions by the nongovernmental political parties that had prevented administrative changes.

Beyond this, university administrators, while publicly opposed to any government legislation, in many cases privately favored actions that would check student violence and prevent serious student participation in university governance. Any protests by administrators and their associations against government action therefore had a rather hollow ring. Finally, the media and the public opinion shaped by it grew increasingly favorable to government action, even if it posed a threat to university autonomy. An organized conservative camp therefore had numerous peripheral allies with which to face a sharply divided opposition. The balance of organization and mobilizational capabilities had shifted from left to right.

A comparison of conservative success in 1969 with earlier failures provides several insights. It also highlights the contrasts between all cases of university administration and other higher educational issues. It would be well, therefore, to sum up the major similarities among all the cases of university administration investigated.

First of all, the fact that the unity of the progressive camp broke down in the 1969 case should not obscure the strongly bipolar pattern of ideological perception, organizational commitment, and policymaking processes common to all issues of university administration. In all cases the broad, affective, nondivisible nature of the issues fixed progressives and conservatives on opposite sides of the Rubicon. Correlatively, each side was quite willing to make reasonably heavy commitments to insure the success of its views and each was willing to take a rather hard line in advocating its position.

Second, the focal point of the policymaking processes most relevant to the issues of university administration was almost always the Diet. That is, attempts to secure or to block some legislative proposal were the focal point of policymaking. This mode itself fostered a highly antagonistic process with little room for and few attempts at compromise. Moreover, the broad political climate within which the specific issues arose was tense,with a variety of highly affective issues further igniting the passions of camp conflict.

As the next two chapters will show, these commonalities in the solution of problems related to university administration contrast sharply with the patterns prevalent in enrollment expansion and specialization. Both of these later issues were settled with neither the overt confrontation nor the same public visibility as matters of administration. Indeed, in one case, enrollment expansion, the entire policy emerged from rather invisible and seemingly unrelated measures, while in the other, specialization, bureaucratic action and pluralistic compromise predominated.

# 6. Incremental Policymaking: Enrollment Expansion

If policymaking in university administration has been dominated by highly ideological confrontational politics, university enrollment expansion represents a near polar opposite. The issue of enrollment expansion has lacked major ideological overtones; its impact has not been perceived as specific; it has been almost infinitely disaggregable in practice despite the size of the constituency affected. Nor has it been an issue of high salience to major political actors. As a result, the policymaking process involved in expansion has been highly incremental and almost totally lacking in controversy. Further, the bureaucracy has perhaps exerted its most significant influence over policymaking in this area.

In most European countries higher education developed as the privilege and prerequisite of the upper classes. For the bulk of the populace, most education ended by the early teens, with the later years of school spent largely in vocational training. Until the 1960s almost no continental European country sent more than 5 or 6 percent of its youth through universities. Elsewhere, the most noteworthy exception to this pattern was the United States, which, with the establishment of land grant colleges after passage of the Morrill Law in the mid-nineteenth century, began to move toward the democratization of higher educational opportunities. The Soviet Union, relying heavily on vocational and evening courses, followed suit, though much later. Given the American orientation, as well as its commitment to democratizing Japan, it was not at all unusual that the Occupation should have sought to make Japanese higher education more accessible.

An elemental aim of the Americans during the Occupation was to insure maximum higher educational opportunities for individual students. Despite limitations on this policy noted in Chapter 3, enrollment in Japanese institutions of higher education has been accelerating. Whereas in 1940 only 4 percent and in 1952 only 7.5 percent of the higher educational age cohort was attending some institution of higher education, by 1974 this figure had skyrocketed to about 25 percent,[1] among the highest in the world. Extrapolating from the expansion rate since 1956, 47.2 percent of the age group will be entering universities or junior colleges in 1980.[2] Nowhere, however, is there evidence to indicate that this post-Occupation expansion was the result of some conscious choice, such as the Morrill Law in the United States or the Robbins Report that recommended the expansion of higher educational opportunities in Britain.[3] Nor is there evidence of the bipolar controversy surrounding policy in adminstration.

Instead, a number of seemingly discrete decisions and actions combined to form a unified policy. In some cases, government authorities carried out actions which seemed to be discrete and independent of one another but which, consciously or not, resulted in a single unidirectional set of changes; in others, authorities simply reacted to an evolutionary trend, by nonaction and activities at the margins of that trend which bolstered its progress.

Regardless, one can isolate no single decision to enact a policy, but the combined actions of the government make it clear that a single course of action has been followed. The term "policy" makes political sense only when such situations are included along with the more conscious and active manipulations of events that are usually associated with the term.

Lack of a formal plan should not be equated with lack of interest by the Japanese government in enrollment expansion, nor can one infer that government actions were in no way responsible for the expansion. In fact, the actions of the government have consistently supported the expansionary trend, and its apparent lack of formal consideration of the problem has subtly bolstered expansion. This encouragement of maximum expansion has satisfied parental pressure for greater educational opportunities and has also provided business and industry with a growing talent pool from which to choose employees. At the same time, the government has managed to minimize the economic and political costs to itself of this expansion by holding down government costs and avoiding any substantial disruption of the country's social structure or dominant values. It has achieved this result by its indirect manipulation of expansion and its reliance on social norms to support this policy.

INDIRECT EFFORTS TO EXPAND ENROLLMENT

The government has used two indirect methods to allow the expansion of higher educational opportunities: the chartering of universities, particularly private universities, and the nonenforcement of minimum legal standards for university conditions. These activities, combined with a reliance on private funding and neglect of government funding, have led to problems of quality and class bias.

## Chartering of Universities

The minister of education has the ultimate responsibility for chartering universities, and no university may be established without a charter.[4] In practice, charters are granted on the basis of investigations of university conditions by the ministry's University Chartering Council, and in the case of private universities additional investigations into the fiscal standing of the "legal person" establishing the university by the ministry's Private Universities Council.[5] Thus, all applicants are subjected to at least one, and in most cases two screenings before the minister of education formally decides whether or not to grant a charter.

An analysis of Figure 6-1 shows the close relationship between the granting of new charters and enrollment expansion. The rate of growth has been far from uniform in either category, with the major expansion of the post-Occupation period starting in 1961 and increasing sharply for the next five years. Between 1953 and 1961 there was relatively little growth in either category, as the Ministry of Education made an initial attempt to stem expansion by making it more difficult to establish and charter a university. (A second attempt to limit growth followed the massive student protests of 1968-69.) Concerned about the need for a period of stability following the tremendous reorganization under the Occupation, the ministry first sought informally to check the growth in the number of four-year universities (two-year junior colleges were allowed to continue expanding at a rapid rate). Then, in August 1955 Minister of Education Matsumura called for specific actions to raise the standards for establishing new universities.[6] By early 1956 the ministry had eliminated conditional charter approval, and that June it announced that no new charters would be granted and that the University Chartering Council would henceforth formally tighten requirements and would conduct more stringent investigations.[7]

FIGURE 6-1

Number of New Universities Established Annually
and Annual Increase in the Number of University Students
(as percent of previous year's total)

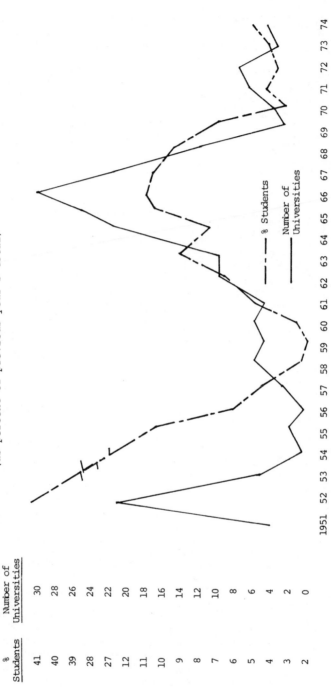

Source: Sōrifu, Nihon tōkei nenkan (Japan Statistical Yearbook) (Tokyo: Prime Minister's Office, annual).

These attempts proved, however, to be short-lived.
Opposition to the policy developed rapidly, particularly within the top levels of the ruling LDP, coming
notably from then-Chief Secretary of the Party Kishi,
Executive-Director Ishii, Party Vice-President Ōno,
and even Parliamentary Vice-Minister of Education
Takeo. They demanded that various groups within their
constituencies be allowed to establish new universities or to upgrade their high schools or junior colleges. The LDP threatened to take budgetary action if
the policy remained inflexible to these political
needs.[8] In October 1956 the standards for chartering
were changed, making the physical and course requirements even more lenient than they had been.[9]

Continual compromise between the LDP and the ministry allowed new university charters to be granted
every year, even while the ministry and the council
sought to constrain the increase through the latter's
investigations. By 1961, however, in part as a response to the postwar "baby boom" and in part to as-
suage business fears of a shortage of skilled labor,
examinations became cursory at best. Even when a
university did not really measure up to the minimum
standards, the council would frequently recommend that
a charter be granted anyhow.[10] The written standards
thus became meaningless. As Ōsawa has complained,
"Despite the fact that these are stated to be the
'minimum standards,' they are applied as if they were
desirable standards or maximum standards."[11]

The natural expansion resulting from the virtual
elimination of all official standards was accelerated
when, in 1962, revisions in the funding of the Private
School Promotion Association implicitly encouraged the
creation of more private universities. In the same
year the ministry dropped its prior requirement that
university authorities consult with the minister of
education when seeking to change the number of students or to create new departments.[12] By 1966 even
members of the University Chartering Council seemed
willing to concede that anyone able to hire an architect to draw up building plans and to borrow sufficient volumes from a friend or from a neighboring
library could acquire a charter.[13]

The results of this more casual attitude toward
expansion and chartering can be seen in Table 6-1.
The sharp rise in the percentage of charter requests
approved in the 1960s reflects the government's increased willingness to grant new charters. The new
charters, in turn, contributed to a major expansion
of enrollment. Most of this expansion took place in
the private universities.

TABLE 6-1

Applications for University Charters

| Year | Number of Applications A | Number Approved B | B/A |
|------|--------------------------|-------------------|------|
| 1949 | 9 | 5 | 56% |
| 1950 | 12 | 6 | 50% |
| 1961 | 8 | 3 | 38% |
| 1962 | 10 | 10 | 100% |
| 1963 | 13 | 10 | 77% |
| 1964 | 24 | 21 | 87% |
| 1965 | 30 | 25 | 83% |
| 1966 | 31 | 28 | 90% |
| 1967 | 37 | 23 | 62% |
| 1968 | 14 | 11 | 78% |
| 1969 | 6 | 3 | 50% |
| 1970 | 5 | 4 | 80% |
| 1971 | 13 | 7 | 54% |
| 1972[a] | 15 | 9 | 60% |
| 1973[a] | 4 | 3 | 75% |
| 1974 | 5 | 4 | 80% |
| 1975 | 9 | 7 | 78% |
| 1976 | 4 | 4 | 100% |

[a]Includes two applications carried over from the previous year and approved.

Source: Unpublished data supplied by the Ministry of Education.

From an administrative standpoint, there are three types of universities in Japan: those under the direct control of the national government; those under the control of local governments, such as prefectures or cities; and finally, those under private administration. The great bulk of university expansion since the end of the Occupation has come in the private sphere. In 1952 there were 221 four-year universities in Japan. Of these, 72 (33 percent) were national, 33 (15 percent) were local public, and 116 (52 percent) were private.[14] In 1975 the total was 420 universities, of which 81 were national (19 percent), 34 were local public (8 percent) and 305 were private (73 percent).[15]

142

In terms of student enrollment a similar shift can be seen. Even though there was a significant increase in the number of students enrolled in public universities, increases there have been far less rapid than in the private institutions. In 1952, 39 percent of the total university student body was enrolled in national universities, 4 percent in local public universities, and 57 percent in private institutions. By 1975 the composition had shifted dramatically, so that about 80 percent of the student body was enrolling in private universities.[16] This preponderant role of the private universities in expanding higher educational opportunities differentiates Japan from most other industrial societies.

## Nonenforcement of Minimum Legal Standards

A second indirect method of expanding higher education was to ignore violations of the written standards for the subsequent operation of chartered universities. The University Chartering Standards set explicit minimum criteria for universities which, according to Article 1, had to be met or exceeded at the time a charter was issued, after which continuing improvements were expected to bring the university above even these levels. This law gives the government the power to revoke the charters of noncomplying institutions, but the Ministry of Education never insisted that universities correct deficiencies found at the time of chartering examination or even that universities at least maintain their inaugural standards.

A twofold deviation regarding these standards was involved. First of all, the standards are based on the so-called student quota, the number of students allowed per faculty or department by the Ministry of Education. This quota bears little relationship to the number of actual entrants, however. A number of "miniversities" found it impossible to attract enough students to meet this quota.[17] On the other hand, a great many institutions vastly exceeded their quotas.[18] One study of 69 major institutions, for example, showed all but one exceeding its quota. Moreover, 47 were in excess by more than 50 percent, and 21 by more than 100 percent.[19] This situation, known and condoned by the Ministry of Education, served as a major contributor to continued expansion. It also meant that any standards based on such quotas were extremely diluted.

Nevertheless, even the diluted standards have not been adhered to. For example, Article 12 of the University Chartering Standards requires that no more than

143

one-half of the faculty members in any university faculty be part-time. Yet a survey of 34 universities for which data were available showed that 16 had more part-time than full-time faculty members. Moreover, many of the remaining 18 had individual faculties in which more than half of the positions were part-time.[20] As a second example, Article 37, clause 4, of the University Chartering Standards[21] provides that libraries shall have seats for at least 5 percent of the students, but a survey of 40 universities showed nearly half to be in violation. One of the most blatant violators had 115 students per library seat.[22] Other legal standards remained similarly unenforced, with the result that it became rather easy to establish, operate, and expand a university and its student enrollment.

Thus, bureaucratic decisions and nondecisions cumulatively sustained and greatly accelerated the trend toward rapid expansion within higher education. Normally, even such a policy of incremental expansion would require major financial and administrative outlays, thereby generating resistance from other sectors of the government concerned about possible budget cuts elsewhere. In the Japanese case, however, the government's reliance on private universities and its funding policies aroused little political opposition, making even easier the incremental enlargement of the universities.

## Funding Policy

The government's indirect methods of encouraging the expansion of higher educational opportunities were accompanied by penury in the funding of higher education. At first glance, funds for higher education in Japan seem to be quite respectable in international terms. Between 1950 and 1973 expenses for higher education rose from 24.8 billion yen to 1,189.6 billion yen, representing a climb from 0.75 percent of national income to 1.28 percent.[23] In view of the large increase in the total number of students and the inflation over the same period, however, the rise is considerably less impressive. Moreover, expenses in 1950 provide a very low base to start from. Only in 1959, for example, did total spending per pupil in higher education reach prewar levels,[24] and current expenses (i.e., direct educational expenses exclusive of capital overhead and expansion costs) only reached prewar levels at the end of the 1960s.[25]

Even more significantly, a decreasing portion of the money spent within Japan for higher education has come from public sources. During the period from 1950 to 1973 government's share of the total bill for higher education shrank from 67.2 percent to 52 percent,[26] and government expenditure per pupil at the beginning of the 1970s was only about two-thirds that of the prewar level.[27] Finally, both as a percent of national income and as a percent of total government spending for education, the Japanese government's outlay for higher education falls far below the levels in other major countries of the world (see Table 6-2). In fact, one survey of government spending for higher education as a percent of total governmental spending in 31 countries showed that only 6 allocated lower percentages to higher education than Japan.[28]

TABLE 6-2

Government Spending for Higher Education
as Percent of Total Government Educational Expense
in Various Countries, 1973

| Country | Percent |
| --- | --- |
| Japan | 13.5 |
| U.K. | 19.7[a] |
| West Germany | 23.4[a] |
| U.S.A. | 23.1 |
| France | 21.0 |

[a]1972

Source: Ministry of Education, Educational Standards in Japan, 1976 (Tokyo: Ministry of Education, 1976), p. 149.

Finally, during the period 1961-70, when Japan's student population was growing faster than that of any other OECD nation except Canada, it was also the only country in the OECD whose expenditures for higher education had failed to keep pace with the rise in total educational expenditures, GNP, or public expenditure. In virtually all other countries during this period, expenditures for higher education rose faster than the other indicators.[29]

This funding situation is tied directly to the fact that enrollment expansion has come about largely

through the private universities.  The Japanese government allocated no significant monies for these universities until the passage of a law in 1970 providing
funding for private institutions.  Until then only
about 3 percent of the total operating budget for private universities in Japan came from government funding, a figure in sharp contrast to funding policies in
most other industrialized countries.  In the Soviet
Union there is, of course, no private funding.  In
West Germany and France more than 80 percent of all
funds come from government sources.  In Britain, even
though all universities are privately administered, 70
percent of the ordinary expenditures and between 90
and 95 percent of the funds for capital needs come
from the government.  In the United States, about one-
third of all private university monies come from the
state or federal governments.[30]
     Thus the Japanese government, while encouraging
the expansion of enrollment in institutions of higher
education by easy charters and nonenforcement of
standards, did so at minimal cost, funding the university system in general and private universities in
particular at a level of niggardliness unmatched in
the industrial world.  More charitably phrased, the
expansion did not force any major reallocations of
funds or personnel.  As a result, no significant
counterpressures to the policy of expansion were
forthcoming from within the government.  But what of
pressures from outside of government?  The consequences of the policy seem to be such as would have
generated vast public resentment.


CONSEQUENCES OF GOVERNMENT ENROLLMENT POLICY

     Two important negative consequences of the expan-
sion policy might have led to some strong external
reaction had other circumstances been different: a
sharp decline in the quality of educational facilities and a class bias to the educational opportunities
that emerged as a result of the expansion.  At first
glance, one might suppose that these would lead to
certain counterpressures, perhaps from students, parents, the lower classes not sharing fully in the expanded opportunities, and so on.  Once these two consequences are examined in the context of other factors, however, particularly organizability, it will be
clear why such counterpressures failed to develop.

## Deterioration of Educational Conditions

A number of statistical indicators point to the
marked decline since 1952 in the physical aspects of
university education in Japan. First of all, the number of students per faculty member rose almost 30 percent between the end of the Occupation and the mid-
1970s, with the major rise coming during the period
of greatest chartering increases.[31] At all other levels of education in Japan, during the same period the
number of students per faculty member declined. The
result is that the number of students per faculty member is higher in universities than at any other level
of education in Japan, in sharp contrast to normal expectations.

The rise in the number of students per faculty
member also contrasts sharply with trends in higher
education throughout the world. It is difficult to
compare various nations' statistics on higher education because definitions vary from country to country.
In absolute terms, however, Japan's poor position in
comparison with other major industrial states can be
documented in figures provided by the white papers of
the Japanese Ministry of Education itself.[32]

Although the number of students per teacher has
been rising, faculty salaries have by no means kept
pace with trends in national income per capita, a
further suggestion of declining quality. For example,
the salaries of teachers in higher education as related to average national income per capita dropped
65 percent between 1950 and 1968, and almost another
30 percent by 1973,[33] again a decline unmatched in any
other country. Moreover, salaries were comparatively
low to begin with, being approximately one-third of
those in the United States, Britain, and West Germany.[34] Even allowing for the differences in per
capita national income, faculty members in Japanese
institutions of higher education receive about one-
half of what their counterparts in these three countries were receiving when their countries were at
similar levels.[35] Part-time employment outside of the
university has become an economic necessity for large
numbers of faculty members, thus making them far less
accessible to students and colleagues.

Figures for such items as research expenditures,[36]
books and libraries,[37] and space per pupil[38] evidence
a similar decline.

These aggregate data mask significant differences
among universities and between national and local universities on the one hand and private universities on
the other.[39] Beyond a doubt, the private universities,

147

where the bulk of the expansion has taken place, suffer most from inferior and declining facilities, as Table 6-3 indicates. Yet, since official policy has relied heavily on the private universities for expanding the enrollment of the entire system, their statistical inferiority establishes even more firmly the tie between government policy and university deterioration.

TABLE 6-3

Comparison of Various Conditions within
National, Public, and Private Universities in Japan

| Condition | Year | National | Public | Private |
|---|---|---|---|---|
| 1) Student-faculty ratio | 1975 | 10.0 | – | 26.8 |
| 2) Percent part-time faculty | 1975 | 29.1 | 36.1 | 47.0 |
| 3) Average books/library (000) | 1967 | 89.0 | 57.0 | 47.0 |
| 4) Students per library seat | 1967 | 9.2 | 9.3 | 15.1 |
| 5) Books per student | 1967 | 96.0 | 67.0 | 25.0 |
| 6) Average space per student (square meters) | 1974 | 83.4 | – | 29.5 |

Sources: 1-2, my calculations from Mombushō, Mombu nempō (Yearbook of the Ministry of Education); Zenkoku Shiritsu Daigaku Kyōjukai Rengō, Zenkoku shiritsu daigaku hakusho, 1976 (White Paper on Japan's Private Universities) (Tokyo: ZSDKR, 1976), p. 229.
3-5, my calculations from Mombushō, Mombu tōkei yōran (Handbook of Educational Statistics), 1970, p. 49.
6, Nihon Shiritsu Daigaku Kyōiku, Jigyō keikakusho (Working Plan), 1970 (Tokyo, 1970), p. 14; Mombushō, Waga kuni no kyōiku suijun (Educational Standards in Japan), 1976, p. 139.


Class Bias

The decline in quality has been accompanied by a strong class bias to the university system. Since nearly 25 percent of the age cohort attend institutions of higher education, the Japanese system could hardly be called "elitist" in the usual sense of the word. Nevertheless, because the expansion of opportunities has occurred largely in the private universities, which are the most expensive for students, it has favored the sons and daughters of families of means.

148

Most private universities in Japan have very little financial equity, either because of the inflation immediately after the war or because of the weak financial requirements when they were chartered. Thus, they depend almost exclusively on tuition, fees, and bank loans for their operating expenses. A vicious cycle exists in which the universities borrow money to establish physical facilities then require high tuition and fees to pay off charges on the bank loans. To maximize total income, they admit more and more students, thereby necessitating further physical expansion, additional bank loans, more servicing charges, and further increases in tuition and in the number of students. Loans underwrite nearly one-quarter of the private universities' budgets,[40] and another 20 percent goes for debt service, a figure that nearly doubled in the decade of the 1960s.[41] In such a poor financial situation, private universities are forced to rely on tuition, fees, and other student "contributions" for 60 percent of their expenditures.[42] The comparable figure in the United States and Great Britain usually falls below 10 percent and rarely exceeds 20 to 30 percent, even in the most impoverished private universities.[43] Moreover, in Japan voluntary student contributions are usually inversely proportional to the attractiveness of a student's academic record, a factor that contributes to the class bias of the system. The costs of entering a private university have become astronomical and have far outstripped increases in the consumer price index, as can be seen from Table 6-4. Furthermore, families must be able to support their offspring for four years once in the university.

As a result of such high costs, the private universities have become prohibitively expensive for the student from lower-middle income families and have become increasingly accessible only to the more well-to-do. A 1968 survey of high school graduates showed, for example, that the most significant factor influencing a student's desire to go on to college was a family income of 1.5 million yen or above. Being male and the son of a professional followed closely, while having very high grades was significantly less important. Of the male students who did not go on to a university, 36 percent cited economic conditions as the reason. The average annual income of parents of those who wished to enter universities was 1.3 million yen for males and 1.46 million yen for females, about twice the income of those who decided not to continue in spite of favorable teacher evaluations of their scholastic achievement and motivation.[44]

149

## TABLE 6-4

Tuition and Fees in Private Universities
Compared to Consumer Price Index

| Year | Tuition | | Entry Fees | | Building Fund Contribution | | Total | | Consumer Price Index |
|---|---|---|---|---|---|---|---|---|---|
| | Yen | Index | Yen | Index | Yen | Index | Yen | Index | |
| 1955 | 20,898 | 65.8 | 7,650 | 42.3 | 8,751 | 41.5 | 37,298 | 52.6 | 92.7 |
| 1960 | 31,773 | 100.0 | 18,074 | 100.0 | 21,078 | 100.0 | 70,925 | 100.0 | 100.0 |
| 1965 | 68,023 | 214.1 | 41,628 | 230.3 | 65,439 | 310.4 | 175,090 | 246.9 | 135.1 |
| 1967 | 77,110 | 242.7 | 48,311 | 267.3 | 75,464 | 358.0 | 200,885 | 283.2 | 147.6 |
| 1969 | 84,048 | 264.5 | 52,028 | 287.9 | 85,798 | 407.1 | 221,874 | 312.8 | 163.9 |
| 1970 | 85,666 | 269.6 | 52,755 | 291.9 | 90,546 | 429.6 | 228,967 | 322.8 | 176.6 |
| 1971 | 90,206 | 283.9 | 53,206 | 294.4 | 91,340 | 433.3 | 234,752 | 331.0 | - |

Source: Ogata Ken, "Shidai no zaisei kiki to shigaku seisaku no 'tenkan'" (Financial Danger to Private Universities and 'Changes' in Private School Policies), Sekai, No 315, February 1972, p. 97.

The limited data available on family income of students entering universities also support the notion of class bias in the system. In 1970 the average family income of students in private universities was 2.10 million yen, or 50 percent higher than the 1.45 million yen for families of students in national universities and 30 percent higher than the 1.63 million for those in local public universities.[45] Moreover, this gap widened significantly with time.

Despite the fact that tuition in national universities is comparatively low and the overall distribution of students in national universities is far more egalitarian than in private universities, in both national and private universities there has been a notable decline in the representation of students from the lower quintiles of the national income brackets, as can be seen from Table 6-5. Under a system of perfectly nonclass-based distribution of university places,

TABLE 6-5

Distribution of University Students by Family Income
and Type of University Attended

| | Lower Quintile | Lower Middle Quintile | Middle Quintile | Upper Middle Quintile | Upper Quintile |
|---|---|---|---|---|---|
| National | | | | | |
| 1960 | 19.8 | 20.6 | 15.4 | 17.6 | 26.9 |
| 1974 | 14.4 | 11.2 | 16.0 | 24.3 | 34.1 |
| Private | | | | | |
| 1960 | 6.4 | 9.2 | 12.3 | 19.5 | 53.6 |
| 1974 | 6.1 | 6.5 | 11.6 | 21.2 | 54.6 |

Source: Mombushō, Nihon no kōtō kyōiku (Higher Education in Japan) (Tokyo: Ministry of Education, 1964), p. 163; Research Institute for Higher Education, Hiroshima University, Statistics on Higher Education in Japan (Hiroshima: RIHE, 1976), p. 9.

all figures should be 20 percent. National universities in 1960 were quite close to such a distribution; private universities never were. There has also been a shift away from equality between 1960 and 1974. The

number of students from the lower two quintiles has
declined in both private and national universities,
and those from the higher two quintiles have increased
their dominance.  While it is difficult statistically
and economically to make legitimate cross-national
comparisons of income distribution and benefits to
social sectors, at least one set of data suggests that
the distribution pattern in Japan is less egalitarian
than that of other industrial societies.[46]

The data on quality and class, therefore, make it
obvious that the government expansion of opportunities
has had two very significant socio-political consequences: general deterioration in university conditions and an increasingly unequal distribution of university places.  Yet no evidence emerges of any significant pressure to contract the expansion, to expand under more democratic circumstances, or to maintain high
standards.  The reasons for this situation are to be
found in the broad social context and values surrounding Japanese higher education.

## SUPPORTING VALUES

No governmental policy is formulated in a valua-
tional vacuum, and the enrollment expansion in Japanese
higher education is no exception.  Three interrelated
values have been strongly congruent with and supportive
of the policy and its consequences throughout the society, namely, the importance of the university diploma, a laissez-faire attitude toward the acquisition of
the degree in both government and private sectors, and
the general governmental policy of rapid economic
growth.

In Japan, as in most countries, there is a high
correlation between a person's level of education and
subsequent economic success.  Thus, in 1967 the starting salary for male university graduates in Japan av-
eraged nearly 70 percent above that for middle school
graduates, 45 percent above that for high school graduates, and 24 percent higher than that for junior college graduates.[47]  Moreover, this gap widens with age
and length of employment, so that even allowing for
the seven years when a middle school graduate is working and a university graduate is in school, the latter's lifetime earnings remain far superior.  Statistically, a university education is a wise investment.[48]
Above and beyond the purely economic "payoff," occupational status and the type of work done are largely
dependent on education, with the most desirable positions tending to demand a university diploma as a prerequisite.

Such differences are not lost on Japanese parents. There is a very high concern among parents for the education of their offspring. A recent survey of parents showed that the topic most frequently discussed in the home was education (52.1 percent), which was also the greatest worry of parents (25.4 percent), nearly double the percentage for the item of next greatest concern. Expectations in the area of education were also very high, with nearly two-thirds of the parents indicating that if they had a son they would want him to finish college.[49]

The relationship between higher education and subsequent success in the minds of Japanese parents is rather blatant. One public opinion poll taken by the Prime Minister's Office indicated that only 22 percent of the parents surveyed who wanted to send their sons to university did so in order for them "to acquire an education," while more than 58 percent sought entry for reasons directly related to the future material success of their offspring, such as "will be advantageous," "want him to acquire a good job," "to acquire technical skills," and so on. An additional 14.5 percent cited the somewhat related reason "because it is generally done."[50]

Parental desires are mirrored in part in the attitudes of the business community. Firms generally will hire their employees only from a limited number of specific schools. Close ties are typically maintained between university officials and various business firms,with mutually acceptable quotas worked out as to the number of graduates a particular firm will hire and what a university will agree to provide for the firm. Thus, career success depends much less on actual skills than on school standing and a school's alumni connections, the entire syndrome suggesting that the university one graduates from is more important than what one learns there.[51]

Numerous writers have described this phenomenon rather cynically as gakureki-shugi, literally "diplomaism," or as a "fixation with the degree."[52] While a diploma per se is important, not all diplomas are equal. Some universities and some faculties offer far more prestigious degrees than others. Indeed, a degree from a particular faculty of a particular university has an almost calculable economic value, both to its recipient and to the firm that eventually employs him. And, if the student "buys" the diploma as the essential passport to future success in government and business, many universities quite clearly can "market" the passports with such factors in mind.

For its part, the government maintains a hands-off attitude toward the relationship between students and private universities as regards funding, tuition raises, deviations from official quotas, and so on. Perhaps the most pertinent facet of this attitude concerns scholarship aid to students, whether in public or in private universities. In this area nothing suggests any sense of government responsibility for insuring that the individual be allowed to acquire a university education regardless of his, or his family's, economic level. The government-sponsored Japan Scholarship Association, which provides 83 percent of all "scholarships" in Japanese universities, provides no scholarship grants whatsoever but merely doles out loans in miniscule sums to a small portion of the student body. Of nearly 1.5 million university students in 1970, the largest group of recipients was the 99,000 (7.6 percent) who received general loans of, in almost all cases, 3,000 yen per month. An additional 88,000 students (6.8 percent) received special allowances of between 5,000 yen and, in very unusual cases, 12,000 yen. Though these amounts were doubled by 1974, the total coverage fell to 11 percent of all students. In fact, Japan has the lowest percentage of students receiving aid, and the lowest amounts received, among the major countries of the world.[53] It seems to be the only such country with no genuine government program of scholarship grants--an indication of the pervasive Japanese attitude that higher education is by and large a private sector relationship beyond the purview of the government.

Such a noninterventionist policy is fully complementary with, and perhaps partly the consequence of, a final element of general attitudes, namely, the dominant consideration given to high-growth economics in the formulation of Japanese governmental priorities. To the extent that conservative political dominance in the postwar period has been at all related to governmental policies, it is fair to say that the LDP has been heavily bolstered by the ability to deliver "peace and prosperity." Beginning with the Hatoyama cabinet's "Six-Year Plan for an Independent Economy," through the Ikeda cabinet's "Plan to Double the National Income in Ten Years," and the industrial development plans in former Prime Minister Tanaka's "Plan to Remodel the Archipelago," the conservatives consistently relied on economic growth and its fallout as a mainstay of their political power. These economic policies were based most fundamentally on the concept of growth through cyclical investment and reinvestment in high and rapid-return items, with the inclusion of such politically profitable exceptions as rice price supports and pork-barrel programs.[54]

For a highly industrialized country like Japan, higher education was not such an item.

Economists differ on the reasons for Japan's phenomenal growth, but one thing is clear: despite the fact that Japan's high level of education may have been a prerequisite to such growth, further investment in education would have produced no appreciable returns in terms of added macrolevel growth. A comparison of the relative importance of several factors to Japan's growth during the period 1944-68 shows the minimal role played by investment in education. In terms of international comparisons, one study showed the role of education to be less significant in Japan than in all but one of the thirteen industrial countries or regions studied.[55] Thus, the weak bargaining position of Ministry of Education officials has had an unmistakably negative effect on standards and funding.

Regardless of the immediate causes of the problems of quality and class bias, deeply rooted values and attitudes have undergirded the policy of rapid incremental expansion of the universities. The importance of the diploma, the notion that higher education is essentially a private business transaction beyond the realm of government intervention, and finally, the dominance of economic growth as a governmental priority must all be seen as the attitudinal props behind the expansion of higher educational enrollment, the decline in the quality of university facilities over the past decade and a half, and the class bias that remains a part of the higher educational system. Despite the clear negative consequences of the government's expansion policy and their tangibility to certain sectors of society, these sectors have been extremely difficult to organize and mobilize, and there has been little political pressure for change.

As far as quality of education is concerned, once a student is admitted, graduation is almost automatic four years later. Few students are dropped for academic reasons, for that would imply a mistake in the admissions procedure, as well as in many cases a surrender of high tuition payments. And since the diploma and one's professors, not the education they purportedly represent, are the critical factors in securing a desirable job, it makes little sense for students to protest declining conditions too loudly, particularly as individuals. Student organizations during the late 1960s began to raise complaints on many campuses, as noted in Chapter 5, in some cases with limited success. Yet student organizations prior to this time,

and student organizations affiliated with Zengakuren
even during this time, devoted the bulk of their activities to more cosmic concerns, scorning as trivial
attention to improvements at the campus level. (Only
with the success of Minsei, which is affiliated with
the Japan Communist Party, Zenkyōtō, and the nonsect
radical movement, did students begin any serious protest against campus conditions.) Whatever pressures
materialized were perforce local and directed at the
campus rather than at the government.

As for the class bias in overall admission, much
of the difficulty in mobilizing opposition stems from
the higher educational system's seeming fairness to
any single individual. There is a good and open system of public education prior to universities, which
graduates roughly 80 percent of the high school age
cohort. Examinations for universities, particularly
for the national and local public institutions, are
open and meticulously protected from whimsical and
personalistically based exceptions. Such apparent
fairness in the examinations masks the fact that only
parents of some means can provide their offspring with
the private tutoring that has become so critical to
success as well as underwrite the living costs, books,
and deferred income attached to higher education, not
to mention the vast tuition bills attendant on private
education.

Parents as a group and lower middle class or
lower class families are difficult to organize politically. Each parent can hope that his or her offspring
will be the one to gain entrance to and graduate from
a high-prestige institution. If and when the child
does not, it is difficult for the parents to organize
with others in the same situation to focus criticism
on a system which exerted no overt discrimination
against any of the children as individuals. Hence,
the success of some exceptional individuals from a
lower socio-economic background who manage to over-
come the systemic hurdles and graduate from a prestigious institution masks the fact that they are exceptions to a rule with a clear and unmistakable bias.

If the comparative inactivity of students and
parents is understandable, what explains the seeming
disinterest with which the so-called proletarian parties view these consequences? An occasional perfunctory criticism of the course of the government's expansion policy can be found in the party platforms of
the JSP and the JCP, but neither has made any great
efforts to correct the situation. The JSP's conduct
can perhaps best be attributed to the party's Talmudic
Marxism: Marx's doctrines in the original are believed

to explain all significant contemporary problems;
those he deals with are significant, while those he
does not can be ignored. Marxism is seen less as a
doctrine from which to begin analysis and more as one
which, if understood "correctly," will provide time-
less answers. Because Marx was not overly concerned
with higher education, neither has been the JSP. At
the organizational level as well, this orientation was
bolstered by the close ties between the JSP and the
major labor federations at the national level. Higher
education (in contrast to primary and secondary education, where the Japan Teachers Union is most active)
has not been a union issue since the end of the Occupation. University administration was interpreted as
a matter of state intervention to enforce ideological
conformity--which would easily be squared with Marx--
and was seen as presenting a threat to leading theore-
ticians for the JSP, many of whom were university
teachers. In contrast, enrollment expansion and its
consequences did not touch directly on key supporters
of the JSP nor on matters with overtly political overtones. The political implications of the government's
incremental policymaking were conservative and anti-
progressive, to be sure, but in a far less open way
than in issues surrounding administration.

In the case of the JCP, the party was first of
all extremely weak during the earliest period of the
expansion policy. But even when its strength grew in
the mid- to late 1960s, it followed a strategy of
localism, treating each campus as a separate entity,
with the result that it, too, was quite lax in pressing for a redirection of national policy.

As a consequence, political pressure for change
was slight and localized at best, almost totally ab-
sent at worst. But the real problem was in the society at large; a core of supporting values in many
ways precluded a broad-scale examination of the policy
and supported incremental expansion regardless of its
cumulative effect.

Lacking the visibility of policy pronouncements
in the area of university administration, enrollment
expansion was instead carried out through a series of
small, related steps. The bureaucracy's readiness to
grant university charters and its reluctance to force
compliance with existing requirements contributed to
this policy. The policy was advanced no less distinctly than policies in university administration,
but its bureaucratic character made it less visible
and controversial.

In essence, the policy provided for an unfunded,
rapid, and uncontrolled expansion, which failed to

maintain educational quality and to enhance the upward mobility of the lower economic classes. Instead
overall physical quality deteriorated markedly and
the lack of public funding restricted admissions to
the more affluent sectors of the population.

Two codas should perhaps be added on this point,
however. First, the lack of governmental funding has
limited to a great extent the government's ability to
exercise control over many universities. Conversely,
the weakness of university organizations and the government's ability to approach the more conservative
university trustees or administrators have mitigated
this limitation somewhat. Second, the expansion policy has not been uniformly beneficial to the government. A good deal of student protest activity during
1968-69 revolved around the poor conditions of universities. Moreover, the government's decision in
1970-71 to increase spending for both private and governmental universities suggested that it had begun to
question the wisdom of its previous policy. Then, in
1975 a law was passed prohibiting the issuance of any
further charters to private universities until 1981,
except in "exceptional circumstances." Thus, some
policy reexamination occurred, but it came largely at
the initiative of the Ministry of Education and the
government bureaucracy and was at best related only
indirectly to broader political currents and controversies. As of 1977, however, there seemed to be
little examination of the class consequences of past
expansion policies, and it seems unlikely that this
problem will receive the same attention as that given
to improving quality.

# 7. Pressure Group Politics: Differentiation and Specialization

All governments are subject to pressures from individuals, groups, or social sectors seeking particularistic benefits. Most governments will respond to demands for what they regard as desirable changes or to pressures that, if ignored, could significantly undermine the regime. The importance of big business to the conservative government in Japan has been so well documented as to need no further elaboration. Its individual members, organizations, and federations have consistently and successfully pressured the Japanese government to make certain changes in the content and structure of higher education.

Since its earliest incarnations, the university has performed some role in professional training and certification. In the twelfth and thirteenth centuries this was limited almost exclusively to the preparation of men for the ministry, medicine, and the law and was distinctly subsidiary to the university's broader role of guarding general knowledge, training the total man, and providing an intellectual oasis for those in search of truth. The development of highly specialized and complex societies, however, forced dramatic changes in this orientation. The business sector in any modern, highly industrialized, and dynamic economy requires a talented and highly educated pool of citizens from which to draw employees; increasingly the universities are being perceived as the key source of that pool. The result has been increased effort in all industrial societies for higher educational systems that will provide the training seen as most useful to subsequent industrial employment. The Japanese business community has been no exception to this pattern; however, the nature of prewar education and the changes introduced by the Americans bolstered efforts to seek government action designed to secure from the universities the kind of graduates business desired.

159

As noted in Chapter 3, the Japanese university is a relatively modern institution, Japan's first being established only in 1877. The political leadership at that time, quite concerned about Japan's weakness vis-a-vis the Western imperial powers and conscious of the need for rapid industrial and technological development so as to defend the integrity of the nation, quite deliberately sought to establish practicality as the guiding principal for all education, including higher learning.[1] A business and political leadership group technically trained to bring about a total economic and social transformation was essential. This orientation went back at least to Satō Shinen, who at the time of the Opium War in China argued that protecting Japan from Western expansionism necessitated specialization and efficiency, with all adults being trained to functionally specific tasks and prohibited from changing occupations, and with a nationally run university to provide the most specialized training. Others, too, prior to the Meiji Restoration, took up the theme of protecting national independence through a combination of "Eastern morals and Western technology," with the result that the earliest emphases in Japanese education were unquestionably specialization and technical skills.

In Western European and U.S. universities, by way of contrast, such concerns were far less central in the earliest days. Only when the Morrill Act of 1862 established the land grant colleges in the United States did the practical application of what was taught become more widespread.[2] Even then the more established liberal arts institutions tended to scorn practicality as exclusively the province of "cow colleges." In Japan, in contrast, even such Western-influenced leaders as Fukuzawa Yukichi called for study which focused on the immediately useful. In his essay "Encouragement of Learning" ("Gakumon no susume"), for example, he wrote:

> Learning does not mean useless accomplishments, such as knowing strange words or reading old and difficult texts, or enjoying and writing poetry. These accomplishments give much pleasure to the human mind and they have their own values. But they should not be slavishly worshipped as the usual run of scholars try to persuade us. There have been precious few scholars in Chinese classics at any time who were good providers, or merchants accomplished in

> poetry and yet clever in business. . . .
> Therefore this kind of unpractical learn-
> ing should be left to other days, and
> one's best efforts should be given to
> practical learning that is close to
> everyone's needs. . . .[3]

Such concerns remained philosophically dominant in
higher education throughout the prewar period.

During the Occupation such specialization and
occupational relevance were the subjects of particular attack. As much the captives of the structure
and ideology of the American higher educational system
as they were devotees of the broad knowledge that had
been its original justification, the Americans sought
to provide a system that minimized, and in some cases
was overtly hostile to, the occupational relevance
and distinctly technical training of the prewar period. Some even paralleled the need for separating
higher education from industrial relevance with the
American penchant for separating church and state.
These goals were to be manifested in a system keyed
to the four-year liberal arts college with a curriculum requiring a heavy two-year program in general
education. This system became the target of business-
initiated pressures for change, the primary thrust of
which sought to force higher education back to the
more occupationally relevant system of diversified
institutions and specialized curriculums of the prewar period.

The prewar history of specialization and differentiation went largely unchallenged at the time by
academics and the political Left. Following the war
the issue has lacked the heightened affect surrounding issues of university autonomy and administration.
Its potential impact has always been seen to be far
less direct and far more specific. No single serious
proposal seeking fundamental changes in all institutions of higher education ever emerged, in contrast
to the issue of university administration. Rather,
the issue has had a reasonably high degree of divisibility and has been quite narrow and specific in its
scope. At the same time, when compared to enrollment
expansion it has been much more diffuse, broader, and
far less disaggregable. Politically, the issue has
never raised constitutional questions and only rarely
has it raised legal ones.[4] For the most part, the
problem has been open to resolution by actions by the
Ministry of Education or some combination of bureaucratic agencies. Yet resolution has necessitated in
most cases far more consciousness, planning, and

161

coordination than enrollment expansion. Incrementalism has not dominated most aspects of the differentiation and specialization question. Finally, the business sector, which has been the most concerned with
the question, has been highly mobilizable and politically influential and has operated in a climate of
official opinion favorable to the economic development to which the issue has constantly been connected,
again separating it from the other two cases.

Similar contrasts with the other issues can be
seen in policymaking. As noted in Chapter 5, in most
matters of university administration, policymaking involved attempts at passing or blocking legislation;
cleavage, total commitment, and vigorous opposition
were almost inevitably present. In the area of educational specialization and differentiation, however,
policymaking was accomplished almost exclusively by
bureaucratic means, such as ordinance revision, quota
changes, encouragement of "independent" university
action, financial inducement, and the like. Confrontations and conflict have been far fewer. In this
area the importance and potential of the overall bureaucratic trends analyzed in Chapter 4 are also
starkly visible.

Government policy toward university administration was largely the result of reaction to such other
specific problems as progressive protest, plus the
somewhat more natural tendency of most governments to
seek control and supervision over ever more diverse
areas of society. Government policies toward enrollment emerged largely as unconscious and incremental
responses to a combination of specific requests by
universities to expand and to the broader climate of
social values. In contrast, its policy toward the
differentiation of higher educational institutions
and the specialization of higher educational training
has been a far more conscious response to clear-cut
and particularistic demands from big business, which
has justified these demands as essential to economic
development.

There have been two related but analytically
distinct components of this problem: structural differentiation among institutions, and specialization
of training to favor certain types of graduates. In
both cases a rather consistent business demand has
led to an almost equally consistent pattern of governmental policy response.

## DEMANDS OF BIG BUSINESS

Japanese big business is represented organizationally in several diverse and autonomous federations. The major ones are the Japan Federation of Employers Associations (JFEA), the Federation of Economic Organizations (FEO), and the Japan Committee for Economic Development (JCED). Of somewhat lesser significance are the Japan Chamber of Commerce and the Kansai Economic Federation.[5] These federations have been the prime articulators and advocates of their members' demands in the area of higher education. While the organizations represent somewhat different perspectives on a variety of economic and other questions, their views on the problems of specialization and differentiation in higher education have been relatively uniform: their central concern has been to make the higher educational system more useful to the manpower needs of the major industries of the country.

Two primary business needs have been expressed: first, functional differentiation of the higher educational structure, and second, increased specialization in courses and the graduation of more science and engineering specialists. The two themes recur constantly in the proposals, plans, suggestions, and demands issued over the entire postwar period by the different business federations. Additional pressure was then invariably applied by, among other things, testimony at public meetings and advisory committee hearings, media lobbying, direct mailings to members, and lobbying by individual businessmen and federation leaders of the government and party officials involved in the decision-making process.

The two themes of specialization and differentiation emerge as early as October 1952. Then the new system of higher education came in for particular criticism in a JFEA document entitled, "Opinion Paper on the Reexamination of the New Educational System." The report criticized "the lack of integration between [general] education courses and specialized courses" and called for increased specialization throughout the higher educational system.[6] One key argument was that, although the bulk of university graduates entered the business world, "the educational perspective" did not treat students as potential employees.

The report went on to declare:

It is imperative that business and industry exercise educational leadership over the learning power of students in postsecondary

education so as to train people who, after
graduation, will use the scientific attainments, techniques, and skills they
have acquired to make positive contributions as employees to society and the
state.[7]

Two subsequent JFEA proposals in December 1954[8]
and November 1956[9] made even more specific criticisms.
Outgrowths of surveys conducted by the association in
March 1953 and March 1955, they showed a great dis-
satisfaction among businessmen with the technical
competence of young graduates of the "new system"
universities, who the businessmen claimed were less
competent than prewar alumni. Both reports sought to
distinguish between "workers and employees" on the one
hand and the "general citizenry" on the other, stressing throughout the business community's need for more
education of the former.[10]
The 1954 report called for a correction of the
"imbalance" between law and literature graduates on
the one hand and science and engineering graduates on
the other. At the time, about 16 percent of the university students were enrolled in programs of science
and engineering, compared to 40 percent in law, politics, commerce, and economics; 13 percent in literature; and 15 percent in teacher training.[11] By way
of contrast, Britain, France, West Germany, and the
Soviet Union all had approximately 35-40 percent of
their student populations in science and engineering,
and several of these countries were seeking to expand
these percentages. (The United States was closer to
the Japanese figure, with approximately 19 percent in
science and engineering.)
The report also demanded "a rationalization of
the education given during the four years of university training" by "coordinating general education
. . . with basic courses of a specialized nature."
It also demanded training for potential employees of
small and medium-sized businesses and for the reestablishment of five-year industrial and technical colleges that would combine three years of high school
and the first two years of college.[12]
The JFEA report two years later expanded upon
these themes, calling again for the five-year technical colleges and demanding as well a long-range plan
to develop more technicians, scientists, and engineers. Better science and engineering facilities at
the university and graduate school level were called
for; provisions to reeducate industry's technical
employees were demanded; and concrete ties between the
university and the industrial world were proposed.[13]

Meanwhile, in January 1955 an FEO set of proposals for "Policies to Encourage Industrial Education in the Schools" raised similar demands.[14]

A November 1960 document of the JCED continued these themes and called for a school system more closely tied to industry to serve the purposes and demands of the industrial world. Part of the proposal was explicitly political: "For the development of a healthy democracy we must train a commonsensical middle class which will serve as a stable social force. . . . In order to bring students into the camp of democracy and capitalism, the financial world must make cooperative moves toward students. For these purposes, it will be most effective to rely on a movement for 'industrial and university cooperation.'"[15]

The Kansai Economic Federation simultaneously reiterated many of the same themes in an "Opinion Paper on the Reform of the University System." The federation claimed that general education was inappropriate and that the university system was not responsive to "the demands of society." It called for greater specialization; for increased emphasis on science and engineering, particularly in the former imperial universities; for the establishment of five-year technical colleges; and for long-range controls over student quotas to meet industrial needs.[16]

JFEA, too, kept up its demand for the five-year technical college, and a special subcommittee issued a further report on its desirability in December 1960.[17] Pressure was also sustained for governmental efforts to increase the number of scientific and engineering graduates. In August 1961 JFEA and FEO issued a joint request to the government and the Diet on this point.[18] Throughout the 1960s JFEA led the business world in pressing for increased functional differentiation of higher educational institutions, for a decrease in the emphasis on general training and education within the university, for increased specialized training, and for more scientists and engineers.

Increasingly the business federations, as they articulated positions calling for more occupationally relevant universities, stressed the somewhat servile position they saw the universities occupying. In 1969, for example, the JFEA declared that "notwithstanding their individual objectives and individual characteristics, today's universities are authorized to exist only insofar as they fulfill their mission by meeting the joint demands of the state and society."[19] It demanded more explicit functional differentiation and even more professional education:

165

It is necessary to diversify the length of
schooling, curriculum, and other matters
and to diversify as well the types of institutions along lines of purpose and
character: graduate schools for high-level
academic studies and research, professional colleges (longer or shorter depending
on their specialties), junior colleges focusing on the acquisition of general education, and special purpose colleges to
train teachers and artists, etc.[20]

Similar demands were issued in two subsequent JFEA reports during the same year and in JCED reports and
proposals.[21]

In general, business and industry wanted a system
of higher education that would provide, at minimal
cost to them, more individuals with at least some
general training for subsequent employment specializa-
tions and that would devote minimal time to subjects
of less occupational significance. The benefits to
business would be clear, narrow, and particularistic,
although in almost all cases the business federations
formulated their demands not in particularistic but
in general terms.

The changes, it was invariably noted, were directed toward meeting "social demand," not business
demands; they would be beneficial to national economic growth, not to big business; they were necessary
to allow Japan to compete internationally, not to
provide the basis for big business expansion overseas; they would provide students with marketable
skills, not bias their total education. Such formulations should not be surprising; particularistic demands are always more readily acceptable when couched
in universalistic terms. To be sure, some aspects
of the demanded changes clearly were of broader utility, particularly given Japan's capitalistic economic
system and the significance of big business in that
system.

The big business community has been an integral
component and the financial mainstay of the conservative camp, with ties to conservative politics that
can be traced back to the Meiji period.[22] The government has been highly responsive to a number of business demands in fields other than education. And,
as noted earlier, to the extent that it perceives any
demands as either meritorious or politically significant, the government seeks to meet them and/or to reconcile the competing demands made upon it.[23] The
fact that there was little opposition to most business

demands made it easy for the government to respond to
most of them.


DIFFERENTIATION AMONG INSTITUTIONS

Under the reorganized American-style system,
Japan initially had only one permanent and legitimate
institution of higher education beyond high school:
the four-year university.  Since 1952 the government,
in response to business demands, has authorized four
entirely new forms of higher educational institution,
has proposed several more, and has encouraged significant differentiation among groups of institutions
within these various categories.
The earliest alteration in the unified system
came with the establishment of junior colleges.  Although actually begun under the Occupation, the junior
colleges were initially granted only temporary status
to provide something of a way-station for those prewar
technical colleges or higher schools that could not
immediately upgrade themselves to four-year universities:

Because conditions of personnel and material
facilities have made it difficult for some
of the old system higher schools and technical schools to shift completely into the new
four-year university system, [the establishment of] two- and three-year universities is
temporarily permitted. [However,] as quickly
as possible they must make plans to qualify
for the new system.[24]

In 1950, the first year they were permitted, 149
junior colleges were established.  During the next two
years 58 were added, while only 2 schools left the
category.[25]  The government meanwhile formalized
standards for the establishment of junior colleges and
set up a special Advisory Committee (later, Council)
on Junior Colleges.  The junior colleges meanwhile
formed a separate Junior College Association.  By 1955
there were 264 junior colleges, and the category was
no longer considered temporary by any but the most
avid devotees of legal literalism.
Initially the government and business considered
the emerging junior college system as a possible way
to meet the demand for more specialization.  The junior colleges went only part way toward meeting the
demands of big business, however.  The primary desire
was to recreate some form of the prewar semmongakkō

167

(technical colleges) that would provide technicians and trained blue-collar personnel, and at first business sought to have the junior colleges fulfill this function. As early as the autumn of 1952 and continuing for the next two years, the JFEA demanded that junior colleges focus their attention on industrial and work-oriented education to meet this need.[26] The junior colleges, however, were slow to respond to this suggestion, and the bulk of their enrollees were in literature, homemaking, law, and economics, with well below 10 percent in science, engineering, agricultural sciences, and nursing.[27] Pressure from the business world continued to mount on the Ministry of Education, and in the fall of 1955 Education Minister Matsumura announced at a press conference that plans were under way to submit to the Central Education Council the question of transforming junior colleges into the institutional form desired by the business world.[28]

The junior colleges quickly perceived this as a threat and fought fiercely to retain their legitimacy and existing character. Following a long debate within the Central Education Council and the Ministry of Education, however, the government proposed in December 1957 to cease recognition of the junior colleges after April 1, 1959, and to establish occupationally oriented specialist colleges (senka daigaku) beginning in 1960.[29]

This plan was submitted to the lower house, where the Education Committee ratified it. The junior colleges and the Junior College Association, however, brought counterpressure upon members of the LDP in the upper house, and some revisions were made in the plans.[30] A second submission was made to the lower house Education Committee that month. Still the positions of the business world, the LDP, the bureaucracy, and the junior college federations were not reconciled. At the end of the month a vector sum compromise emerged that provided for the creation of a five-year higher technical school system to begin in 1962 and that allowed junior colleges to continue in their existing character but stipulated that they were to aim explicitly at providing specialized education as preparation for employment.[31]

The junior colleges continued to oppose this explicit change in their goals, and a final compromise provided that junior colleges would serve to "provide [both] general and professional education for secondary school graduates and [also] to develop the intellectual and practical abilities required for their future careers and practical life."[32]

In accord with the compromise, the government drafted a bill to create the desired five-year technical colleges. With the opposition from the junior colleges assuaged, with the conservative camp almost uniformly committed, and with the progressive camp almost totally uninterested, the bill sailed through the Diet meeting only perfunctory opposition. The technical schools went into effect on April 1, 1962.

Both the junior colleges and the higher technical schools have since come to occupy significant positions in Japanese higher education. In 1950 there were 149 junior colleges; in 1975 there were 513, of which 434 were privately administered.[33] Student enrollment increased during the same time from 15,000 to nearly 350,000.[34] A startling 90 percent of all junior college students are enrolled in private institutions, an even higher proportion than that for four-year colleges, and an almost equally high 85 percent are women, well over half of whom are in homemaking or literature. Only about one-quarter of the students could be said to be in occupationally related fields of study, and almost all of these are either women enrolled in the education division or men attending evening courses in engineering or commerce.[35]

The higher technical schools are quite distinct, being five-year institutions that combine the last three years of high school with two years of college, with explicitly technical and vocational aims. The system has been primarily under national administration, in contrast to the generally private junior colleges: 54 of the 65 higher technical schools are national, while only 4 are local public and 7 are private.[36] With only one exception, there have been no new local public and private technical schools established since 1963, whereas there have been 25 national institutions created since then. In 1975 there were 48,000 students, up from an initial 3,375 in 1962.[37] Fewer than 800 of these students were women, and virtually the entire enrollment is in the technical fields of industrial or mercantile engineering.[38] In short, the government has taken the primary fiscal and administrative responsibility for the development and maintenance of the system most explicitly demanded by the business community, a system that in turn has come to occupy a major role in Japanese higher education, while meeting simultaneously the counterdemands of the junior colleges for an autonomous existence.

Quite clearly the junior college and the higher technical school have extremely different characters and serve rather separate purposes. The junior colleges act primarily as finishing schools for women, while the higher technical schools train middle and low-level technicians and engineers for industry. The social classes served by the two are also quite different. Junior colleges, being privately administered, are generally expensive and thus available primarily to the more well-to-do, while the technical schools are government-operated and rather inexpensive, attracting many of their students from middle and lower income groups, many of whom are unable to afford the four-year colleges or have not qualified academically for the limited financial aid available there. Both types of institution have grown rapidly, however, and both represent significant differentiations within higher education and major deviations from the pattern of a higher educational system based on the four-year college.

Even further institutional differentiation was proposed by the Central Education Council in its comprehensive 1963 evaluation of the higher educational system, and in the late 1960s two components were added; these were national training institutes for industrial arts teachers and for nursing teachers, both of which began in 1966. Both were three-year institutes, again created and maintained by the government. At one point there were nine of the former institutes, with an enrollment of 2,300; these, however, were discontinued in 1969, when the government determined that a sufficient number of industrial arts teachers had been trained.[39] In 1975 there were nine institutes for nursing teachers, all affiliated with national universities. These had a combined enrollment of just over 1,000.[40] Although numerically insignificant, these institutes were part of the broader trend toward increasing functional differentiation of higher educational institutions through national government support.

The trend toward functional differentiation manifested in the establishment of these diverse institutions of higher education is likely to persist. For example, in 1967 the Economic Planning Agency in its Economic and Social Development Plan for 1967-71 proposed a three-group distinction among higher educational institutions: "a group mainly for general culture; a group mainly for training special workers; a group mainly for higher-level scientists and researchers."[41] This theme was further developed in 1971, when the government adopted a proposal by the Central Education Council to specialize educational institutions even more.[42]

The latter report urged that five distinct categories of higher educational institutions be established. Two categories, those of the junior college and the higher technical school, would not represent significant deviations. The three other categories, however, would require major structural changes. One category would be for "universities" of three specific types, each with a substantially different curriculum following roughly the earlier outlines suggested by the Economic Planning Agency. There would be a comprehensive curriculum "providing professional knowledge and skills for those careers which are not particularly specialized." An academic curriculum would "provide basic academic knowledge and skills," while an occupational curriculum would "provide the theoretical and technical training required for particular professional occupations so as to provide students with the qualifications or abilities for those occupations." The comprehensive curriculum would aim at training white-collar workers, the academic curriculum at training scholars, and the occupational curriculum would seek to develop technical professionals.

Beyond the university a further differentiation would take place. "Graduate schools" would provide two or three years of academic education in specific fields--essentially the equivalent of an M.A.-granting institution--while "research centers" would provide opportunities for training for the Ph.D. The plan would bring about a major change from the unified graduate schools attached to universities offering both the M.A. and Ph.D. and would also meet partially the business demand for institutions receptive to the retraining of technical employees. This report makes it clear that the earlier steps to differentiate institutions along functional lines indicate a continuing trend in official thinking toward a return to the prewar system of widespread institutional differentiation and high occupational relevance in higher education.

The government has also taken a number of steps to differentiate the four-year universities under its control according to their primary orientations as either teaching or research institutions.[43]

Theoretically, all national universities have equal status in law, and the early Occupation had sought to minimize any vast differences in quality among them. These efforts met with sharp resistance from the Ministry of Education and the more privileged of the universities, and by the end of the Occupation a clear hierarchy of prestige and quality among the national universities could be perceived. Quality differentiation is inevitable among educational institutions, but since 1952 the government has reinforced, among the national universities under its control, the normal processes of improvement and regression. The key aspect in the government's role has been the distinction between the "chair system" and the "course system" as the basis for internal organization of national universities.

The distinction is rooted in the structure of prewar Japanese higher education, when "chairs" were established as the organs for research and "courses" were designed for general education and teaching.[44] The formal discrimination between the two functions was eliminated during the Occupation, but no specific changes were mandated in the organizational format of the universities. The result was that the existing systems in individual universities tended to be perpetuated.

The chair system, particularly in the experimental and clinical fields, provides for more faculty at the junior level than does the course system. As a result, it often gives immense power to senior faculty, while limiting the upward mobility of junior faculty.[45] Moreover, as institutionalized bureaucratically within the Ministry of Education, the difference between the two systems has become the basis for distinctions between research and teaching, and subsequently for important distinctions among universities.

Separate chair and course systems have emerged primarily as the outgrowth of subtle, almost invisible, bureaucratic steps, rather than as the result of any dramatic legislative struggle. As early as March 1951 the government was seeking to reestablish a fundamental difference between research and teaching institutions.[46] In 1954 an administrative directive further spelled out the government's perception of these differences, establishing the chair system as the exclusive unit for research and then specifying which institutions would be allowed to have chairs.[47] An additional directive in 1956 made the distinctions formal and set up the chair as the basic unit for research and the course as the unit for teaching.[48] This distinction has become institutionalized, and the 1963 and 1971 reports of the Central Education Council encouraged its continuance.[49] As a result, universities have been categorized as either "comprehensive universities" (sōgō daigaku) engaged in both research and teaching or "ordinary universities" (tanka daigaku or daigaku), whose faculties simply teach. The 1971 report made an even more rigid distinction between teaching and

172

research as regards the functions of the distinct
"graduate schools" and "research centers,"[50] which
it proposed should be established. It was implicit
as well in the sections dealing with the undergradu-
ate university. This fundamental distinction between
teaching and research has led to additional discrimi-
nations in such areas as allocation of budgets and
faculties, student entry quotas, educational programs,
graduate training facilities, and so on.

As far as budgeting is concerned, the two systems
were essentially equal in 1949. By 1951 chair-system
personnel were receiving twice the funding per person
as course-system faculty. By 1965 this figure was
three times as much, and the gap continued to increase
thereafter.[51] Amano, relating these factors to the
geographical distribution of incoming students and employment patterns following graduation, distinguishes
three fundamentally different types of national university: central, national, and local.[52]

The so-called central universities represent the
most prestigious educational institutions in Japan,
consisting of the seven prewar imperial universities
plus three others. These institutions are organized
almost exclusively on the chair system; they have the
bulk of the graduate programs and research facilities;
they attract students from throughout the country and
train them in all fields; and their graduates hold
prestige positions throughout society.

There are also ten universities of the so-called
national type. Most trace their ancestry to arts and
language institutions of the prewar period. They are
now organized on a course rather than a chair basis
and have limited graduate facilities. They retain
some truly national character in student body and
alumni, however, even though the latter group remains
primarily in the fields of literature and art.

Finally, the category that Amano labels local
universities is made up of institutions that draw
students primarily from, and return them to, the geographical areas in which they are situated. Their
prime function has been training such individuals for
local white-collar posts, most notably in the teaching field. These, too, are organized on the basis of
courses, not chairs; they offer limited programs and
have disproportionately few graduate and research
facilities. Table 7-1 indicates some of the more
significant statistical distinctions among the three
types, with the powerful position of the ten central
universities being most clear.

Consequently, the distinction between the teaching and research functions forms a link in the broader

policy of differentiating higher educational institutions along functional lines. This particularization of institutions has led to a tracking system for higher educational institutions in which each track corresponds to some occupational or vocational category, quite in accord with business demands.

These combined policies of institutional specialization have been only one base of the government's policy of increasing occupational relevance and specialization within higher education and represent only a partial, primarily bureaucratic response to the demands of big business. Government policies toward specialized training have been the additional aspect of its overall response.

TABLE 7-1

Internal Comparison of National Universities

|  | Central | National | Local | Total |
|---|---|---|---|---|
| 1) No. of schools | 10 | 10 | 55 | 75 |
| % of total | (13.3) | (13.3) | (73.4) | (100.0) |
| 2) Annual no. of students (entry quota 1967) | 17,647 | 3,344 | 42,940 | 63,931 |
| % of total | (27.6) | (5.2) | (67.2) | (100.0) |
| 3) No. of educational personnel | 42,245 | 4,205 | 53,384 | 99,834 |
| % of total | (42.3) | (4.2) | (53.5) | (100.0) |
| 4) No. of graduate courses | 75 | 11 | 89 | 175 |
| % of total | (42.8) | (6.3) | (50.9) | (100.0) |
| 5) Annual no. of graduate students (entry quota 1967) | 7,653 | 536 | 3,788 | 11,977 |
| % of total | (64.0) | (4.5) | (31.5) | (100.0) |
| 6) No. of research institutes | 55 | 2 | 13 | 70 |
| % of total | (78.5) | (2.9) | (18.6) | (100.0) |
| 7) Budget (billions ¥) | 115.5 | 10.4 | 120.0 | 246.0 |
| % of total | (47.0) | (4.2) | (48.8) | (100.0) |

Sources: 1, 3, 4, 7 are 1969 figures calculated on the basis of data in Mombushō, Mombushō dai 97 nempō, pp. 204-209; 2, 5, 6 from Amano Ikuo, "Kokuritsu daigaku," in Shimizu Yoshihiro, ed., Nihon no kōtō kyōiku, p. 191.

SPECIALIZATION OF TRAINING

Specialization has been the watchword for changes
both among institutions and within them.  The business
community, as was noted earlier, made consistent demands during the 1950s and 1960s for more specialized
training within higher educational curriculums and for
more graduates in scientific and technical fields.
The establishment of the higher technical schools and
the specific national training institutions went part
way toward meeting these demands institutionally, as
did the functional distinctions that emerged among
national universities.  The government, however, moved
in two other areas to meet business demands: it increased specialized course requirements, and it dramatically augmented the number of graduates in science and
engineering.  The bulk of this policymaking involved
conscious bureaucratic and intraministerial changes,
brought about with minimal intercamp conflict and only
limited public visibility.

As noted earlier, the de facto regulations for
the new system of higher education set up by the Occupation were the University Standards formulated in 1947
by the University Accreditation Association under the
direction of SCAP and CIE officials.  These standards
were the basis for a university's membership in the
association, that is, its accreditation.  Although
technically private regulations, they were accepted
and used by the Ministry of Education as the basis on
which to charter universities as well.

As originally drawn up in July 1947 and revised
in June 1953, the standards provided for two years of
broad liberal arts education with specific credit requirements in the areas of foreign language, physical
education, specialized courses, and general education.
All universities were required to offer two or more
foreign languages and to establish general education
programs with a minimum of fifteen courses, three or
more to be offered in each of the three major subfields
of humanities, natural sciences, and social sciences.[53]
Students were required to earn 36 of their required 124
credits in the three major subfields.  In short, all
graduates had to have had some exposure, usually three
or four courses, within each subfield and to have devoted most of their first two years to the general education program, foreign language training, and physical
education.  During their final two years they could
take more specialized work in their major fields.

There was strong opposition to this arrangement
from the major business federations, who charged that
the general education program was too broad, lacked

integration with subsequent specialized programs, and repeated much of what was done or should have been done in high schools. It was even argued that general education was irrelevant in an age of specialization.[54]

The government responded to these charges by reducing the official requirements for general education. In June 1954 two governmental directives exempted medical and dental programs from the University Standards. Then, in 1956 a ministerial directive called the University Chartering Regulations affected all courses of study.[55] The new requirements accepted the existing three-field division for general education programs; however, they allowed a university to offer 20 percent fewer courses in each than did the old standards. Moreover, geography, education, and astronomy were dropped from the possible course offerings for general education, while psychology and statistics courses were added.[56] Meanwhile, although universities were still expected to offer two foreign languages in principle, they could offer only one "if there were special circumstances related to the type of faculties or courses set up in the university."[57] Furthermore, the notion of "basic education" courses was introduced. Courses eligible for this category were introductory courses for subsequent specialization;[58] as many as eight could be offered in fulfillment of the 36 general education credits needed for graduation. These new regulations thereby weakened considerably general education and foreign language requirements and allowed specialized courses to be included among the general education requirements needed for graduation.

Business pressures against the general education program continued despite these changes, some of which were echoed by official government investigative reports. The 1963 report of the Central Education Council contained heavy criticisms of even the revised version of the general education program, for example. In that year, too, a special research committee was established to investigate the University Chartering Standards, and after two years it submitted a report on the problem to the minister of education,[59] stressing the need to strengthen specialized and basic education and to eliminate any minimum standards for general education.[60] Academic groups were quick to criticize such a totalistic proposal,[61] and it was never implemented. In August 1970, however, the Ministry of Education put out a second major set of revisions, less total than that proposed in 1963, but again by the use of a ministerial directive.[62]

176

These revisions dropped the requirement that a university offer a minimum number of courses in general education. Instead, they allowed each university to determine its own required courses and the number of units it would offer in general education. The graduation requirement of 36 credits in general education was retained, but these credits no longer had to be divided equally among three subfields, making it possible for a student to take almost all courses within a single subfield. Moreover, the new regulations allowed students to substitute up to 12 credits of "basic" courses in their specialization for portions of the general education requirement. Even these requirements were loosened for foreign students and for those in medical and dental programs. In addition, the library requirements for holdings in general education were reduced.[63]

These two government directives drastically cut the general education requirements for both universities and students. Because the process involved primarily the allowance of exceptions to existing rules rather than the governmentally directed enforcement of new rules, the changes were of a much more divisible nature and individual universities could respond in an ad hoc manner. These changes were thus qualitatively different from those in the area of university administration, where changes were mandated throughout the entire system.

Beyond their immediate and visible impact on general education requirements, the changes allowed by the government also legitimated the thrust toward specialization within the university. The upwardly oriented student, faculty member, or administrator was not too subtly made aware that big business and the government were strongly committed to specialization, and many trimmed their academic sails accordingly.[64] General education thus became a secondary hurdle to clear rather than an essential element in a serious intellectual "race."

These changes in the content of higher education were matched by attempts to increase the number of graduates in the fields of science and engineering. The earliest efforts in this area were undertaken exclusively by the Ministry of Education, primarily through its power to establish entry quotas for each faculty of each institution of higher education. According to a 1964 Ministry of Education document, "An increase in the number of enrollees in science and engineering departments . . . has been attempted every year since the inauguration of the new schools system."[65] This entry quota proved at best a rough

177

approximation of the number of students entering a particular faculty, and the results of the early and annual efforts, while not insignificant, by no means met business needs for massive expansion and economic growth. A more systematic, coordinated, and long-range plan was developed in 1957; its key aim was to increase by 8,000 the number of freshmen enrolled in science and engineering departments over a five-year period.[66]

During the first three years of the plan the quotas were generally met; even these figures, however, proved to be well below the needs foreseen by industry and economic planners. A more coordinated and massive effort was demanded, and in February 1959 the government established the Science and Technology Council as an organ of the Prime Minister's Office. The council, which consisted of the prime minister, the ministers of finance and education, and the ministers of state for economic planning and for science and technology, and others, was to coordinate the actions of the various government agencies and to provide for comprehensive development of the government's policies for science and technology.[67] This step marked an intensification of governmental concern to meet the demands of big business, not only for increased numbers of scientists and technicians but more generally throughout the science field.[68]

One and a half years later the council issued an extensive plan that became the keystone for a variety of coordinated government activities in science and technology. Among other things, the proposal, entitled "A Comprehensive Plan for the Advancement of Science and Technology in the Next Ten Years," contended that between 1960 and 1970 Japan would face estimated manpower shortages of 170,000 in science and technology, of 50,000 in medicine, and of 440,000 in engineering.[69] In the same month the Economic Advisory Council, a committee affiliated with the Economic Planning Agency of the Prime Minister's Office, issued a document that was to become the basis for Japan's phenomenal growth during the 1960s, "A Plan for the Doubling of the National Income." This document declared, among other things, that "the most important thing in long-term planning for economic growth involves a numerical guarantee of and an increase in the quality of our scientists and technicians."[70] In March 1961 the Science and Technology Agency issued a series of recommendations, concluding with a statement that the universities must increase the number of students in the sciences and engineering and must consider policies to alleviate quickly the

178

pending shortages that could be a key impediment to economic growth.[71] The responsibility for alleviating these shortages was placed on the Ministry of Education and on the individual universities, both public and private. The need for substantial government aid to reach these goals was recognized in all the reports.

A number of coordinated steps were taken by the relevant government agencies to achieve the expansion targets. Several of these necessitated Diet action; most were handled exclusively within the bureaucracy. In March 1961 a bill was passed to set up temporary national institutes for training science and technology teachers.[72] This bill ran into some opposition, particularly from the Japan Science Council, but passed rather easily; it provided for three-year programs affiliated with nine of the major national universities and sought to alleviate some of the teaching needs that would be met by the proposed increases.

The necessary funds for the overall increases in facilities and enrollment were budgeted by the Finance Ministry in coordination with the various other governmental agencies, and in September 1961 the Ministry of Education issued a plan to increase the number of students in science and technology departments by 16,000 per year starting in 1961.

This shift in the departmental enrollment pattern was achieved again through essentially bureaucratic means: changes in the entry quota for specific university departments, encouragement of and ready permission to establish or expand existing science and engineering departments, and financial inducements. Special accounts were established for private university expansion in the sciences,[73] and subsidies were made available under the Budget Execution Rationalization Law. Under this, faculties of universities could apply for subsidies to one or more ministries or government agencies; once funds were granted, the reviewing agency would receive periodic reports on the basis of which they could modify or revise the subsidies.[74] Many of the actions taken by the Ministry of Education were carried out exclusively through directives or internal decisions; the subsidies were part of the budget process and went through the Diet along with the entire national budget; the comparatively small sums involved and the limited nature of Diet debate and refinement of the budget virtually isolated the process from significant public debate.[75]

The main outlines of the expansion were formulated in 1960-61; subsequent refinements, however, took place. As noted, for example, the initial increase sought by the Ministry of Education was 16,000 per year. The business federations subsequently declared that such an increase would be insufficient,[76] and eventually a goal of an increase of 20,000 per year was established for the years 1961-64. This, too, was subsequently raised almost annually.

Beyond this, additional government groups reformulated in minor ways certain aspects of the proposed increases or took, or sought to take, steps that would further advance and legitimate the overall policy. The Economic Advisory Council, in a 1963 proposal entitled "Countermeasures toward the Problem of Developing Human Talents for Economic Growth," refined many of the proposals and rearticulated the need for increasing the numbers and quality of Japan's science and engineering personnel.[77] The Committee to Investigate the Constitution in 1964 issued a report that called for some constitutional statement on the desirability of close cooperation between education and industry.[78] In 1969 a Labor Ministry survey contended that the number of technicians in the area of manufacturing was only 84 percent of the requirement and urged greater efforts to fulfill this need.[79] On balance, however, despite the minor revisions and further urgings, the basic policy set in 1960-61 was the key operative policy for the decade, one that was quite successful in increasing the numbers of scientists and technicians.

From 1960 to 1970 the coordinated government efforts resulted in more than a doubling of the number of science and engineering faculties and in a 2.6-fold increase in the number of science and engineering graduates.[80] Moreover, there was a significant shift in the fields in which students were enrolled. In 1960, 18.2 percent of the total student enrollment was in the fields of science and engineering; by 1975 this figure was up to 23.2 percent. Even more significant, within the national universities, where the government efforts were most direct, the figure rose from 24 percent to 33 percent in these fields.[81]

Thus, conscious government policy altered the structure and content of the higher educational system to make it increasingly specialized, occupationally oriented, and responsive to the demands of big business. The policy has involved the increased differentiation and specialization of higher educational institutions and curriculums and the increased graduation of science and engineering specialists. Bureaucratic directives have been the key to most of the shifts in the general education requirements, to the differentiations made between universities on the chair system and those on the course system, and to many of the proposals to differentiate further among higher educational institutions. Bureaucratic action increasing entry quotas and offering financial inducements was a substantial force in increasing the number of science and engineering departments, as well as the number of scientists and engineers, during the 1960s. In nearly all cases, bureaucratic advisory committees were a key device in the generation of concrete policy proposals.

In virtually all of these cases, the government policies were effected with minimum opposition. The only significant opposition came from the Junior College Association over the attempt to force the junior colleges into the mold of prewar technical colleges. Like most studies of pressure group politics, this case was resolved by a compromise in which both sides received a substantial component of what they wanted.

Opposition in most other cases was blunted or virtually nonexistent. Financial measures, for example, could be argued in the annual budget hearings, but only on the basis of ad hoc appeals on highly disaggregable matters that could be dealt with on an individualistic basis. No substantial collective movement ever emerged around the problem of the government's financial measures.

Entry quotas too were ad hoc. Bargaining between individual universities and the Ministry of Education occurred on most occasions, but again agreements could be made on a case-by-case basis. And to the extent that the government's desire for university expansion in science and engineering was congruent with the desires of most private universities, there was little argument from the universities about these inducements.[82]

General education had never been very popular with those trained under the prewar system and never really gained public support; government efforts to reduce these requirements were opposed primarily by liberal educators. Insofar as the changes involved exceptions to rules rather than mandated changes, though, few universities or administrators protested, for they could always retain stricter requirements.

The specific proposals to expand the number of science and engineering facilities and graduates often came in for general criticism from the political Left in the form of opposition to the close ties between industry and the university (sangaku kyōdō). But the Left was less concerned with the broad changes taking place and much more worried about specific ties between the universities and projects with military overtones.[83] The broader aspects of the shifting

181

policies on specialization were given minimal attention.

At the time of the 1956 administrative directive establishing the new University Chartering Standards, for example, the academic community and the political Left were curiously silent. The only public statement of opposition appears to have been that of the Japan Teachers Union denouncing the directive as reactionary and claiming that "it essentially prohibits research activities in the new system universities, reducing the bulk of the national universities to the status of [prewar] technical colleges." The union took no further action, however.[84] Throughout the postwar period, progressive groups have denounced most statements or actions by which the Ministry of Education or the Central Education Council sought to foster ties between university and industry. Rarely, if ever, have these attacks gone beyond pro forma charges that all such activities are being made exclusively in response to "the demands of monopoly capital."[85]

Much of this apathy must clearly be attributed to the nature of the issues involved: low affect, high specificity, explicit scope, and high divisibility. Furthermore, in almost all cases the changes in policy have been carried out through almost invisible administrative processes, with little opportunity for non-conservative groups to exert an early, formal, and visible impact on decisions. Lastly, most of the policies have been pushed by big business federations having a great deal of internal political strength and intimate connections to the major organs of the LDP and the government. These groups have also formulated their demands in very general terms that stressed their contribution to national economic growth and were thus difficult to oppose. Japan's progressive camp, in general, found it exceptionally difficult to argue with the phenomenal growth achieved under LDP governments during the late 1950s and the 1960s, and the business community, legitimately or not, was able to convince both the government and large sectors of the public that its demands for specialization and differentiation were necessary for the continuance of that growth. The result was that issue definition was far less dichotomous than was the case in issues of university administration. Moreover, the government's policy of responding to business demands by increasing specialization and institutional differentiation was effected rather easily by the bureaucratic devices over which the conservatives exercise almost total control. At the same time, the process

was more conscious and to some extent more conflictual than the incrementalism of enrollment expansion.
In short, it was characterized by features rather
midway between the other two cases.

# 8. Conclusions

The most striking characteristic of Japanese policymaking which emerges from this study is its diversity. At the same time, this diversity is neither random nor sui generis to each policymaking case. In contrast to those case studies of decision-making or policymaking which analyze single decisions or policies made at specific times and places and argue for the uniqueness of each, and in contrast to the broader macrotheoretical approaches which formulate broad generalizations about policymaking regardless of time and place, this study has concentrated on a limited number of cases over a broad, but distinct and finite time period. As a result, it has been possible to analyze specific decisions in some depth, recognizing their discrete and individual characteristics, while at the same time highlighting certain commonalities and patterns. The result has been a portrayal of both similarities and mutabilities in Japanese policymaking. There are clearly broad and distinct patterns to policymaking, while at the same time each specific case within these broad patterns shows its own distinctness and modulation.

While it makes no claim to presenting a totally comprehensive typology of policymaking patterns, this study suggests that at least three clearly identifiable patterns can be found in postwar Japan: policymaking by camp conflict, policymaking by incrementalism, and pressure group policymaking. These patterns differ from one another in terms of the degree of manifest conflict, in the open or closed nature of the policymaking process, and in the relative weight of different governmental and nongovernmental organs in the formulation of policy. Which pattern is most nearly approximated in any individual case is a function of the interaction and combination of two different sets of variables. One set of functional variables involves the affect, scope, and divisibility of the particular issue; the other set of structural variables involves the relevant legal requirements governing the policymaking process and the organizational strength and mobilizability of the political actors most heavily involved in it.

The limited number of cases here prevents any mathematically precise analysis of the contributions made by each of the individual variables to the process of policymaking. What is striking is that in the cases examined the variables are highly synchronized with one another. At the one extreme of policymaking by camp conflict, for example, the issue of university administration was clearly the most highly affective of those studied, as well as the broadest in scope and the most difficult to disaggregate. In addition, it almost always arose in the context of legislative proposals that required Diet action and would clearly and directly affect the fortunes of large numbers of significant and comparatively easily mobilizable political actors. The result was always a publicly visible process involving high participation and mutual conflict between Japan's two political camps. At the same time, significant variations occurred among all three of the major cases of administration studied, with only one resulting in the successful passage of legislation altering relations between the universities and the government.

Representing something of a polar opposite was incremental policymaking. The issue of enrollment expansion lacked meaningful historical affect and was broad, unspecific, and easily disaggregable. Never requiring any specific legislation and influencing no major organizations or political actors in significant and particularistic ways, expansion was almost exclusively dealt with through bureaucratic devices, in the form of easy processing of charter applications, non-enforcement of certain minimum legal standards concerning quality, discretionary funding flexibilities, and a heavy reliance on private-sector universities and market mechanisms. Almost no clear-cut decision to expand enrollments seems ever to have been made; however, this area shows how easily policy can result from the combination of several discrete decisions, each one of which has come about slightly differently, no one of which independently has the scope or comprehensiveness to merit the term policy.

Occupying a midpoint on most of the variables and in the policymaking process as well was the case of specialization and differentiation of higher education. The issue was distinctly more affective than enrollment expansion, but in no way as emotional as administrative issues; it was far less disaggregable than enrollment, but again not so comprehensive as administrative issues; and its scope was both narrower and more specific than enrollment but not so broad as administration. Structurally as well, specialization and differentiation occupied a midpoint of sorts: the issue affected the well-organized and mobilizable big business community quite specifically, but because few other groups saw any immediate consequences for themselves, business pressure on the government for action tended for the most part to go unopposed. When it was opposed in the case of the efforts to make the junior colleges more occupationally relevant, the government solution was a pluralistic compromise, with both sides winning large measures of what each had sought. And finally, most of the steps demanded some, but only limited, legislative action, being solvable for the most part through bureaucratic means, although more conscious and directed means than those used to expand enrollments.

These cases make clear the necessity to analyze both structural variations and particular issue content in order to predict with any degree of accuracy the type of policymaking process that is most likely to occur in any empirical situation. Clearly, the interaction of function and structure, rather than either in isolation, determines the nature of policymaking. And these interact in regularized, mutually reinforcing ways that tend toward patterned rather than random policymaking procedures.

No claim of exclusivity or totality is advanced for the three patterns analyzed; their value lies in representing ideal types that set the outer limits and possibilities of policymaking rather than in predicting in detail all individual policymaking situations. Yet the close empirical fit of the several specific cases examined within the area of higher education suggests that the three patterns are useful and distinct as more than abstractions. Moreover, their congruence and close comparability with existing studies of Japanese policymaking suggest their applicability outside the area of higher education.

As in all usages of ideal or pure types, sensitivity to the fact that individual cases may prove to vary somewhat from the precise patterns is important. As Bacchus has suggested:

> To claim the existence of separate and parallel processes is to invite the same distortion involved in classifying a process into phases or stages, namely the failure to recognize that they may merge into hybrid

varieties, and are in fact most frequently encountered in that form.[1]

Nonetheless, given existing theory and empirical studies, the three patterns are clearly significant bases from which to examine other cases for confirmation or disconfirmation of their utility. The isolated hybrid in no way reduces the utility of broad patterns; in fact, explaining why a particular case has shown such muted characteristics is in itself intellectually profitable. At the same time, the appearance of a sufficient number of comparable hybrids suggests the emergence of a new entity, either in addition to the existing patterns or as a replacement for one or more of them.

Although the broad thrust of this study has been an analysis of policymaking processes, certain limited conclusions about the substance and evolution of Japanese higher educational policies as well as about the relationship between policymaking and public policy outcomes can also be advanced. It is useful to begin by noting that major changes were fostered in higher education by the U.S. Occupation in all three areas under investigation. The Americans sought to bring about a more open, autonomous, and generalist system than that which existed in the prewar period. Close government controls were to be checked, as was the functional differentiation of institutions and specialization of educational content which had dominated the prewar system. At the same time, more equal opportunities for students and more equality among institutions were sought. Not all of these goals were achieved under the Occupation, but there has been a substantial movement away from several of the Occupation-induced changes.

In a sense, the policy area that has shown the greatest continuity with American aims and changes has been the democratization of enrollment opportunities. There, the changes induced by the Occupation were not so great as is often imagined. Nevertheless, substantial democratization has taken place; more than one-quarter of the college-aged population was, by the early 1970s, receiving some higher education, giving Japan one of the highest ratios in the industrial world. This conclusion emerges despite widespread differences in the quality of institutions, unequal access of both sexes and social classes to the opportunities available, substantial decline in the quality of educational facilities in most areas of higher education, and heavy reliance on impoverished private institutions and the minimal commitment of governmental funds to higher education.

At the same time, it is clear that these emerging opportunities have been for an education substantially different from the very general training in four-year liberal arts college that was envisioned by the Occupation. The establishment of the junior college and higher technical school systems, plus the expectation that new types of functionally differentiated institutions will continue to emerge, makes this clear. Changing opportunities are also visible in the differentiation that the government has fostered among the national universities by heavily funding a few institutions to support their high-level research and graduate facilities and relegating most others to less prestigious functions.

An equally visible trend, and another reversal of Occupation policies, has been the shift toward a more specialized system of higher education. Institutions have become more functionally specialized, and the general education courses offered have declined in proportion to the increased demands for technically trained graduates. A massive program, begun in 1960 and continued into the 1970s, increased substantially the number and proportion of graduates in the fields of science and engineering, leading to a decline in the relative importance of general education, social science, and the humanities. All this has been in response to demands from industrial sectors for a more occupationally relevant system than that which was set up between 1946 and 1952. The trend itself is unmistakable, although it is difficult to evaluate normatively: one of the great problems of the university in any industrial society involves striking a sensible balance between legitimate but inherently one-sided occupational needs and the university's own historical, but often dangerously ivory-towered, responsibility to serve society as something more than a processing plant for technocrats. How well the Japanese system has fared in this delicate balancing act must remain largely a matter of debate by those with competing visions of the ideal equilibrium.

It is in the area where the greatest political battles have been fought that it is most difficult to assess any particular trend. Japanese progressives have been quick to suggest that the "reverse course" during the Occupation was the starting point for an unrelenting effort by the government to increase its control over all actions on campus, to abridge the autonomy of the university, and to check particularly the powers of the faculty conference. Unquestionably, many such government efforts can be cited; on the other hand, most of these efforts, prior to 1969,

were singularly unsuccessful in the face of persistent
and unified opposition by the academic community and
the progressive camp.  At the same time, the successful passage of the 1969 University Control Act signaled a greater government willingness and ability to
exercise far stricter controls over the universities
than it had been able to in the past.

The impact of the law in practice, however, has
been rather minimal.  The law was to be only a five-
year temporary measure, and its provisions allowing
the minister of education to close universities undergoing sustained violence were never used.

From another perspective, however, the formal
provisions and implementation of the law represent
its least significant aspects.  The law's real impact
lay in its practical effect on the centralization of
powers within the individual university, in the cur-
tailment of student protest, and in the bolstering of
a new willingness of the Ministry of Education to exercise powers over universities not affected in any
way by the law.

The law had the desired effect on campus protests.  University presidents, faced with the alternative of ending protests on their campuses or coming
under the provisions of the law that would allow the
minister of education to suspend all university operations, almost unanimously chose the former course of
action.  Police on campus, once an event capable of
generating flames of protest among even relatively
conservative academicians, became a relatively common
occurrence throughout the country during late 1969
and early 1970.  In October 1969, 77 universities
were undergoing major protests, but with the passage
of the law, university administrators began to call
in police at the slightest indication of student activism, and such actions dropped off sharply.  By
December protests were under way at 38 universities,
by January at 15, and in February only 8 universities
were undergoing significant protests.[2]  By mid-1970
virtually all protests had ceased and quiet settled
over the campuses.  The willingness of university administrators to act against protesting students under
the threat of closure obviated any need for the minister of education to use the powers given him.  The
law therefore served to centralize power on campus,
both in its provisions and in the rapid assumption
by administrators of positions of initiative and control.

Such centralizing by the government can also be
seen in the increased willingness of the Ministry of
Education, soon after the law's passage, to take

190

strong action against individual universities acting
in ways that displeased it. For example, the ministry began refusing to appoint university presidents
selected by procedures legal within the universities
but at odds with ministerial orientations. In many
cases, such refusals were based on the fact that
students or student organizations in some way participated in the selection or veto of certain choices.[3]
At Kyushu University, for example, Inoue Seiji was
duly elected by the faculty, only to find that his
outspoken criticisms of the government and of police
actions on campus resulted in the ministry's refusal
to accredit his election.[4]

Additionally, the ministry began to hold up
funds for some universities whose actions it opposed.
In the summer of 1970, for example, in the spirit of
university reform that followed the protests of the
late 1960s, Toho University selected a temporary faculty chairman and named two assistant professors,
rather than full professors, to head affiliated hos-
pitals. The Ministry of Education quickly suspended
all research and construction funds to the school on
the grounds that this constituted an illegal action.[5]

How directly such microcosmic actions by the
Ministry of Education can be attributed to changes in
the power relations between the government and the
universities is difficult to establish. Obviously
none of them is based on powers granted by law. The
law, however, in addition to the formal changes it
made, represented a significant symbolic shift in
the balance of power between government and university, and it would appear that this symbolism trans-
formed relations even more than the law itself.
These few actions may not warrant the conclusion
that the government has dramatically increased its
powers over the university and will continue to do so.
On the other hand, they are significant enough to foster concern that even further alterations in the power
balance between the universities and the government
may be forthcoming, particularly if and when violent
student protest against the government reemerges. If
this were to happen, it could signal a significant
weakening of the autonomy of the Japanese universities, a renewed cry for legislative measures, and,
not inconceivably, a return to many of the awesome
controls of the 1930s and 1940s.

In this regard it is especially interesting to
note that in 1974, when the law was due to expire,
the Cabinet Legislative Bureau provided a strange legal interpretation that since the law had not been explicitly repealed after five years, its provisions

remained in effect. As of early 1978, this interpretation remained, and it is conceivable that the government could rely upon it to close universities where protests occur in the future.

The study makes it also possible to advance several broader comments on the nature of postwar Japanese politics. What emerges most strongly is the need for refinement of many assumptions about the common or unique aspects of Japanese politics. This is particularly true for policymaking, but it holds too for statements about the political roles of the Diet, the bureaucracy, other government institutions, big business, LDP factions, and the opposition parties. It is clear that meaningful generalization depends largely on the issue involved. For example, the Diet was a focus of action in most areas of university administration but was totally irrelevant to enrollment expansion. LDP factional politics were hardly involved in any of the cases; big business was significant only in differentiation and specialization; and the opposition parties played very different roles from one issue to the next. The study therefore forces recognition of some of the great diversity in Japanese political life.

Overarching such diversity, however, is the hegemonic pluralism examined in Chapter 4 but visible in all of the case studies. The bureaucratic influence over policymaking is rather constant, especially in the reliance on bureaucratically dominated advisory committees and bureaucratic directives and communications. Moreover, the ability of the conservative camp to achieve its policy ends has been quite demonstrable. This has been particularly so in areas where it could rely on closed, bureaucratic processes such as prevailed in enrollment expansion and to a lesser extent in differentiation and specialization. But it was true as well in the more public 1969 passage of the University Control Act.

This leads to discussion of a more fundamental political question. What, if anything, is the relationship between policymaking process and public policy outcome? Surely the relationship is more complex than any implication that policy is simply the residual of process. It should be clear that certain structural and functional limits exist on policy choices and on policymaking process. But beyond this, one can ask whether particular types of policymaking process lead to certain identifiable types of outcomes. Do policies which emerge, for example, as a consequence of camp conflict differ in some significant way from those which emerge through pressure group interaction or through governmentally directed incrementalism? Do conflict-laden processes make it more possible for larger numbers of groups, sectors, or individuals to be meaningfully involved, for example, and if so, does this lead to any significant differences in outcomes? Are the policies thus arrived at more inherently democratic in content than those which are not the result of camp conflict? Conversely, are bureaucratic processes inherently more conservative in outcome than confrontational politics? Does pressure group policymaking lead to policies inherently biased against a more publicly generated and participatory version of the national interest?

These questions are not susceptible to easy answers based on the cases investigated here. Yet certain tentative conclusions are possible. First of all, it does seem that the squeaky hinge gets the oil, in Japan as elsewhere. Japanese progressives have been far more successful in the area of university administration, where policymaking has been conflictual and open, than in the areas of enrollment expansion and of differentiation and specialization. Where they have been most uproarious, they have been most successful. Similarly, junior colleges and the peak business federations were as successful through a completely different process related to the specialized and differentiated system of higher education.

A more striking conclusion relates to Japanese educational policy and to the relationship between policymaking and policy outcomes: differences in process seem not to have resulted in discontinuities among the various components of the Japanese government's higher educational policy. Despite the wide variations in process, the government has carried out policies that could truly be called integrated. Enrollment expansion, specialization, and differentiation, despite the different ways in which they were formulated, are highly compatible. Enrollment expansion has been partially responsible for the success in meeting manpower development quotas in science and engineering. Aspects of the differentiation among institutions and departments have made it possible for the broad enrollment to take place, as certain institutions and departments remained insulated from the general expansion and declining quality and could focus on meeting particular high quality goals while at the same time other institutions and fields could absorb the bulk of the new enrollees. Meanwhile, the controversies that arose over university governance and administration did not impede general policy developments in both these areas; in fact, the government succeeded generally in keeping down student protest activities that might have obstructed them. Moreover, elements of government enrollment expansion and specialization policies were seen by some politicians and Ministry of Education bureaucrats as conducive to the reduction of student protests and to an increase in the reliance of institutions on the government. Increased government control over administration since the 1969 legislation has also bolstered the government's informal capabilities to exercise direction over microlevel decisions about enrollment expansion and differentiation and specialization. In sum, therefore, differences in the mechanics of policymaking for component issues seem not to have interfered significantly with the integration of higher educational policy, suggesting that differences in process do not necessarily lead to mutually contradictory or incompatible policy outcomes.

Striking too is the social and political impact of the policies that have been handled bureaucratically and quietly and the lesser significance of the most visible political issues. There seems to be no direct relationship between the degree to which any issue is publicly resolved and its social or political significance. The magnitude of Japanese enrollment expansion and the increased specialization and differentiation would clearly appear to be of far greater moment for Japanese higher education and Japanese society than shifts in administrative oversight and governance. This is not to say that what is significant will not occur publicly; nor conversely, that what does not happen publicly is most significant; nor that open policymaking is less significant than closed. The simple explanation for such differences may lie in the fact that the Japanese opposition has been concerned more with an issue of limited significance, namely, university administration, than with other truly important aspects of Japanese higher education. The ideological generals of the progressive camp, like their military counterparts throughout the world, may well be so concerned with fighting the battles of the last war that they lose sight of the unique and significant features of the present. By focusing all of their higher educational concern on the protection of university autonomy and the independence of the faculty conference, Japan's progressives may well have ignored the truly significant changes that have been occurring in the entire system of higher education through increased specialization, differentiation, and enrollment. And by not recognizing such changes, they may have abdicated their influence over the course of such activities.

Still, the evidence suggests at least the tentative conclusions that a good deal of what is significant in a society is not subject to broad public debate and that major changes in policies can occur without passing through a process of broad public debate.

In this regard, the structural features of Japanese bipolarity and conservative hegemony may have had more significance for policy outcomes than did the differences in policymaking processes they permitted. The integrated nature of Japanese higher educational policies is clearly conservative and favors the upper and middle classes and the major industrial sectors, as opposed to the lower classes, smaller industry, or students as a group. Enrollment expansion, differentiation, and specialization, as well as increased government control over university administration, all have distinctly conservative hues, and it is this conservative integration that is most uniform about Japanese higher educational policy. This in turn is conspicuously aided by the fact that some of the more fundamental issues in Japanese higher education have been resolved through bureaucratic processes outside wide public scrutiny and by bureaucratic organs closely tied to the ruling Liberal Democratic Party and its conservative supporters.

At the same time, emphasis on the hegemonic nature of much of Japanese policymaking and policy consequences should not obscure the fact that Japan remains pluralistic. If different groups in Japan lack the unfettered participation in the policymaking process that is so readily presumed to be a component of open pluralism, many areas of policymaking still remain significantly open to nonconservative groups and parties. These groups often set the outer limits on what the government can achieve without causing major fissures in social serenity.

Ironically, the power of these groups has seemed to be the greatest in the areas where the conservatives seemed to care the most, notably in the efforts to alter the university administrative system. Certainly, the ability of the Japanese progressives to join academics in successfully blocking government efforts in this area in 1953-54 and 1960-63 proved them to have significant political capabilities. This occurred despite the fact that the Diet, which was the focal point of policymaking efforts, was under the clear majoritarian rule of the conservative

LDP. Although Japanese progressives are also able to operate quietly behind the policymaking scenes to influence the government, in the cases examined they were largely uninfluential in those areas of policy dominated by bureaucratic policymaking, where their channels of effective communication were minimal.

Finally, while the hegemony of the conservative camp is well tempered by elements of pluralism, there are also disadvantages to open choice on all issues of public policy, as the immobilisme of France under the Fourth Republic or Italy since the end of World War II makes clear. The conservative camp has exerted increased control over the organs of public policymaking, even as their electoral totals continue to ebb. Yet their political leadership and control have met many of the major challenges facing the country in the area of higher education. At times their policies have proved favorable to democratic principles, such as enrollment expansion. And such actions, emerging from a very closed process, raise a question about the importance of claims made for the necessity of "open" policymaking to achieve democratic aims. Nevertheless, this policy has been only superficially egalitarian, while many other areas of government policy, particularly in administration, specialization, and differentiation, have provided either direct and particularistic benefits to limited sectors of society or else have the potential for direct abridgment of such democratic essentials as academic freedom. On balance, therefore, the greatest potential for democracy in policymaking and in policy is still likely to result from the more open, not the more closed, processes.

# Notes

Chapter 1.  Introduction.

1.  See inter alia, Robert A. Scalapino and Junnosuke
Masumi, Parties and Politics in Contemporary Japan
(Berkeley: University of California Press, 1962);
Nathaniel B. Thayer, How the Conservatives Rule Japan
(Princeton: Princeton University Press, 1969); Chito-
shi Yanaga, Big Business in Japanese Politics (New
Haven: Yale University Press, 1968); Nihon Seiji Gak-
kai, ed., Nihon no atsuryoku dantai (Pressure Groups
in Japan) (Tokyo: Iwanami Shoten, 1967); Haruhiro
Fukui, "Studies in Policymaking: A Review of the Lit-
erature," in T.J. Pempel, ed., Policymaking in Contemporary Japan (Ithaca, N.Y.: Cornell University
Press, 1977), reviews the major literature expounding
this viewpoint.

2.  Kawashima Takeyoshi, "Kindai Nihon no shakaigaku-
teki kenkyū" (Sociological Research on Modern Japan),
Shisō, No. 442, April 1961.

3.  See the sources cited in note 1.  In addition,
see George O. Totten and Tamio Kawakami, "The Func-
tions of Factionalism in Japanese Politics," Pacific
Affairs, Vol. 38, Summer 1965, pp. 109-22; Hans H.
Baerwald, Japan's Parliament (London: Cambridge Uni-
versity Press, 1974), Ch. 2; Watanabe Tsuneo, Habatsu
--Hoshutō no kaibō (Factions--A Dissection of the
Conservative Party) (Tokyo: Kōbundō, 1958); Watanabe
Tsuneo, Habatsu--Nihon hoshutō no bunseki (Factions--
Analysis of the Japanese Conservative Party) (Tokyo:
Kōbundō, 1962); Yomiuri Shimbun Seiji-bu, ed., Seitō
--Sono soshiki to habatsu no jittai (Political Par-
ties--Their Organizational and Factional Realities)
(Tokyo: Yomiuri Shimbunsha, 1966); Asahi Shimbun
Seiji-bu, ed., Seitō to habatsu (Parties and Fac-
tions) (Tokyo: Asahi Shimbunsha, 1968).

4. The "emperor system" is a standard tool of the Kōza-ha of Japanese Marxism. Most noteworthy in this school is Hattori Shiso. See the discussion of Hattori and the Kōza-ha in James W. Morley, "Introduction: Choice and Consequence," in Morley, Dilemmas of Growth in Prewar Japan (Princeton: Princeton University Press, 1971), pp. 18ff. But see also Ishida Takeshi, Kindai Nihon seiji kōzō no kenkyū (Studies in the Structure of Modern Japanese Politics) (Tokyo: Miraisha, 1956), for reliance on the term by a non-Kōza member. While cultural interpretations tend to be widespread, one of the more persuasive remains that of Chie Nakane, Japanese Society (Berkeley: University of California Press, 1970).

5. Among some of the better works in this area, see Karl Deutsch, The Nerves of Government (New York: Free Press, 1966); David Easton, A Systems Analysis of Political Life (New York: Wiley, 1965); Talcott Parsons and Edward Shils, eds., Toward a General Theory of Action (Cambridge, Mass.: Harvard University Press, 1966); Herbert Spiro, "Comparative Politics: A Comprehensive Approach," American Political Science Review, Vol. 56, September 1962, pp. 517-95; Herbert Spiro, Government by Constitution (New York: Random House, 1959); Robert Dahl and Charles Lindblom, Politics, Economics and Welfare (New York: Harper, 1953); Anthony Downs, An Economic Theory of Democracy (New York: Harper and Row, 1957).

6. A particularly useful approach to this problem in the context of the United States is William C. Mitchell, Public Choice in America (Chicago: Markham, 1971). See also Arnold J. Heidenheimer, Hugh Heclo, and Carolyn Teich Adams, Comparative Public Policy (New York: St. Martin's, 1975); Harold Wilensky, The Welfare State and Equality (Berkeley: University of California Press, 1975).

7. See inter alia, Richard Rose, "Comparing Public Policy: An Overview," European Journal of Political Research, Vol. 1, April 1973, pp. 67-93; Ira Sharkansky, ed., Policy Analysis in Political Science (Chicago: Markham, 1970); Hugh Heclo, "Review Article: Policy Analysis," British Journal of Politics, Vol. 2, January 1972, pp. 83-108; Theodore J. Lowi, "Decision Making vs. Policy Making: Toward an Antidote for Technocracy," Public Administration Review, Vol. 30, May/June 1970, pp. 314-25; R.H. Haveman and J. Margolis, eds., Public Expenditures and Policy Analysis (Chicago: Markham, 1970); Austin Ranney, ed.,

Political Science and Public Policy (Chicago: Markham, 1968).

8. Joseph A. Schumpeter, Capitalism, Socialism and Democracy, 3rd ed. (New York: Harper, 1950), Ch. 12.

9. See, for example, Philips Cutright, "Political Structure, Economic Development, and National Security Programs," in Charles F. Cnudde and Dean E. Neubauer, eds., Empirical Democratic Theory (Chicago: Markham, 1969), pp. 429-48.

10. A useful assessment of this point can be found in Charles W. Anderson, "System and Strategy in Comparative Policy Analysis: A Plea for Contextual and Experiential Knowledge," in William B. Gwyn and George C. Edwards III, eds., Perspectives on Public Policymaking (New Orleans: Tulane University, 1975), pp. 219-41.

11. OECD, Towards Mass Higher Education (Paris: OECD, 1974), p. 24.

Chapter 2.  Framework for Analysis.

1. E.E. Schattsneider, The Semi-Sovereign People (New York: Holt-Rinehart, 1960).

2. See Aaron Wildavsky, The Politics of the Budgetary Process (Boston: Little, Brown, 1964); Guy Lord, The French Budgetary Process (Berkeley: University of California Press, 1973); John Creighton Campbell, Contemporary Japanese Budget Politics (Berkeley: University of California Press, 1977), and "Japanese Budget Baransu," in Ezra Vogel, ed., Japanese Organization and Decision Making (Berkeley: University of California Press, 1975), pp. 71-100.

3. Charles F. Hermann, Crises in Foreign Policy (Indianapolis and New York: Bobbs-Merrill, 1969); James A. Robinson, "Crisis Decision-Making: An Inventory and Appraisal of Concepts, Theories, Hypotheses, and Techniques of Analysis," Political Science Annual, Vol. 2 (Indianapolis and New York: Bobbs-Merrill, 1969), pp. 111-48; Richard C. Snyder, et al., Foreign Policy Decision-Making (New York: Free Press, 1962); Joseph Frankel, The Making of Foreign Policy (London: Oxford University Press, 1963), inter alia.

4. Theodore Lowi, "Four Systems of Policy, Politics,

and Choice," Public Administration Review, Vol. 32,
July/August 1972, pp. 298-310.

5.  William Zimmerman, "Issue Area and Foreign-Policy
Process," American Political Science Review, Vol. 67,
December 1973, pp. 1204-12.

6.  William H. Riker, The Theory of Political Coalitions (New Haven: Yale University Press, 1962).

7.  Lewis A. Froman, Jr., "An Analysis of Public Policies in Cities," Journal of Politics, Vol. 29, February 1967, pp. 94-108; "The Categorization of Policy
Contents," in Austin Ranney, ed., Political Science
and Public Policy (Chicago: Markham, 1968), pp. 41-52.

8.  Murray Edelman, The Symbolic Uses of Politics
(Urbana: University of Illinois Press, 1967); Heinz
Eulau and Robert Eyestone, "Policy Maps of City Councils and Policy Outcomes: A Development Analysis,"
American Political Science Review, Vol. 62, March
1968, pp. 124-43; James Q. Wilson, Political Organizations (New York: Basic Books, 1973).

9.  Theodore J. Lowi, "American Business and Public
Policy, Case Studies and Political Theory," World
Politics, Vol. 16, July 1964, pp. 677-715.  See also
his "Decision Making vs. Policy Making: Toward an
Antidote for Technocracy," Public Administration Re-
view, Vol. 30, May/June 1970, pp. 314-25; and his
"Four Systems of Policy."

10.  Zimmerman, "Issue Area."

11.  Riker, Political Coalitions.

12.  On the Security Treaty controversy, see: George
R. Packard III, Protest in Tokyo (Princeton: Prince-
ton University Press, 1966); Robert A. Scalapino and
Junnosuke Masumi, Parties and Politics in Contempo-
rary Japan (Berkeley: University of California Press,
1962); "Japanese Intellectuals Discuss American-
Japanese Relations," Far Eastern Survey, Vol. 29,
October 1960, pp. 145-60, inter alia.  On constitu-
tional revision, see: Haruhiro Fukui, Party in Power
(Berkeley: University of California Press, 1970),
Ch. 8; and Dan Fenno Henderson, The Constitution of
Japan (Seattle: University of Washington Press,
1968).  On the right to strike, see Ehud Harari, The
Politics of Labor Legislation in Japan (Berkeley:
University of California Press, 1973).

13. Fukui, Party in Power, Ch. 9; Chitoshi Yanaga, Big Business in Japanese Politics (New Haven: Yale University Press, 1968); Campbell, "Japanese Budget Baransu" and Budget Politics; K. Bieda, "Economic Planning in Japan," Economic Record, Vol. 45, June 1969, pp. 181-205; Haruhiro Fukui, "Economic Planning in Postwar Japan: A Case Study in Policy-Making," Asian Survey, Vol. 12, April 1972, pp. 327-48, inter alia.

14. Lowi, "Four Systems of Policy," p. 300.

15. Fukui, Party in Power, Ch. 7; John Creighton Campbell, "Compensation for Repatriates: A Case Study of Interest-Group Politics and Party-Government Negotiations in Japan," in T.J. Pempel, ed., Policymaking in Contemporary Japan (Ithaca, N.Y.: Cornell University Press, 1977).

16. William Steslicke, Doctors in Politics: The Political Life of the Japan Medical Association (New York: Praeger, 1973); "Doctors, Patients, and Government in Modern Japan," Asian Survey, Vol. 12, November 1972, pp. 913-31; "The Political Life of the Japan Medical Association," Journal of Asian Studies, Vol. 31, August 1972, pp. 841-62.

17. Naoki Kobayashi, "The Small and Medium-Sized Enterprises Organization Law," in Hiroshi Itoh, ed., Japanese Politics--An Inside View (Ithaca, N.Y.: Cornell University Press, 1973), pp. 49-67; and "Interest Groups in the Legislative Process," ibid., pp. 68-87.

18. An excellent comparative study of the problem of race relations in the two countries is Ira Katznelson, Black Men, White Cities (New York: Oxford University Press, 1973).

19. Robert A. Dahl, ed., Regimes and Oppositions (New Haven: Yale University Press, 1973), p. 1.

20. Among the more prominent works in the so-called elitist tradition, see: C. Wright Mills, The Power Elite (New York: Oxford University Press, 1956); Floyd Hunter, Community Power Structure (New York: Anchor, 1963, orig. 1953); G. William Domhoff, Who Rules America? (Englewood Cliffs, N.J.: Prentice-Hall, 1967) and The Higher Circles (New York: Vintage, 1970). The pluralist perspective is presented in: Robert A. Dahl, Who Governs? (New Haven: Yale University Press, 1961); Nelson W. Polsby, "How to Study Community

Power: The Pluralist Alternative," Journal of Politics, Vol. 22, August 1960, pp. 474-84, and Community Power and Political Theory (New Haven: Yale University Press, 1963), inter alia.

21. A particularly useful assessment of the elitist vs. pluralist interpretations in studies in Japanese politics is Haruhiro Fukui, "Studies in Policymaking: A Review of the Literature," in Pempel, Policymaking.

22. Ibid.

23. Campbell, "Compensation for Repatriates"; Steslicke, Doctors in Politics, "Doctors, Patients, and Government," and "The Political Life of the JMA"; George DeVos and Hiroshi Wagatsuma, Japan's Invisible Race (Berkeley: University of California Press, 1967); Scalapino and Masumi, Parties and Politics; Yanaga, Big Business; Michael Donnelly, "Setting the Price of Rice: A Study of Political Decision-Making," in Pempel, Policymaking; Nihon Seiji Gakkai, ed., Nihon no atsuryoku dantai (Pressure Groups in Japan) (Tokyo: Iwanami Shoten, 1967), inter alia.

24. See note 12. On citizens' movements, see: Yokohama-shi Jūmin Undō Rengō, ed., Jūmin undō tanjō (Birth of the Citizens' Movement) (Tokyo: Rōdō Jumposha, 1969); Matsushita Keiichi, Shimin sanka (Citizen Participation) (Tokyo: Tōyō Keizai Shimpōsha, 1971); Asukata Ichio, Kakushin shisei no tembō (Prospects for Progressive City Politics) (Tokyo: Shakai Shimpō, 1967); Margaret A. McKean, "Pollution and Policymaking," in Pempel, Policymaking.

25. See U.S., Department of Commerce, Japan: The Government-Business Relationship (Washington, D.C.: U.S. Government Printing Office, 1972); Dan Fenno Henderson, Foreign Enterprise in Japan (Chapel Hill: University of North Carolina Press, 1973); Chalmers Johnson, "MITI and Japanese International Policy," in Robert A. Scalapino, ed., The Foreign Policy of Modern Japan (Berkeley: University of California Press, 1977).

26. Most generally, the Ministry of Finance, the Ministry of International Trade and Industry, the Science and Technology Agency, and the Economic Planning Agency.

27. For example: Wildavsky, Budgetary Process; Aage Clausen, How Congressmen Decide: A Policy Focus

(New York: St. Martin's, 1973); Robert A. Dahl and Charles E. Lindblom, Politics, Economics and Welfare (New York: Harper, 1953).

28. See the sources cited in note 15.

29. Donald Hellmann, Japanese Domestic Politics and Foreign Policy (Berkeley: University of California Press, 1969).

30. See the sources cited in notes 16 and 17.

Chapter 3. Nature of the Issues.

1. This is only one of many possible translations of this article of the Charter Oath. For the oath, its background, and its possible implications, see Robert M. Spaulding, Jr., "The Intent of the Charter Oath," in Richard K. Beardsley, ed., Studies in Japanese History and Politics (Ann Arbor: University of Michigan Press, 1967), pp. 3-36.

2. See inter alia, R.P. Dore, "The Legacy of Tokugawa Education," in Marius B. Jansen, ed., Changing Japanese Attitudes toward Modernization (Princeton: Princeton University Press, 1965), pp. 99-131; and R.P. Dore, "Education: Japan," in Robert E. Ward and Dankwart Rustow, eds., Political Modernization in Japan and Turkey (Princeton: Princeton University Press, 1964), pp. 176-204.

3. Herbert Passin, Society and Education in Japan (New York: Columbia University Teachers College, 1965), pp. 209-10.

4. Dore, "Education: Japan," p. 189.

5. Asō Makoto, Eriito to kyōiku (Elites and Education) (Tokyo: Fukumura Shuppan, 1967); Ronald P. Dore, "The Future of Japan's Meritocracy," International House of Japan Bulletin, October 1970, pp. 30-50.

6. See especially Ivan Parker Hall, Mori Arinori (Cambridge: Harvard University Press, 1973); Michio Nagai, Higher Education in Japan (Tokyo: University of Tokyo Press, 1971), pp. 166-96.

7. Nagai, Higher Education, p. 31.

8. Ikazaki Akio, Daigaku no jichi no rekishi (The

History of University Autonomy) (Tokyo: Shin Nihon Shinsho, 1965), pp. 25-31.

9.  Henry D. Smith II, Japan's First Student Radicals (Cambridge: Harvard University Press, 1972).

10.  Nagai, Higher Education, pp. 40-41.

11.  Passin, Society and Education, pp. 122-25; Koya Azumi, Higher Education and Business Recruitment in Japan (New York: Columbia University Teachers College, 1969).

12.  Based on Smith, Japan's Student Radicals; Passin, Society and Education, p. 104.

13.  Smith, Japan's Student Radicals, pp. 1-2.

14.  Shimizu Yoshihiro, Shiken (Examinations), p. 110, as cited in R.P. Dore, "Mobility, Equality, and Individuation in Modern Japan," in Dore, ed., Aspects of Social Change in Modern Japan (Princeton: Princeton University Press, 1967), p. 123. One of the main instruments of this merotocratic elitism was the rigid examination system.

15.  SCAP, General Headquarters, Civil Information and Education Section, Education in the New Japan (Tokyo: GHQ, SCAP, 1948), Vol. 2, p. 26.

16.  Terasaki Masao, "Sengo daigaku kaikaku no rinen to jōken" (Theory and Reality in Postwar University Reform), in Ikazaki Akio and Nagai Kenichi, eds., Daigaku no jichi to gakusei no chii (University Autonomy and the Position of Students), Vol. 1 (Tokyo: Seibundō, 1970), pp. 1, 5.

17.  Report of the United States Education Mission to Japan (Washington, D.C.: U.S. Government Printing Office, 1946).

18.  Ibid., p. 47.

19.  Ibid., p. 50. This was more a reflection of the American ideal than of realities.

20.  Ibid., p. 50.

21.  Ibid., p. 57.

22.  Ibid., p. 62.

23. Ibid., pp. 47-48.

24. Ibid., p. 62.

25. Mombushō, Waga kuni no kōtō kyōiku (Higher Education in Japan: Ministry of Education White Paper) (Tokyo: Mombushō, 1964), p. 24 (hereafter 1964 White Paper). A translation of this report is in John J. Blewett, S.J., Higher Education in Postwar Japan (Tokyo: Sophia University Press, 1965), pp. 16-17.

26. Report of the U.S. Education Mission, pp. 48, 52.

27. Mombushō, Mombu hōrei yōran (Handbook of Laws and Ordinances in Education) (Tokyo: Teikoku Chihō Gyōsei Gakkai, annual), 1971, p. 11.

28. Ibid., pp. 1-10, 15-32, for both the constitution and the School Education Law. These are variously reproduced in other collections of documents. The Ministry of Education has a pamphlet translation of the School Education Law. It appears as well in SCAP, Education in the New Japan, Vol. 2, pp. 112-30, although this has only the initial version of the law and not its subsequent revisions.

29. Mombushō, Kyōiku Sasshin Iinkai yōran (Handbook of the Education Reform Committee) (Tokyo: Mombushō, 1949) (hereafter KSI yōran).

30. Interview with Harada Taneo, National Institute for Educational Research, February 3, 1971.

31. Chartering involves the process of being established as a legal person or a corporation; accreditation involves peer evaluation by other universities to determine if a university's facilities warrant recognition by other academic associations. Kaigo Tokiomi and Terasaki Masao, Daigaku kyōiku (University Education) (Tokyo: Tōkyō Daigaku Shuppankai, 1969), pp. 62-88.

32. Mombushō, 1964 White Paper, p. 267.

33. Mombushō, ed., Waga kuni no kyōiku no ayumi to kongo no kadai: Chūō Kyōiku Shingikai chūkan hōkoku (The Course of Japanese Education and Future Problems: Interim Report of the Central Education Council) (Tokyo: Ōkurashō Insatsukyoku, 1969), p. 380 (hereafter CEC 1969 Report).

34.  Compiled from data in Mombushō, <u>1964 White Paper</u>, pp. 266-69.

35.  Mombushō, <u>CEC 1969 Report</u>, p. 381.

36.  But it is reported that CIE went so far as to ban participants from both the Ministry of Education and Tokyo University, and only these two, from the organizational meeting of the University Accreditation Association.  Terasaki, "Sengo daigaku kaikaku," p. 21.

37.  Terasaki Masao, "Sengo daigakushi no magarikado" (Crossroads in the History of Postwar Universities), <u>Bōsei</u>, Vol. 2, June-July 1971, p. 55.

38.  Robert K. Hall, <u>Education for a New Japan</u> (New Haven: Yale University Press, 1949), pp. 421-23.

39.  Mombushō, <u>CEC 1969 Report</u>, pp. 170-73.

40.  Kaigo and Terasaki, <u>Daigaku kyōiku</u>, pp. 97-99. Of particular interest is <u>Kobe Jōgakuin</u>, which in its early history, <u>Kōbe Jōgakuin hachijūnenshi</u>, specifically attributes its early reestablishment to Dr. Holmes of CIE, who had once been a teacher there. <u>Ibid.</u>, p. 98.

41.  Mombushō, <u>Kyōiku tōkei shiryōshū</u> (Collected Statistical Source Materials on Education) (Tokyo: Mombushō, 1970), pp. 71-76.

42.  SCAP, <u>Education in the New Japan</u>, Vol. 1, p. 171.

43.  Article 10.

44.  SCAP, <u>Education in the New Japan</u>, Vol. 1, p. 171.

45.  This was similar to a February 1947 plan offered at Hokkaido University.  On this, see Kaigo and Terasaki, <u>Daigaku kyōiku</u>, pp. 578-80.

46.  Suzuki Eiichi, "Kyōiku gyōsei no enkaku" (Development of Educational Administration), in Yamamoto Toshio, ed., <u>Kyōiku gyōsei gaisetsu</u> (Outlines of Educational Administration) (Tokyo: Ochanomizu Shobō, 1967), p. 11.

47.  Hall, <u>Education</u>, p. 58.

48.  <u>Tōkyō shimbun</u>, November 4, 1947.

49. Daigaku Kijun Kyōkai, Daigaku Kijun Kyōkai jūnenshi (Ten-Year History of the University Accreditation Association) (Tokyo: DKK, 1957), pp. 136ff
(hereafter DKK, Jūnenshi).

50. Mombushō, KSI yōran, pp. 105-106; Tōkyō shimbun,
January 29, 1948.

51. Sekai jihō, January 8, 1948.

52. Kaigo and Terasaki, Daigaku kyōiku, p. 96; Yamanaka Akira, Sengo gakusei undōshi (History of the
Postwar Student Movement) (Tokyo: Aoki Shoten, 1961),
p. 38.

53. The plan is reproduced in Kaigo and Terasaki,
Daigaku kyōiku, pp. 651-57; and in Tabata Shigejirō
et al., eds., Sengo no rekishi to kihon hōki (History
and Fundamental Regulations of the Postwar Period),
Vol. 1 of Daigaku mondai sōshiryōshū (Comprehensive
Collection of Documents on the University Problem)
(Tokyo: Yūhikaku, 1970), pp. 13-17.

54. SCAP, Education in the New Japan, Vol. 2, p. 27.

55. "Daigaku no jichi" (University Self-Government),
Hōritsu jihō, Vol. 42, January 1970, pp. 232-34, for
text of speech. See also Nomura Hyōji, Daigaku seisaku: Daigaku mondai (University Policies: University
Problems) (Tokyo: Rōdō Jumpōsha, 1969), pp. 487-91.

56. Walter Crosby Eells, Communism in Education in
Asia, Africa and the Far Pacific (Washington, D.C.:
American Council on Education, 1954), p. 29.

57. Ibid., p. 22. In addition to the overt adoption
of anticommunism as an aim of the Occupation, U.S.
attitudes toward higher education changed regarding
the relative weight of the several purposes of higher
education. Increasingly, the initial aims of developing a university system geared to the abstract search
for truth and knowledge, and of the substantive development of broadly educated, critical citizens
gave way to that of developing a university system
that would meet the economic and political needs of
the state (and, not completely incidentally, one unlikely to support political radicalism among faculty
and students). Here too the report of the second
Education Mission to Japan marks the shift. The report of the second mission contrasts sharply with
that of the first in stressing throughout the rela-

tionship between the system of higher education and
the achievement of tangible social and political goals.
"The final character of the country's higher education," the report maintained, "must be determined by
the kinds of highly educated people needed to carry
out the national objectives." Report of the Second
U.S. Education Mission to Japan (Washington, D.C.:
U.S. Government Printing Office, 1950), p. 9.

58. Robert A. Fearey, The Occupation of Japan, Second
Phase: 1948-1950 (New York: Macmillan, 1950), p. 45.
In July 1951, for example, CIE sent a pamphlet to universities and to the Ministry of Education entitled
"Advice in the Reform of Higher Education," which
among other things urged the complete elimination of
Communist influences from the faculty and from student
groups within the university. Terasaki, "Sengo daigakushi," p. 55.

59. Ibid.

60. Ibid.

61. Ikazaki, Daigaku no jichi, p. 103.

62. Asahi shimbun, August 6, 1949. The Assembly of
National University Presidents (Kokuritsu Daigaku Gaku-
chō Kaigi) is not to be confused with the Association
of National University Presidents (Kokuritsu Daigaku
Kyōkai).

63. Nihon keizai shimbun, September 7, 1949.

64. Ōhara Seiji, "Daigaku hōan no suii" (Developments in the Plan for a University Law), Refarensu,
No. 44, September 1954, pp. 73-85.

65. Ibid., pp. 79-80; Kaigo and Terasaki, Daigaku
kyōiku, p. 612.

66. The two final plans are reproduced in Nomura,
Daigaku seisaku, pp. 498-509. Section 2, clause 8
contains the critical phrases in both cases.

67. One might cite the 1918 University Ordinance as
a possible exception.

Chapter 4. Nature of Political Structures.

1. Maurice Duverger, Political Parties (New York:
Wiley, 1954), p. 214.

2.   Otto Kirchheimer, "The Waning of Opposition in
Parliamentary Regimes," Social Research, Vol. 24,
Summer 1957, pp. 127-56.

3.   See especially Giovani Sartori, "European Political Parties: The Case of Polarized Pluralism," in
Joseph LaPalombara and Myron Weiner, eds., Political
Parties and Political Development (Princeton: Princeton University Press, 1966), pp. 137-76; also Robert
A. Dahl, ed., Political Oppositions in Western Democracies (New Haven: Yale University Press, 1966)
and Regimes and Oppositions (New Haven: Yale University Press, 1973).

4.   Nishihira Shigeki, Nihon no senkyō (Japan's Elections) (Tokyo: Shiseido, 1972).  The shifting balance
in the party system is dealt with in T.J. Pempel,
"Political Parties and Social Change: The Japanese
Experience," in Louis Maisel and Joseph Cooper, eds.,
The Development of Political Parties (Berkeley: Sage,
1978).

5.   The U.S. Occupation in its earliest days sought to
limit many of the powers held by the prewar bureaucracy.  In some limited respects they were successful;
in most, their reforms were at best limited.  Ide
Yoshinori, "Sengo kaikaku to Nihon kanryōsei" (Postwar
Reform and the Japanese Bureaucratic System), in Tōkyō
Daigaku Shakai Kagaku Kenkyūjo, ed., Sengo kaikaku
(Postwar Reform) (Tokyo: Tōkyō Daigaku Shuppankai,
1974), pp. 143-229.  In no way, however, should the
argument that the Japanese state is increasing its
powers be taken to mean that it is now as powerful,
or more powerful, than its prewar counterpart.

6.   Chitoshi Yanaga, Big Business in Japanese Politics
(New Haven: Yale University Press, 1968); Haruhiro
Fukui, Party in Power (Berkeley: University of Cali-
fornia Press, 1970); Robert A. Scalapino and Junnosuke
Masumi, Parties and Politics in Contemporary Japan
(Berkeley: University of California Press, 1962);
Nathaniel B. Thayer, How the Conservatives Rule Japan
(Princeton: Princeton University Press, 1969); Junno-
suke Masumi, "The Political Structure in 1955," Jour-
nal of Social and Political Ideas in Japan, Vol. 2,
December 1964, pp. 29-36; Misawa Shigeo, "Seisaku
kettei katei no gaikan" (Outline of the Policymaking
Process), Nihon Seiji Gakkai nempō 1967 nen (1967 An-
nual of the Japan Political Science Association)
(Tokyo: Iwanami Shoten, 1967), pp. 14-15.

7. All appointments at this level are made by the cabinet, and before cabinet approval is granted, the LDP screens all candidates. Under unusual circumstances a Leftist might be appointed, but this is rare. My thanks go to several Japanese sources who prefer anonymity and to Gerald Curtis for explaining this point.

8. See *inter alia*, Henry Steck, "Power and the Policy Process: Advisory Committees in the Federal Government," paper delivered at the annual meeting of the American Political Science Association, Washington, D.C., 1972; George T. Sulzner, "The Policy Process and the Uses of National Governmental Study Commissions," *Western Political Quarterly*, Vol. 24, September 1971, pp. 438-48.

9. Nihon Kyōshokuin Kumiai, "Kyōiku kankei shingikai no jittai" (Realities of Advisory Committees Concerned with Education) (Tokyo: Unpublished 2-volume manuscript of the Japan Teachers Union, 1968), Vol. 1, pp. 22-23. See also Rinji Gyōsei Chōsakai, Daiichi Semmon Bukai, Daiichihan, *Hōkokusho* (Report) (Tokyo: Rinji Gyōsei Chōsakai, 1963), passim; Ōgita Tumotsu, "Shingikai no jittai" (Realities of the Advisory Committees), *Nempō gyōsei kenkyū* (Administrative Research Annual), Vol. 7 (Tokyo: Iwanami Shoten, 1969), pp. 21-71; Ebata Kiyoshi, "Kōmuin seido shingikai" (The Advisory Committee in the Bureaucratic System), *Jurisuto*, No. 360, December 15, 1966), pp. 56-58; Okabe Shirō, "Seisaku keisei ni okeru shingikai no yakuwari to sekinin" (The Role and Responsibilities of Deliberative Councils in Policymaking), *Nempō gyōsei kenkyū*, Vol. 7, pp. 1-19; Satō Isao, "Shingikai" (Advisory Committees), in *Gyōsei soshiki* (Administrative Organization), Vol. 4 of *Gyōseihō kōza* (Lectures on Administrative Law) (Tokyo: Yūhikaku, 1965), pp. 97-117; Ebata Kiyoshi, "Kore ga seifu shingikai da" (These Are the Government's Advisory Committees), *Jiyū*, August 1965, pp. 131-41; Young Ho Park, "The Government Advisory Commission System in Japan," *Journal of Comparative Administration*, Vol. 3, pp. 436-37.

10. Okabe, "Seisaku keisei ni okeru shingikai," pp. 1-2.

11. Rinji Gyōsei Chōsakai, *Hōkokusho*, p. 270; 1975 data supplied by the Administrative Management Agency of the Prime Minister's Office.

12.  Interview with Nishida Kikuo, former director of Planning and Research, Ministry of Education, June 17, 1971.

13.  Mombushō Chōsakyoku, "Chūō Kyōiku Shingikai yōran" (Handbook of the Central Education Council) (Tokyo: Unpublished volume for internal use in the Ministry of Education, 5th ed., 1966).

14.  Mombushō, Waga kuni no kyōiku no ayumi to kongo no kadai: Chūō Kyōiku Shingikai chūkan hōkoku (The Course of Japanese Education and Future Problems: Interim Report of the Central Education Council) (Tokyo: Ōkurashō Insatsukyoku, 1969). The final report is entitled Kongo ni okeru gakkō kyōiku no sōgōteki na kakujū seibi no tame no kihonteki shisaku ni tsuite: Tōshin (Report: On the Basic Policies for the Comprehensive Expansion and Consolidation of Future School Education) (Tokyo: Ōkurashō Insatsukyoku, 1971).

15.  Terms of reference for the 1968 case and the report are in Yamamoto Tokushige, ed., Daigaku mondai shiryō yōran (Handbook of Source Materials on the University Problem) (Tokyo: Bunkyū Shorin, 1969), pp. 424-39. This report, but not the terms of reference, is in most standard collections of sources.

16.  Nishida interview.

17.  The seven committees investigated were: the Educational Reform Committee (Kyōiku Sasshin Iinkai) later named the Educational Reform Council (Kyōiku Sasshin Shingikai), the Central Education Council (Chūō Kyōiku Shingikai), the University Chartering Council (Daigaku Setchi Shingikai), the Private Universities Council (Shiritsu Daigaku Shingikai), the Higher Technical Schools Council (Kōtō Semmongakkō Shingikai), the Science Council (Gakujutsu Shingikai), and the Investigating Committee on Preparations for the Establishment of Tsukuba University (Tsukuba Shindaigaku Sōsetsu Jumbi Chōsakai). All committees deal with the functional area of education, and generalization to other committees is difficult. The low number of businessmen may be atypical. Data were compiled from Jinji kōshin roku (Who's Who). Where possible, missing data were supplied from other sources such as Asahi nenkan (Asahi Yearbook).

18.  Perhaps the most egregious case of a bureaucrat engaged in interlocking advisory committees was Ishino Shinichi, vice-minister of finance, who in 1964 was on

211

no less than 57 different councils simultaneously.
Numerous counterparts from other ministries have
served on 30 or more committees at the same time.
Committees considered as general policy are the Cen-
tral Education Committee, the Educational Reform
Council, and the Investigating Committee on Prepara-
tions for the Establishment of Tsukuba University.
The technical group includes the University Charter-
ing Council, the Private Universities Council, the
Higher Technical Schools Council, and the Science
Council. Ebata, "Kore ga seifu shingikai da," p. 132.

19. Lewis J. Edinger and Donald D. Searing, "Social
Background in Elite Analysis: A Methodological In-
quiry," American Political Science Review, Vol. 61,
June 1967, pp. 428-45.

20. The usual phrase used is kakuremi, literally, "a
cloak to hide behind." See, for example, an article
in the series "Gyōsei kaikaku" (Administrative Reform) in Mainichi shimbun, July 15, 1967. Also
Okabe, "Seisaku keisei ni okeru shingikai," pp. 10-11;
Ebata, "Kore ga seifu shingikai da." For a partial
retort to the charge, see Hayashi Shūzō, "Shingikai
no kōyō to sono genkai" (The Efficiency and Limits of
the Advisory Councils), Toki no hōrei, No. 586, November 3, 1966, pp. 15-18.

21. See, for example, Grant McConnell, Private Power
and American Democracy (New York: Vintage, 1966);
Henry W. Ehrmann, "Interest Groups and the Bureaucracy in Western Democracies," in Mattei Dogan and Richard Rose, eds., European Politics: A Reader (Boston:
Little, Brown, 1971), pp. 333-53; Theodore J. Lowi,
The End of Liberalism (New York: Norton, 1969); Andrew
Shonfield, Modern Capitalism (New York: Oxford University Press, 1966).

22. The entire plan is reproduced in Hirahara Haru-
yoshi, "Kyōiku seisaku no ritsuan kikō toshite no
Chūkyōshin" (The Central Education Council as a
Drafting Organ in Educational Policies), Jurisuto,
No. 459, August 15, 1970, pp. 28-29.

23. Article 20 of Shiritsu gakkō hō (Private Schools
Law) in Mombushō, Mombu hōrei yōran (Handbook of Laws
and Ordinances in Education) (Tokyo: Teikoku Chihō
Gyōsei Gakkai, annual), 1971, pp. 389-90.

24. Interview with Ōtake Hakase, January 7, 1971;
Japanese University Accreditation Association,

Japanese Universities and Colleges (Tokyo: Japanese University Accreditation Association, 1967), p. 5. This practice is the outgrowth of certain competitive relations between the University Accreditation Association and the University Chartering Council existing when the latter was formed. Daigaku Kijun Kyōkai, Daigaku Kijun Kyōkai jūnenshi (Ten-Year History of the University Accreditation Association) (Tokyo: Daigaku Kijun Kyōkai, 1957), pp. 99-108 (hereafter DKK, Jūnenshi).

25. Shiritsu gakkō hō, clause 18.

26. Ōsaki Jin, "Shiritsu daigaku" (Private Universities), in Shimizu Yoshihiro, ed., Nihon no kōtō kyōiku (Japanese Higher Education) (Tokyo: Daiichi Hōki, 1968), pp. 150-53.

27. Kaigo Tokiomi and Terasaki Masao, Daigaku kyōiku (University Education) (Tokyo: Tōkyō Daigaku Shuppankai, 1969), pp. 516-34.

28. DKK, Jūnenshi, pp. 81-107; Daigaku Kijun Kyōkai, Tekikaku hantei ni tsuite (Concerning University Accreditation) (Tokyo: Daigaku Kijun Kyōkai, 1951).

29. The actual standards established are in Mombushō, Mombu hōrei yōran, 1957, pp. 96-109; the original standards can be found in pre-1956 editions, or in Daigaku Kijun Kyōkai, Daigaku Kijun Kyōkai kijunshū (Collection of the Standards of the University Accreditation Association) (Tokyo: Daigaku Kijun Kyōkai, 1969), pp. 1-7. On the comparison and significance of the two different sets of standards, see Kaigo and Terasaki, Daigaku kyōiku, pp. 543-47; and Terasaki Masao, "Daigaku setchi kijun" (The University Chartering Standards), Asahi jānaru, Vol. 12, August 2, 1970, pp. 39-44.

30. Mombushō, Mombu hōrei yōran, 1971, pp. 177-91.

31. Daigaku Kijun Kyōkai, Kaihō, No. 19, pp. 17-21.

32. Its administrative personnel are primarily from the Ministry of Education. Interview with Nishiyama Masazumi, September 2, 1970; interview with Miyazawa Bunji, September 2, 1970. See also Nihon gakujutsu kaigi hō (Law No. 121, July 10, 1948), Articles 3-6.

33. Science Council of Japan, General Description of the Science Council of Japan (Tokyo: Science Council

of Japan, 1951). "Scientists" is a term broadly defined to include humanistic and social scientists as
well as natural and applied scientists, and the council's 210 members are elected by the various sectors
of Japanese science. The bulk of Japan's university
teachers and researchers are eligible to elect these
members, and in practice nearly 90 percent of the members at any one time are chosen from these two groups.
My calculations from data provided by the Science
Council of Japan.

34. T. Dixon Long, "Policy and Politics in Japanese
Science: The Persistence of a Tradition," Minerva,
Vol. 7, Spring 1969, p. 439.

35. Ogose Sunao et al., "Yanaihara kara Kaya e, I"
(Tokyo University from Presidents Yanaihara to Kaya,
Part 1), Asahi jānaru, Vol. 12, November 22, 1970,
p. 32.

36. Long, "Policy and Politics," p. 440.

37. Interview in Tōkyō shimbun, August 17, 1969.

38. On the Japan Teachers Union, see Donald Thurston,
Teachers and Politics in Japan (Princeton: Princeton
University Press, 1973); and Benjamin C. Duke, Japan's
Militant Teachers (Honolulu: University of Hawaii
Press, 1973).

39. Interview with Nagai Michio, May 29, 1971; interview with Fukushima Akio, July 12, 1971; interview
with Amagi Isao, April 19, 1971. The two met finally
in 1972, thereby breaking the ice between them.

40. The exclusion of outside groups may be more characteristic in higher educational policymaking than in
certain other areas such as business where the corpor-
atist pattern is far more in evidence. Since the bulk
of the business community is closely identified with
the conservative camp, however, such a pattern suggests the importance of ideological considerations in
the delegation of responsibilities, much the same as
in the delegation of power to bureaucratic agencies.
One important question that cannot be dealt with here
is whether groups have influence because they are in
on the earliest stages of policymaking, or whether
they are included because they are influential.

41. Misawa, "Seisaku kettei katei," pp. 24-25; also
Masumi Junnosuke, "Jiyū Minshutō no soshiki to kinō"

(Organization and Functions of the Liberal Democratic
Party), in Nihon Seiji Gakkai nempō 1967 nen; Thayer,
How the Conservatives Rule, pp. 207-36.

42.  P.H. Levin, "On Decisions and Decision Making,"
Public Administration, Vol. 50, passim, but esp. pp.
24-25, deals with this problem at the theoretical
level.

43.  The theme of legislative decline as seen through
the apparent waning of the "independent" legislator
has been particularly prevalent in the United States
and Britain and can be traced at least to the nine-
teenth century with James Bryce's classic, The American Commonwealth (New York: Macmillan, 1891).

44.  These figures would appear to be somewhat below
those for Britain where, despite difficulties of introduction, private member bills still make up over
56 percent of all bills introduced during the period
1962-65.  R.M. Punnett, British Government and Politics (New York: Norton, 1968), p. 231.  See also his
footnote on p. 228 regarding private member bills.
In France and West Germany it is even easier for private members to introduce legislation.  Arnold J.
Heidenheimer, The Governments of Germany (New York:
Crowell, 3rd ed., 1971), p. 178; Nicholas Wahl, "The
French Political System," in Samuel H. Beer and Adam
B. Ulam, eds., Patterns of Government (New York: Random House, 1958), pp. 424-27.

45.  The role of private member bills in Japan seems
to be of far less importance, therefore, than in either Britain or Germany, although not quite so low
as in France.  In Britain, for example, the passage
rate of private member bills from 1962 to 1965 was
more than 30 percent and has been rising.  Moreover,
67 of the 239 successful bills (28 percent) during
this period were private member bills.  Punnett,
British Government and Politics, p. 231.  Figures for
the German Bundestag are roughly comparable.  In the
second Bundestag (1953-57), for example, about one-
quarter of the 483 successful bills were introduced
by individual members; in the fifth Bundestag (1965-
69) this figure was about one-fifth.  Heidenheimer,
Governments of Germany, pp. 176-77.
      Overall, the Japanese figures would appear to
be more comparable to those of France, where under
the constitution of the Fifth Republic the government
has the initiative in setting the legislative calen-
dar despite the ease with which private members can

215

introduce legislation. Between 1959 and 1968 just
under 90 percent of the total bills voted were submitted by the government. It should be noted that the
trend in France is in the opposite direction from
that in Japan. Thus, from 1959 to 1962 the figure
was 93.1 percent; between 1962 and 1967 it was 87.4
percent; and from 1967 to 1968 it was down to 79.3
percent. François Goguel, "Parliament under the
Fifth French Republic," in Gerhard Loewenberg, ed.,
Modern Parliaments (Chicago: Aldine, 1971), pp. 93-95.

46. Takagi Ikurō, "Gendai Nihon no kokka kenryoku"
(State Power in Contemporary Japan), in Sakisaka Itsu-
rō, ed., Gendai Nihon no seiji to ideorogii (Politics
and Ideology in Contemporary Japan) (Tokyo: Kawade
Shobō Shinsha, 1971), pp. 117-18.

47. Misawa, "Seisaku kettei katei," p. 25.

48. Takagi, "Gendai Nihon no kokka kenryoku," p. 118.

49. Misawa, "Seisaku kettei katei," p. 26.

50. Seijigaku jiten (Political Dictionary) (Tokyo:
Heibonsha, rev. ed., 1969), pp. 663, 775.

51. Kurt Steiner, Local Government in Japan (Stanford:
Stanford University Press, 1965), p. 315.

52. A recent examination of this problem can be found
in Takeshi Ishida, "Interest Groups under a Semipermanent Government Party: The Case of Japan," The Annals
May 1974, pp. 1-10.

53. For an elaboration, see T.J. Pempel, "The Dilemma
of Parliamentary Opposition in Japan," Polity, Vol. 8,
Fall 1975, pp. 63-79.

54. Interview with Yamanaka Gorō, June 2, 1971.

55. Misawa, "Seisaku kettei katei," p. 25; also Koya
Azumi, "Political Functions of Soka Gakkai Membership,"
Asian Survey, Vol. 11, September 1971, p. 920. From
1967 to 1971 the JSP voted in support of 67 percent
of the government-sponsored proposals that came to a
vote; the JCP supported over 33 percent; the Clean
Government Party, 75 percent; and the DSP, 82 percent.

56. Interview with Kobayashi Takeshi, July 9, 1971.

Chapter 5. Policymaking through Camp Conflict.

1. See, for example, Kōsaka Masaaki, Hirakareta dai-gaku no tame ni (Toward Open Universities) (Tokyo: Nansōsha, 1969) and Daigaku mondai to gakusei undō (The University Problem and the Student Movement) (Tokyo: Nansōsha, 1968), pp. 145-55. Morito Tatsuo, "Bijon toshite no 'hirakareta daigaku'" (A Vision of the 'Open University'), Daigaku jihō, March 1970, pp. 14-20; "Daigaku no 'kōgakuka' ni tsuite" (On Making University Education 'Public'), Shigaku shinkō, Vol. 19, pp. 6-14; and "Hatten suru shakai to daigaku no arikata" (The Way Universities Should Be in an Open Society), in Jiyū Minshutō, ed., Kokumin no tame no daigaku (Universities for the People) (Tokyo: Jiyū Minshutō Kōhō Iinkai, 1969), pp. 43-58.

2. For example, see Tōkyō Daigaku Shimbunsha, Daigaku mondai (The University Problem) (Tokyo: Minami Kikaku-shitsu, 1969), Ch. 3; Takizawa Katsumi, Hakai to sōzō no ronri: Shisō no jiyū kara jiyū naru shisō e (The Logic of Destruction and Creation: From the Freedom of Thought to Thinking of Freedom), Bessatsu Ushio, April 1969, special issue.

3. Arai Tsuneyasu, Kiki no gakusei undō (The Student Movement in Crisis) (Tokyo: Meiji Shoin, 1952), pp. 231-32; Lawrence H. Battistini, The Postwar Student Struggle in Japan (Rutland, Vt.: Tuttle, 1956), pp. 79-81.

4. Arai, Kiki no gakusei undō, pp. 232-47. For left-wing interpretations of this incident, see Shiryō: Sengo gakusei undō (Sources: The Postwar Student Movement) (Tokyo: Sanichi Shobō, 1969), Vol. 2, pp. 405-19.

5. Arai, Kiki no gakusei undō; Ōhara Seiji, "Daigaku hōan no suii" (Developments in the Plan for a Univer-sity Law), Refarensu, No. 44, September 1954, p. 82.

6. On the Popolo Incident, see Ikazaki Akio, Daigaku no jichi no rekishi (The History of University Auton-omy) (Tokyo: Shin Nihon Shinsho, 1965), pp. 121-37; Kaigo Tokiomi and Terasaki Masao, Daigaku kyōiku (University Education) (Tokyo: Tōkyō Daigaku Shuppan-kai, 1969), pp. 35-40. The decision of the Tokyo court is in Daigaku Mondai Kenkyūkai, Daigaku mondai: Shiryō yōran (Handbook of Source Materials on the Uni-versity Problem) (Tokyo: Bunkyū Shorin, 1969), pp. 208-64.

217

7.  *Mainichi shimbun*, August 6, 1953.

8.  Kaigo and Terasaki, *Daigaku kyōiku*, pp. 627-28.

9.  "Kokuritsu daigaku no hyōgikai ni kansuru zantei sochi o sadameru kisoku" (Regulations to Establish Temporary Measures Regarding a University Council in the National Universities), in Nomura Hyōji, *Daigaku seisaku: Daigaku mondai* (University Policies: University Problems) (Tokyo: Rōdō Jumpōsha, 1969), pp. 519-21.

10.  For actual plans, see *ibid.*, pp. 521-24. For an analysis of their implications, see Ōhara, "Daigaku hōan," pp. 83-84; Kaigo and Terasaki, *Daigaku kyōiku*, pp. 628-32; and Ienaga Saburō, *Daigaku no jiyū no rekishi* (History of Academic Freedom) (Tokyo: Kōshobō, 1962), pp. 127-28.

11.  Ōhara, "Daigaku hōan," p. 83.

12.  For example, see *Shakai taimusu*, June 11, 1953.

13.  All students in a particular faculty are automatically enrolled in the self-governing association of the faculty, and the elected leaders of the association choose to make or not to make any outside affiliations.

14.  That is not to suggest that total apathy had earlier been the mood, as the Sunakawa demonstrations of June 1957 and protests in the fall of 1958 against the Police Duties Bill would clearly indicate. On the upsurge, see in particular George R. Packard III, *Protest in Tokyo* (Princeton: Princeton University Press, 1966).

15.  Mombushō, *Gakusei mondai ni kansuru daijin danwa oyobi tsūtatsu nado* (Communications Statements of the Minister of Education, etc. on the Student Movement) (Tokyo: Mombushō, 1970), p. 31.

16.  Newspapers of this period carried the comment; but see also Nomura, *Daigaku seisaku*, p. 830.

17.  Full text in *ibid.*, p. 538.

18.  As in Kaigo and Terasaki, *Daigaku kyōiku*, p. 634.

19.  *Ibid.*, pp. 633-34.

20. Mombushō, Mombu nempō (Yearbook of the Ministry of Education) (Tokyo: Ōkurashō Insatsukyoku, annual), 1960, pp. 213-15.

21. Mainichi shimbun, September 14, 1960.

22. Ikazaki, Daigaku no jichi, pp. 156-57.

23. The entire speech is in Nomura, Daigaku seisaku, pp. 540-42.

24. Tabata Shigejirō et al., eds., Sengo no rekishi to kihon hōki (History and Fundamental Regulations of the Postwar Period), Vol. 1 of Daigaku mondai soshiryō-shū (Comprehensive Collection of Documents on the University Problem) (Tokyo: Yūhikaku, 1970), pp. 77-79.

25. School Education Law, Article 58, Clause 3.

26. Munakata Seiya, "The Task of Universities and the State," Journal of Social and Political Ideas in Japan, Vol. 1, August 1963, p. 93.

27. Asahi shimbun, June 24, 1962.

28. For a catalog of the major protest activities and the groups involved between April and September 1962, see Yomiuri shimbun, October 8, 1962. For Zengakuren activities, see Shiryō: Sengo gakusei undō, Vol. 6, pp. 188-250.

29. Asahi shimbun, August 3, 1962.

30. Ibid.

31. Ibid., September 8, 1962.

32. See, for example, ibid., August 2, 1962.

33. Mainichi shimbun (evening edition), September 17, 1962.

34. Asahi shimbun, August 3, 1962.

35. The counterplan offered by the Japan Science Council was most acceptable to the more extreme elements of the antigovernment forces and represented little change from the existing situation, but the Association of National University Presidents plan was considered by most academics, including the more moderate progressives, as the more "practical"

219

alternative. For the plans and how they differed, see the very helpful chart in Ikazaki, Daigaku no jichi, pp. 165-69.

36. Asahi shimbun (evening edition), June 23, 1962.

37. Asahi shimbun, August 1, 1962.

38. The full text of the report is given in Nomura, Daigaku seisaku, pp. 550-59; and in Tabata, Rekishi to hōki, pp. 83-90.

39. Section 4, clause 8.

40. It is interesting that neither the chairman of the Central Education Council, Amano Teiyū, nor the chairman of the committee that drafted the universities' plan, Kyoto University President Hirasawa Kō, was present. However, Hiroshima University President Morito Tatsuo and Tokyo University President Kaya Seiji, both members of the Central Education Council, attended as university delegates.

41. Asahi shimbun, October 8, 1962.

42. See, for example, those reported in Asahi shimbun November 1, 1962 (evening edition), and November 2, 1962; and in Nihon keizai shimbun, December 1, 1962.

43. Asahi shimbun (evening edition), January 21, 1963.

44. Nihon keizai shimbun, December 3, 1962.

45. Ibid., December 27, 1962.

46. See the article by Ōkōchi Kazuo, in Asahi shimbun, October 29, 1962.

47. Asahi shimbun, October 16, 1962.

48. Ibid., November 10, 1962. This "power" had always involved a mere ratification of university-level choices.

49. Asahi shimbun, November 3, 1962.

50. Nihon keizai shimbun, November 2, 1962, inter alia.

51. On this, see, for example, Hans H. Baerwald, "Ikeda's Low Posture," New Republic, Vol. 149, November 23, 1963, pp. 9-10.

52. For the text of the major bill, see Daigaku Mondai Kenkyūkai, Daigaku mondai yōran, pp. 109-12.

53. Notably the School Education Law and the Law of Special Regulations on Educational Personnel. Asahi shimbun (evening edition), January 11, 1963; Mainichi shimbun, January 11, 1963.

54. Asahi shimbun, January 19, 1963; Mainichi shimbun, January 23, 1963; Nihon keizai shimbun, January 23, 1963.

55. Nihon keizai shimbun, January 25, 1963.

56. Asahi shimbun (evening edition), January 25, 1963.

57. Asahi shimbun, January 26, 1963.

58. Ōhashi Hisatoshi, Shiryo: Daigaku no jichi (Source Materials: University Autonomy) (Tokyo: San-ichi Shobō, 1970), p. 265 (from data provided by the Ministry of Education).

59. To seasoned American radicals the number of police actions and arrests in 1968 may seem surprisingly low; however, they reflect primarily a general policy of noninterference by police in university affairs through the first half of 1969 and a policy of making as few arrests as possible when on campuses. See the police statement of policy at this time in Asahi shimbun (evening edition), February 13, 1968; and Mainichi shimbun (evening edition), February 13, 1968. On relations between police and the university community, see, inter alia, Inoue Seiji, "Daigaku jichi to keisatsuken" (University Autonomy and Police Authority), Hōritsu jihō, special issue, January 1970, pp. 108-17; Okudaira Yasuhiro, "Daigaku to keisatsu" (Universities and Police), Jurisuto, No. 426, June 1969, pp. 63-70.

60. Mainichi Shimbun, ed., Ampō to Zengakuren (The Security Treaty and Zengakuren) (Tokyo: Mainichi Shimbunsha, 1969).

61. For a causal analysis of the earlier disputes, see chart compiled in Jurisuto, No. 347, June 1966, pp. 46-51. Later, see the listings in Shūkan asahi, September 13, 1968; Sandee mainichi, February 20, 1969; Sankei shimbun, July 3, 1968. For a related analysis which attempts to deal with the specific catalysts to student protest and the issue of university alienation see Nagai Michio, Daigaku no kanōsei (Possibilities fc the Universities) (Tokyo: Chūō Kōronsha, 1969), pp. 11-

62. This was in contrast to the existing theory of the student role, characterized as eizobutsu, long dominant among university administrators and political conservatives, which holds that universities, like libraries and museums, are public institutions with certain fixed rules. The very use of these facilities by patrons (students, in the case of universities) implies a contractual acceptance of all existing institutional rules and no right to challenge them. Those who disagree in any way with such rules need not use the facilities. This concept as it relates to universities has been expounded best by Yamanaka Gorō, JSP member of the lower house, and is drawn from the German administrative concept of Anstalt. Interview with Yamanaka Gorō, June 2, 1971. See also the communication of the minister of education on January 16, 1963, "Gakusei no higōhō undō ni tsuite" (On the Illegal Activities of Students), in Mombushō, Gakusei mondai, p. 31.

63. Fukashiro Junrō, "Chian toshite no daigaku rippō" (The University Law for Public Peace), Asahi jānaru, Vol. 11, June 8, 1969, pp. 115-16.

64. Ibid.; see also the history of cooptation of U.S. universities by the federal and state governments as seen by James Ridgeway in The Closed Corporation (New York: Ballantine, 1968).

65. Mombushō, Gakusei mondai, p. 38.

66. Ibid., pp. 38-39.

67. Ibid., p. 40.

68. Tabata, Rekishi to hōki, pp. 144-52, has the entire report of this committee.

69. Ibid., Part 1, No. 1.

70. Ibid.

71. Ibid., Part 3, No. 1.

72. Ibid., Part 1, No. 1.

73. Mombushō, Gakusei mondai, pp. 41-45.

74. The communication is in Daigaku Mondai Kenkyūkai, Daigaku mondai yōran, pp. 149-52.

75. Mombushō, Gakusei mondai, p. 43.

76. Asahi shimbun, December 2, 1967.

77. Asahi shimbun (evening edition), January 10, 1968.

78. Asahi shimbun, December 2, 1967.

79. "Saikan no gakusei undō ni kansuru iken" (Opinion on the Current Student Movement), in Tabata, Rekishi to hōki, pp. 157-59; Nomura, Daigaku seisaku, pp. 186-87.

80. Ibid.

81. Asahi shimbun, April 14, 1968.

82. Asahi shimbun (evening edition), April 15, 1968.

83. Asahi shimbun, May 3, 1968.

84. Mombushō, Daigaku mondai, p. 46.

85. In Daigaku Mondai Kenkyūkai, Daigaku mondai yōran, p. 424.

86. Ibid.

87. Sankei shimbun, February 15, 1968; Yomiuri shimbun, February 18, 1968.

88. On the Nihon University disturbances, see, "Nichidai--Horobi to saisei no kiro" (Nihon University--Crossroads of Ruin and Rebirth), Asahi jānaru, Vol. 11, February 23, 1969, pp. 4-13; on the collective bargaining session, see "Nichidai taishū dankō, 1968.9.30" (Collective Bargaining at Nihon University, September 30, 1968), Chūō kōron, No. 975, November 1968, special issue, pp. 259-84.

89. Stuart Dowsey, Zengakuren: Japan's Revolutionary Students (Berkeley: Ishi Press, 1970), p. 112.

90. Sankei shimbun, February 15, 1968.

91. Asahi shimbun, December 20, 1968, as in Dowsey, Zengakuren, p. 112.

92. Sankei shimbun, February 15, 1968.

93. Yomiuri shimbun (evening edition), October 1, 1968.

94. Asahi shimbun (evening edition), October 1, 1968; Yomiuri shimbun (evening edition), October 1, 1968; Mainichi shimbun, October 3, 1968; Sankei shimbun, October 3, 1968; Tōkyō shimbun, October 3, 1968.

95. Such is the prestige of Tokyo University that a public opinion survey ranked the president of Tokyo University just below the prime minister, ahead of members of the cabinet and representatives of both the upper and lower house. See Nishihira Shigeki, "Sori ika kyūjūhachi no shokugyō saiten" (An Evaluation of Ninety-eight Occupational Positions from the Prime Minister on Down), Jiyū, No. 6, November 1964, pp. 120-27.

96. On the Tokyo University strike, see especially Ogose Sunao, Tōdai: Daigaku funsō no genten (Tokyo University: Origins of the University Disturbances) (Tokyo: Sanichi Shobō, 1968). The literature on the Tokyo disturbances is voluminous. For some of the more important works, see the entries in Kokusai Bunka Shinkōkai, Higher Education and the Student Problem in Japan (Tokyo: University of Tokyo Press, 1972), pp. 185-97.

97. On this note and its relation to the Tōdai strike, see Tōkyō Daigaku Shimbunsha, Daigaku mondai, pp. 106-18.

98. Tōkyō shimbun, January 14, 1969.

99. Yomiuri shimbun (evening edition), January 21, 1969.

100. "Tōkyō daigaku nana gakubu shūkai (nana gakubu 'dankō') ni okeru kakuninsho ni tsuite" (On the Note of Confirmation Regarding the Seven Departments Conference [the Seven Departments of Collective Bargaining]), text in Nihon keizai shimbun, February 9, 1969, section 1, paragraph 2.

101. Ibid., section 1, paragraph 5.

102. Ibid., section 2, paragraph 1, clause 1.

103. Ibid., section 2, paragraph 1, item 3.

104. Ibid., section 2, paragraph 2, item 3.

105. Fukashiro Junrō, "Daigaku mondai ni taisuru seitō no taishitsu" (The Predispositions of the

Political Parties toward the University Problem),
*Gendai seiji*, June 1969, pp. 6-7.

106. These various plans are contained in most docu-
ment collections. See Daigaku Mondai Kenkyūkai,
*Daigaku mondai yōran*; Tabata, *Rekishi to hōki*; and
Nomura, *Daigaku seisaku*; also Daigaku Mondai Kenkyū-
kai, *Nihon no daigaku mondai* (The Japanese University
Problem) (Tokyo: Sekai Shisōsha, 1970), 2 vols.

107. At one point ninety-six university administrators issued a declaration of opposition to the proposal. See *Asahi shimbun*, July 11, 1969.

108. *Asahi shimbun*, May 29-30, 1969, as in Daigaku
Mondai Kenkyūkai, *Nihon no daigaku mondai*, Vol. 2,
p. 23.

109. The report is reproduced in Nomura, *Daigaku
seisaku*, pp. 84-97; Daigaku Mondai Kenkyūkai, *Daigaku
mondai yōran*, pp. 425-39; Tabata, *Rekishi to hōki*,
pp. 20-32; Daigaku Mondai Kenkyūkai, *Nihon no daigaku
mondai*, Vol. 2, pp. 52-63.

110. *Sankei shimbun*, March 6, 1969.

111. *Yomiuri shimbun*, April 12, 1969.

112. The text is in Nomura, *Daigaku seisaku*, pp. 99-
100.

113. Fukashiro, "Seitō no taishitsu," p. 113.

114. In fact, of course, bringing forth the bill at
such a time was politically advantageous. With university administrators almost uniformly committed to
the conservative position on curbing students, with
public opinion growing more restive, and with even
the Communist Party denouncing any continuance of
student violence, opposition strong enough to stop
the bill was highly unlikely. Moreover, even if the
bill did not pass, the government could easily shift
the blame for any continued student violence onto
those opposition parties that had blocked it. *Ibid.*,
pp. 114-15.

115. The text is in Tabata, *Rekishi to hōki*, pp.
239-44.

116. Nomura, *Daigaku seisaku*; Nagai Kenichi, *Kempō
to kyōiku kihonken* (The Constitution and Bases of

Authority in Education) (Tokyo: Keisō Shobō, 1970).

117. See, for example, Nagai Michio, Daigaku no kanō-sei, pp. 27-28.

Chapter 6. Incremental Policymaking.

1. Mombushō, ed., Waga kuni no kyōiku no ayumi to kongo no kadai: Chūō Kyōiku Shingikai chūkan hōkoku (The Course of Japanese Education and Future Problems: Interim Report of the Central Education Council) (Tokyo: Ōkurashō Insatsukyoku, 1969), p. 380 (here-after CEC 1969 Report).

2. Mombushō, Kongo ni okeru gakkō kyōiku no sōgōteki na kakujū seibi no tame no kihonteki shisaku ni tsuite: Tōshin (Report: On the Basic Policies for the Compre-hensive Expansion and Consolidation of Future School Education) (Tokyo: Mombushō, 1971) (hereafter cited as Mombushō, Tōshin 1971).

3. On the Robbins Report, see Richard Layard, John King, and Claus Moser, The Impact of Robbins (Middle-sex, England: Penguin, 1969).

4. Mombushō, Mombu hōrei yōran, 1971 (Handbook of Laws and Ordinances in Education) (Tokyo: Teikoku Chihō Gyōsei Gakkai, annual).

5. Mombushō, Setchi shinsa yōran (Handbook for Chartering Investigations) (Tokyo: Mombushō, 1970); interview with Ōyama Yoshitoshi, former member of the University Chartering Council, July 15, 1971.

6. Mainichi shimbun, August 13, 1955; and Sangyō keizai shimbun, September 15, 1955 (evening edition).

7. Ministry of Education, Education in Japan (Tokyo: Ministry of Education, annual), 1955, p. 87, and 1956, p. 58; Asahi shimbun, September 9, 1956.

8. Ibid.

9. These standards are in Mombushō, Mombu hōrei yōran, 1957, pp. 96-109; the original standards can be found in pre-1956 editions, or in Daigaku Kijun Kyōkai, Daigaku Kijun Kyōkai kijunshū (Collection of the Standards of the University Accreditation Associ-ation) (Tokyo: Daigaku Kijun Kyōkai, 1969), pp. 1-7. On the comparison and significance of the two different

sets of standards, see Kaigo Tokiomi and Terasaki Masao, Daigaku kyōiku (University Education) (Tokyo: Tōkyō Daigaku Shuppankai, 1969), pp. 543-47; and Terasaki Masao, "Daigaku setchi kijun" (The University Chartering Standards), Asahi jānaru, Vol. 12, August 2, 1970, pp. 39-44.

10. Ōyama interview.

11. Ōsawa Masaru, Nihon no shiritsu daigaku (Private Universities in Japan) (Tokyo: Aoki Shoten, 1968), p. 155.

12. Mombushō, Waga kuni no kōtō kyōiku (Higher Education in Japan: Ministry of Education White Paper) (Tokyo: Mombushō, 1964), pp. 37-38 (hereafter 1964 White Paper)

13. Sasaki Yoshio, "Daigaku setchi shinsa ni tazusawatte omou" (Participating in and Thinking about Investigations for University Chartering), Daigaku shiryō, July 1966, pp. 10-15.

14. Mombushō, Zenkoku daigaku ichiran (Japanese Universities at a Glance) (Tokyo: Ōkurashō Insatsukyoku, 1968).

15. Mombushō, Mombu tōkei yōran (Handbook of Educational Statistics) (Tokyo: Ōkurashō Insatsukyoku, annual), 1976, pp. 54-55.

16. Mombushō, Kyōiku tōkei shiryōshū (Collected Statistical Source Materials on Education) (Tokyo: Mombushō, 1970), pp. 9-10, 71-82; and supplemental data supplied by the Ministry of Education. Similar shifts have also occurred at the junior college level.

17. Ogata Ken, "Zokuzoku tōsan o yosō sarete iru abunai daigaku" (Precarious Universities: Bankruptcies Increasingly Expected); Shuppan gendai, March 8, 1970, special issue.

18. Mombushō, Zenkoku daigaku, gives entry quotas by faculty, while actual entrants are given in Mombushō, Mombu nempō (Yearbook of the Ministry of Education) (Tokyo: Ōkurashō Insatsukyoku, annual). If other figures are accepted, it may be that even the Mombu nempō figures understate the actual number of entrants. Publishers of the university entry manual Keisetsu jidai (Study Time) (Tokyo: Ōbunsha, annual) maintain that their surveys indicate this is the case.

227

19.  Hōsei Daigaku Daiichi Daini Keizai Gakubu Ogata Zeminaaru, "Shiritsu daigaku no kenkyū jōken oyobi zaisei" (Research Conditions and Finance in Private Universities) (Tokyo: Seiyūsha, 1970, for private distribution), Vol. 2, pp. 94-95 (hereafter Ogata Seminar).

20.  Ibid., pp. 59-66.

21.  Mombushō, Mombu hōrei, 1976, p. 184.

22.  Ogata Seminar, pp. 79-80.

23.  My calculations from Sōrifu, Nihon tōkei nenkan (Japan Statistical Yearbook) (Tokyo: Prime Minister's Office, annual), for various years.

24.  Mombushō, CEC 1969 Report, p. 381.

25.  Ibid., p. 382.

26.  My calculations from ibid., p. 286; Hiroshima International Seminar on Higher Education, "Reference Material No. 1," April 1976, unpublished, p. 2; and Ministry of Education, Educational Standards in Japan, 1970 (Tokyo: Ministry of Education, 1971), p. 240. There are several volumes with this title, or the Japanese equivalent, Waga kuni no kyōiku suijun, published in 1959, 1964, 1970, and 1976.  Not all have been translated into English.  Subsequent references, cited as Mombushō, Standards, will be to the Japanese-language editions for 1959 and 1976 and to the English editions for 1964 and 1970.

27.  See sources cited in note 26; prewar figures are in Mombushō, Waga kuni no kōtō kyōiku (Higher Education in Japan: Ministry of Education White Paper) (Tokyo: Mombushō, 1964), pp. 304-305.

28.  Friedrich Edding and Dieter Berstecher, International Developments of Educational Expenditure, 1950-1965 (Paris: UNESCO, 1969), p. 40.

29.  OECD, Towards Mass Higher Education (Paris: OECD, 1974), pp. 180-82.

30.  Ōsaki Jin, "Shiritsu daigaku" (Private Universities), in Shimizu Yoshihiro, ed., Nihon no kōtō kyōiku (Japanese Higher Education) (Tokyo: Daiichi Hōki, 1968), p. 146; Mombushō, CEC 1969 Report, p. 119; Barbara Burn, et al., Higher Education in Nine

<u>Countries</u> (New York: McGraw-Hill, 1971), p. 181. The
new law allows the government to pay up to 50 percent
of private university faculty salaries, but such sums
are not automatic and will still leave Japan with a
very low proportion of government support.

31. Mombushō, <u>Kyōiku tōkei</u>, pp. 9-10, 57-72; and
<u>Standards, 1976</u>, p. 95. This increase becomes even
more significant when seen in the light of the changing relationship between full-time and part-time faculty. The number of part-time faculty has increased
from approximately one out of four in 1951 to one out
of three in 1975, with the greatest jump again coming
during the 1960s. <u>Ibid.</u>, p. 108.

32. Mombushō, <u>Standards, 1964</u>, p. 91; <u>ibid.</u>, <u>1970</u>,
pp. 99-100; also Hiroshima International Seminar,
<u>Reference Material No. 2</u>, p. 3.

33. Based on data in Mombushō, <u>CEC 1969 Report</u>, p.
447; <u>Standards, 1970</u>, p. 109, and <u>1976</u>, p. 115.

34. Mombushō, <u>CEC 1969 Report</u>, p. 447.

35. <u>Ibid.</u>, p. 135.

36. In 1964, for example, research expenditures in
national universities were about two-thirds of the
prewar level for experimental chairs and had not yet
reached one-third of the prewar figure for nonexperi-
mental chairs. Moreover, the amounts in other national as well as in public and private universities were
and remain even lower. Ichikawa Shōgo, "Daigaku wa
kore de ii ka?" (Does This Mean the Universities Are
Good?), <u>Kyōiku hyōron</u>, November 1964, pp. 15-17.

37. Nearly one-half of the universities in Japan
(46.3 percent) have libraries with fewer than 50,000
volumes; two-thirds have fewer than 100,000, a condi-
tion that has grown worse over time. In 1963, for
example, the figures were 38.5 percent and 61.1 percent respectively. Additionally, in many of the larger libraries there have been drastic declines in the
number of books per pupil. Mombushō, <u>Mombu nempō</u>.

38. Building space per pupil has declined 47 percent
since the end of the Occupation. Based on figures in
Jiyū Minshutō, Bunkyō Seido Chōsakai, <u>Kokumin no tame</u>
<u>no daigaku</u> (Universities for the People) (Tokyo: Jiyū
Minshutō Kōhō Iinkai, 1969), part 3, p. 19, for data
to 1965; and in Mombushō, <u>Gakkō kihon chōsa hōkokusho</u>

(Report on the Basic School Survey) (Tokyo, Ōkurashō Insatsukyoku, annual), for years after 1965.

39. Ōsawa, Nihon no shiritsu daigaku, pp. 222-68; and Nihon Gakujutsu Kaigi, "Shiritsu daigaku no jōsei ni tsuite" (On Aid to Private Universities), a recommendation to the prime minister dated May 11, 1965, reprinted in Nihon Gakujutsu Kaigi, Kankoku seimeishū (Collected Recommendations and Declarations of the Japan Science Council) (Tokyo: Gakujutsu Kaigi, 1966), Vol. 4, p. 117.

40. Ogata Ken, "Jinkenhi hojo no imi suru mono" (The Meaning of Subsidies for Personnel Expenditures), Keizai shirin, Vol. 39, October 1971, special issue, p. 15.

41. Ibid., p. 15. Also Ōsaki, "Shiritsu daigaku," pp. 167-77; Ogata Ken, "Shiritsu daigaku keiei no jittai to mondaiten" (Realities and Problems in the Management of Private Universities), Jurisuto, No. 411, December 1, 1968, pp. 69-75. "Debt service" includes payment on both principle and interest; interest constitutes about one-seventh of total debt service.

42. Hiroshima International Seminar, Reference Material No. 1, p. 9.

43. Ogata, "Shiritsu daigaku keiei," p. 73.

44. Having very low grades, being a female, or having parents of limited education, low income, or from an agricultural or blue-collar background were negative factors. Mombushō, CEC 1969 Report, pp. 50-53.

45. Mombu kōhō, No. 545, February 13, 1972, p. 4. The class pattern of Japanese higher education exists in other capitalist societies. In the Soviet Union offspring of apparatchiki apparently also have a better chance for higher education, although economic class per se is less relevant. Gerhard Lenski, Power and Privilege (New York: McGraw Hill, 1966). One study, however, contends that the Japanese pattern is significantly more biased toward upper-class students than is that of either the U.S. or the USSR. See Herbert Passin, Society and Education in Japan (New York: Columbia University Teachers College, 1965), p. 121.

46. Hiroshima University, Research Institute for Higher Education, International Comparison of Higher Educational Statistics (Hiroshima: RIHE, 1976), p. 3.

47. Sumiya Mikio, Kyōiku no keizaigaku (An Economic Study of Education) (Tokyo: Yomiuri Shimbunsha, 1970), p. 96.

48. Ibid., p. 228; Ogata Ken, "Kyōiku keizairon no kadai to hōhō" (Problems and Methods in Educational Economics), Keizai shirin, Vol. 38, January 1971, special issue, p. 83.

49. Sumiya, Kyōiku no keizaigaku, pp. 12-18.

50. Mombushō, CEC 1969 Report, p. 36. For further analysis of those going on, see Mombushō, Kōtō gakkō sotsugyōsha no shinro jōkyō (The Circumstances of Advancement of High School Graduates) (Tokyo: Mombushō, 1969).

51. See Koya Azumi, Higher Education and Business Recruitment in Japan (New York: Columbia University Teachers College, 1969).

52. Shimbori Michiya, Gakureki--jitsuryokushugi o habamu (Academic Background--Thwarting the Merit System) (Tokyo: Daiyamondosha, 1966); Fukaya Masashi, Gakureki-shugi no keifu (Genealogy of Diplomaism) (Tokyo: Reimei Shodō, 1966).

53. Mombushō, Standards, 1970, pp. 133-34, 233-34; and Standards, 1976, p. 157; OECD, Higher Education, p. 215.

54. In a study of the impact of economics on policy, Itō concludes that at least in the ten-year period 1955-65 "politics was discussed exclusively in economic terms." Itō Masaya, Ikeda Hayato--sono sei to shi (Ikeda Hayato--His Life and Death) (Tokyo: Shiseido, 1966), pp. 90-91, as quoted in Daiichi Ito, "The Bureaucracy: Its Attitudes and Behavior," The Developing Economies, Vol. 6, December 1968, p. 451.

55. Kanamori Hisao, "Nihon no seichōritsu wa naze takai ka?" (Why is Japan's Growth Rate High?), Ekonomisuto, Vol. 48, November 24, 1970, pp. 29-30. See also Tsunehiko Watanabe, "Improvement of Labor Quality and Economic Growth--Japan's Postwar Experience," Economic Development and Cultural Change, Vol. 21, October 1972, pp. 33-53.

Chapter 7. Pressure Group Politics.

1. Herbert Passin, Society and Education in Japan
(New York: Columbia University Teachers College,
1965), pp. 92-99; Nagai Michio, Kindaika to kyōiku
(Modernization and Education) (Tokyo: Tōkyō Daigaku
Shuppankai, 1969), passim, but especially Ch. 2;
Ministry of Education, Japan's Growth and Education
(Tokyo: Ministry of Education, 1963); Nagai Michio,
Higher Education in Japan: Its Takeoff and Crash
(Tokyo: University of Tokyo Press, 1971).

2. Nagai, Kindaika, p. 35.

3. In Passin, Society and Education, p. 206.

4. Some critics of the government, however, contend
that any government direction over the universities
is a violation of Article 23 of the constitution,
which guarantees academic freedom. As will be seen,
a few items of the government's policy changes in the
area of specialization and differentiation also were
based on legal changes that passed the Diet.

5. On the political role of big business in Japan,
see, for example, Chitoshi Yanaga, Big Business in
Japanese Politics (New Haven: Yale University Press,
1968); Frank C. Langdon, "The Political Contributions
of Big Business in Japan," Asian Survey, Vol. 3, Octo-
ber 1963, and "The Attitudes of the Big Business Com-
munity," in James William Morley, ed., Forecast for
Japan (Princeton: Princeton University Press, 1972);
Nathaniel B. Thayer, How the Conservatives Rule Japan
(Princeton: Princeton University Press, 1969); and
Yomiuri Shimbunsha, Zaikai (The Financial World)
(Tokyo: Yomiuri Shimbunsha, 1972).

6. Plan as in Daigaku Mondai Kenkyūkai, Daigaku mondai: Shiryō yōran (Handbook of Source Materials on the
University Problem) (Tokyo: Bunkyū Shorin, 1969), pp.
475-76.

7. As cited in Terasaki Masao, "Sengo daigakushi no
magarikado" (Crossroads in the History of Postwar
Universities), Bōsei, Vol. 2, June-July 1971, p. 56.

8. "Futatabi kyōiku seido no kaizen ni tsuite" (A
Second Proposal on the Reform of the Educational System). The plan is analyzed in Kaigo Tokiomi and Terasaki Masao, Daigaku kyōiku (University Education)
(Tokyo: Tōkyō Daigaku Shuppankai, 1969), pp. 447-49,

and is reproduced in Daigaku Mondai Kenkyūkai, Daigaku mondai yōran, pp. 477-78, under the title "Kyōiku seidi kaizen ni kansuru yōbō" (Demands for the Reform of the Educational System).

9. "Shinjidai no yōsei ni taiō suru gijutsu kyōiku ni kansuru iken" (An Opinion on Scientific Education to Respond to the Demands of a New Age), reproduced in Daigaku Mondai Kenkyūkai, Daigaku mondai yōran, pp. 479-82.

10. Kaigo and Terasaki, Daigaku kyōiku, pp. 126-27.

11. Mombushō, Kyōiku tōkei shiryōshū (Collected Statistical Source Materials on Education) (Tokyo: Mombushō, 1970), pp. 39-40.

12. Daigaku Mondai Kenkyūkai, Daigaku mondai yōran, pp. 477-78.

13. Ibid., pp. 479-82; Kaigo and Terasaki, Daigaku kyōiku, pp. 130-31, 447-49.

14. "Gakkō kyōiku ni okeru sangyō kyōiku no shinkō hōsaku."

15. Asahi shimbun, July 10, 1960; also in Nomura Hyōji, Daigaku seisaku: Daigaku mondai (University Policies: University Problems) (Tokyo: Rōdō Jumpōsha, 1969), p. 666.

16. Ibid., pp. 670-71.

17. Ibid., p. 671.

18. Ibid., pp. 682-83; Daigaku Mondai Kenkyūkai, Daigaku mondai yōran, pp. 483-84.

19. Nihon Keieisha Dantai Remmei, "Chokumen suru daigaku mondai ni kansuru kihonteki kenkai" (Basic Views of the University Problem We Are Facing), reproduced in Nomura, Daigaku seisaku, pp. 172-77.

20. Nomura, Daigaku seisaku, p. 175.

21. Nihon Keieisha Dantai Remmei, "Kyōiku mondai ni taisuru sangyōkai no kenkai" (Opinions of the Industrial World Concerning the Basic Problems of Education), September 1969, and "Sangaku kankei ni kansuru sangyōkai no kihon ninshiki oyobi teigen" (Basic Understandings and Proposals of the Industrial World

Regarding Industrial Education); Nihon Keizai Dōyūkai, Kyōiku Mondai Iinkai, "Daigaku no kihon mondai" (The Basic Problems in Education), November 15, 1968, and "Kōji fukushi shakai no tame no kōtō kyōiku seido" (A Higher Educational System for a Highly Productive Society), July 18, 1969.

22.  Robert A. Scalapino, Democracy and the Party Movement in Prewar Japan (Berkeley: University of California Press, 1953); Peter Duus, Party Rivalry and Political Change in Taishō Japan (Cambridge: Harvard University Press, 1968); Tetsuo Najita, Hara Kei and the Politics of Compromise, 1905-1915 (Cambridge: Harvard University Press, 1967); Arthur E. Tiedemann, "Big Business and Politics in Prewar Japan," in James William Morley, Dilemmas of Growth in Prewar Japan (Princeton: Princeton University Press, 1971), inter alia.

23.  The political currency of the pressure group is not always the same.  John C. Campbell ("Compensation for Repatriates: A Case Study of Interest-Group Politics and Party-Government Negotiations in Japan," in T.J. Pempel, ed., Policymaking in Contemporary Japan [Ithaca, N.Y.: Cornell University Press, 1977]), Haruhiro Fukui (Party in Power [Berkeley: University of California Press, 1970], Ch. 7), and William Steslicke (Doctors in Politics: The Political Life of the Japan Medical Association [New York: Praeger, 1973], for example, all deal with groups whose primary political currency is a presumed ability to deliver or withhold large numbers of votes.  In the case of business, the political currency is clearly money and ideology.

24.  School Education Law, supplement to articles 109-10; subsequently deleted by Law 110, 1964.

25.  Mombushō, Tanki daigaku ichiran (Outline on Junior Colleges) (Tokyo: Mombushō, 1970).

26.  See Asahi shimbun (evening edition), October 26, 1952; Mainichi shimbun, October 31, 1954, and November 15, 1954; Asahi shimbun, November 1, 1954, and November 5, 1954.

27.  My calculations, from Mombushō, Kyōiku tōkei.

28.  Mainichi shimbun, September 14, 1955; Asahi shimbun, September 15, 1955.  The proposal was related to the ideas of tanka daigaku and senka daigaku, both of which terms were applied at the time to the newly proposed institutions.

234

29. _Mainichi shimbun_, December 9, 1957.

30. _Asahi shimbun_, November 1, 1958; _Tōkyō shimbun_, March 3, 1959; _Yomiuri shimbun_, March 9, 1959.

31. _Tōkyō shimbun_, April 1, 1959.

32. School Education Law, Article 69.

33. Mombushō, _Mombu tōkei yōran_ (Handbook of Educational Statistics) (Tokyo: Ōkurashō Insatsukyoku, annual), 1976, pp. 56-57.

34. _Ibid._, p. 58.

35. Ministry of Education, _Educational Standards in Japan, 1970_ (Tokyo: Ministry of Education, 1971), p. 209 (hereafter Mombushō, _Standards_); Mombushō, _Mombu nempō_ (Yearbook of the Ministry of Education) (Tokyo: Ōkurashō Insatsukyoku, annual), 1968, p. 341. It should also be noted that all national junior colleges are attached to four-year national universities as evening facilities. Clyde Vroman, _Japan: A Study of the Educational System of Japan and Guide to the Academic Placement of Students from Japan in United States Educational Institutions_ (n.p.: American Association of Collegiate Registrars and Admissions Officers, 1966), p. 62.

36. Mombushō, _Kōtō semmongakkō ichiran_ (Outline on Higher Technical Schools) (Tokyo: Mombushō, 1970); Mombushō, _Mombu tōkei yōran_, 1976, p. 52.

37. Mombushō, _Standards, 1970_, p. 34; Kōtō Kyōiku Kondankai, _Kōtō kyōiku no kakujū seibi keikaku ni tsuite_ (On the Plans for the Expansion and Consolidation of Higher Education) (Tokyo: Kōtō Kyōiku Kondankai, 1974), p. 18; Mombushō, _Mombu tōkei yōran_, 1976, p. 53.

38. Mombushō, _Kōtō semmongakkō_, p. 115; Mombushō, _Standards, 1970_, p. 34.

39. Mombushō, _Mombu nempō_, 1968, p. 210.

40. Mombushō, _Mombu tōkei yōran_, 1976, pp. 14-17.

41. Economic Planning Agency, _Economic and Social Development Plan, 1967-1971_ (Tokyo: Economic Planning Agency, 1967), p. 114.

42. Mombushō, Kongo ni okeru gakkō kyōiku no sōgōteki na kakujū seibi no tame no kihonteki shisaku ni tsuite: Tōshin (Report: On the Basic Policies for the Comprehensive Expansion and Consolidation of Future School Education) (Tokyo: Mombushō, 1971) (hereafter Mombushō, Tōshin 1971); an abbreviated English version of the plan is in Mombushō, Standards, 1970, pp. 179-91; and a full translation was published as Basic Guidelines for the Reform of Education (Tokyo: Ministry of Education, 1972).

43. An additional differentiation made among the national universities that is not discussed here is that which occurs in the national university entrance examinations. The national universities are grouped into two categories: the prestige schools and all the others. Students may take both tests but must indicate the school of their choice on each exam; failing the high-prestige exam leaves most with a choice between one year as a rōnin or attendance at an explicitly designated low-prestige institution. This system has been under attack in the mid-1970s and is likely to be reexamined.

44. Interview with Amano Ikuo, March 2, 1971; Kaigo and Terasaki, Daigaku kyōiku, pp. 145-46.

45. OECD, "Education Committee, Reviews of National Policies for Education: Japan," unpublished report, 1970, pp. 42-43; Amano interview; interview with Kitamura Kazuyuki, October 28, 1970.

46. A Ministry of Education document entitled "Daigaku no kōza nado ni kansuru yōkō" (Plans Relating to Chairs in the Universities) was formulated at this time. Kaigo and Terasaki, Daigaku kyōiku, p. 149.

47. "Kokuritsu daigaku no kōza ni kansuru shōrei" (Administrative Directive on Chairs in the National Universities), Administrative Directive No. 23, 1954, Ministry of Education.

48. "Daigaku setchi kijun" (Standards for University Chartering), Administrative Directive No. 28, 1956, Article 5, sections 2 and 3. On this, see Terasaki Masao, "Daigaku setchi kijun" (The University Chartering Standards), Asahi jānaru, Vol. 12, August 2, 1970, pp. 39-44.

49. See Part 2, section 2, subsection 3.

50.  Mombushō, Tōshin 1971, Part 3, section 2, subsection 5.

51.  Mombushō, Waga kuni no kōtō kyōiku (Higher Education in Japan: Ministry of Education White Paper) (Tokyo: Mombushō, 1964), pp. 54-55 (hereafter 1964 White Paper); Kaigo and Terasaki, Daigaku kyōiku, p. 150; Amano Ikuo, "Kokuritsu daigaku" (National Universities), in Shimizu Yoshihiro, ed., Nihon no kōtō kyōiku (Japanese Higher Education) (Tokyo: Dai-ichi Hōki, 1968), p. 200.

52.  Amano, "Kokuritsu daigaku," passim.

53.  Daigaku kijun, Article 7.  See Nomura, Daigaku seisaku, pp. 456-57.

54.  On the problem of general education, see, inter alia, Inō Keigo and Nishibori Michio, "Daigaku ni okeru ningen keisei ni kansuru iken chōsa, III" (Opinion Survey Concerning the Personality Development of Students in Higher Education, Part 3), in Kokuritsu Kyōiku Kenkyūjo, Kiyō (Bulletin of the National Institute for Educational Research), No. 69, December 1969, pp. 41-54.  In a survey of employers concerning the strong and weak points of university graduates, the authors found only 72 of 355 who had a favorable opinion of the educational system.  Of these, only 40 cited as desirable such items as breadth of knowledge, diversity, and wide perspectives.  In contrast, 162 of 353 cited major criticisms, such as lack of specialized knowledge, weakness in basics, poor general education, and so on.  See also Yoshimura Tōru, "Ippan kyōiku" (General Education), in Shimizu, Nihon no kōtō kyōiku, pp. 101-44; Murakami Yasuaki and Himai Osamu, "Kyōiku" (Education), in Uchida Tadao and Etō Shinkichi, eds., Atarashii daigakuzō o motomete (In Search of a New Image of the University) (Tokyo: Nihon Hyōronsha, 1969), pp. 139-48.

55.  "Daigaku setchi kijun."

56.  Article 20, clauses 2 and 3.

57.  Article 21.

58.  Article 19, clause 2; Article 23.

59.  For the composition of the committee, see Mombushō, Mombu nempō, 1963, p. 104.  For the report, see Mombushō, Atarashii daigaku setchi kijun: Ippan kyōiku

(The New University Chartering Standards: General
Education) (Tokyo: Mombushō, 1970), p. 192.

60.  See Section 5, clause 2 of the report, in ibid.,
p. 128.

61.  For the reaction of the Nihon Kyōiku Gakkai Daigaku Seido Kenkyū Iinkai (Research Committee on the
University System of the Japan Educational Association) to the draft report, see Kyōikugaku kenkyū,
Vol. 33, March 1966, pp. 91-95; the reaction of the
Association of National University Presidents is in
Mombushō, Atarashii daigaku setchi kijun, pp. 137-54;
that of the University Accreditation Association is in
ibid., pp. 155-62.

62.  Directive No. 21, 1970.

63.  Mombushō, Atarashii daigaku setchi kijun; see
also Zadankai, "Kaizensareta daigaku setchi kijun"
(The Revised University Chartering Standards), Tōki no
ugoki, October 1, 1970, pp. 4-17.

64.  See, for example, Ogose Sunao et al., "Yanaihara
kara Kaya e, I" (Tokyo University from Presidents
Yanaihara to Kaya, Part 1), Asahi jānaru, Vol. 12,
November 22, 1970.

65.  Mombushō, 1964 White Paper, p. 100.

66.  Mombushō, Standards, 1964, p. 25.

67.  Council for Science and Technology, Outline of
the Council for Science and Technology (Tokyo: Council
for Science and Technology, 1970), p. 103.  The entire
organizational plan is in Tabata Shigejirō et al.,
eds., Daigaku mondai sōshiryōshū (Comprehensive Collection of Documents on the University Problem) (Tokyo: Yūhikaku, 1970), Vol. 8, pp. 147-49.

68.  A key concern in Japanese industrial circles at
the time was the preservation of national control over
critical areas of industry, and IBM's acquisition of
the French computer firm Machines Bull and the American company's consequent dominance of the French computer industry were viewed as a warning of what might
happen to Japan if its science and technology were
not developed and protected from foreign influence.
The impact was similar to that of Sputnik in the United States.

238

69. Science and Technology Agency, Governmental and Administrative Organization in the Field of Scientific Research (Tokyo: Science and Technology Agency, 1971), p. 32 (hereafter STA, Organization of Scientific Research).

70. Nomura, Daigaku seisaku, p. 667.

71. Tabata Shigejirō et al., eds., Sengo no rekishi to kihon hōki (History and Fundamental Regulations of the Postwar Period), Vol. 1 of Daigaku mondai sōshiryō-shū (Comprehensive Collection of Documents on the University Problem) (Tokyo: Yūhikaku, 1970), p. 71.

72. Tabata, Daigaku mondai sōshiryōshū, Vol. 8, pp. 434-35.

73. A special subsidy to encourage science education in private universities was begun in 1956. See Mombu-shō, 1964 White Paper, p. 133.

74. STA, Organization of Scientific Research, pp. 40-41.

75. On the Japanese budget process, see John C. Campbell, Contemporary Japanese Budget Politics (Berkeley: University of California Press, 1977).

76. "Gijutsu kyōiku no kakkiteki shinkō saku no kakuritsu suishin ni kansuru yōkō" (Demands in Regard to the Establishment and Promotion of a Policy for Epochmaking Advances in Technological Education), in Nomura, Daigaku seisaku, pp. 682-83.

77. Ibid., pp. 683-700.

78. Nagai Kenichi, Kempō to kyōiku kihonken (The Constitution and Bases of Authority in Education) (Tokyo: Keisō Shobō, 1970), p. 247.

79. STA, Organization of Scientific Research, p. 33.

80. Kagaku Gijutsuchō, Kagaku gijutsu hakusho (Science and Technology White Paper) (Tokyo: Ōkurashō Insatsukyoku, 1971), p. 101; STA, Organization of Scientific Research, p. 33.

81. Mombushō, Standards, 1970, pp. 27-29; Mombushō, Mombu tōkei yōran, 1976, pp. 58-59.

82. Lax government supervision over the funds appropriated for science and engineering faculties frequently enabled universities to use the money for other purposes. Interview with Harada Taneo, National Institute for Educational Research, February 3, 1971.

83. See, for example, Tōkyō Daigaku Shimbunsha, Daigaku mondai (The University Problem) (Tokyo: Minami Kikakushitsu, 1969), Ch. 5.

84. Terasaki, "Daigaku setchi kijun," pp. 41-42.

85. Nihon Kyōshokuin Kumiai, Kokumin no tame no daigaku (Universities for the People) (Tokyo: Nihon Kyōshokuin Kumiai, 1970), p. 29.


Chapter 8. Conclusion.

1. William Bacchus, Foreign Policy and the Bureaucratic Process (Princeton: Princeton University Press, 1974), pp. 30ff.

2. Ministry of Education, Educational Standards in Japan, 1970 (Tokyo: Ministry of Education, 1971), p. 39.

3. In regard to the refusal to appoint the elected president of Kobe University, see Mainichi shimbun, February 16, 1971. The ministry's refusal to appoint Sunazawa as chairman of education at Hokkaido University might also be cited; see Ōhashi Hisatoshi, Shiryō: Daigaku no jichi (Source Materials: University Autonomy) (Tokyo: Sanichi Shobō, 1970), pp. 42-55.

4. On this, see ibid., pp. 17-42.

5. "Kyōiku kaizō" (Educational Restructuring series), Asahi shimbun, June 17, 1971.

# Index

241

243

# Studies of the East Asian Institute

THE LADDER OF SUCCESS IN IMPERIAL CHINA, by Ping-ti Ho.
Columbia University Press, 1962.

THE CHINESE INFLATION, 1937-1949, by Shun-hsin Chou.   Columbia
University Press, 1963.

REFORMER IN MODERN CHINA:   CHANG CHIEN, 1853-1926, by Samuel
Chu.   Columbia University Press, 1965.

RESEARCH IN JAPANESE SOURCES:   A GUIDE, by Herschel Webb with
the assistance of Marleigh Ryan.   Columbia University Press, 1965.

SOCIETY AND EDUCATION IN JAPAN, by Herbert Passin.   Teachers
College Press, Columbia University, 1965.

AGRICULTURAL PRODUCTION AND ECONOMIC DEVELOPMENT IN JAPAN, 1873-
1922, by James I. Nakamura.   Princeton University Press, 1966.

JAPAN'S FIRST MODERN NOVEL:   UKIGUMO OF FUTABATEI SHIMEI, by
Marleigh Ryan.   Columbia University Press, 1967.

THE KOREAN COMMUNIST MOVEMENT, 1918-1948, by Dae-Sook Suh.
Princeton University Press, 1967.

THE FIRST VIETNAM CRISIS, by Melvin Gurtov.   Columbia University
Press, 1967.

CADRES, BUREAUCRACY, AND POLITICAL POWER IN COMMUNIST CHINA, by
A. Doak Barnett.   Columbia University Press, 1967.

THE JAPANESE IMPERIAL INSTITUTION IN THE TOKUGAWA PERIOD, by
Herschel Webb.   Columbia University Press, 1968.

HIGHER EDUCATION AND BUSINESS RECRUITMENT IN JAPAN, by Koya
Azumi.   Teachers College Press, Columbia University, 1969.

245

THE COMMUNISTS AND CHINESE PEASANT REBELLIONS:  A CASE STUDY IN
THE REWRITING OF CHINESE HISTORY, by James P. Harrison, Jr.
Atheneum,1969.

HOW THE CONSERVATIVES RULE JAPAN, by Nathaniel  B. Thayer.
Princeton University Press, 1969.

ASPECTS OF CHINESE EDUCATION, edited by C. T. Hu.  Teachers
College Press, Columbia University, 1969.

DOCUMENTS OF KOREAN COMMUNISM, 1918-1948, by Dae-Sook Suh.
Princeton University Press, 1970.

JAPANESE EDUCATION:  A BIBLIOGRAPHY OF MATERIALS IN THE
ENGLISH LANGUAGE, by Herbert Passin.  Teachers College Press,
Columbia University, 1970.

ECONOMIC DEVELOPMENT AND THE LABOR MARKET IN JAPAN, by Koji
Taira.  Columbia University Press, 1970.

THE JAPANESE OLIGARCHY AND THE RUSSO-JAPANESE WAR, by Shumpei
Okamoto.  Columbia University Press, 1970.

IMPERIAL RESTORATION IN MEDIEVAL JAPAN, by H. Paul Varley.
Columbia University Press, 1971.

JAPAN'S POSTWAR DEFENSE POLICY, 1974-1968, by Martin E. Weinstein.
Columbia University Press, 1971.

ELECTION CAMPAIGNING JAPANESE STYLE, by Gerald L. Curtis.  Columbia University Press, 1971.

CHINA AND RUSSIA:  THE GREAT GAME, by O. Edmund Clubb.  Columbia
University Press, 1971.

MONEY AND MONETARY POLICY IN COMMUNIST CHINA, by Katherine Huang
Hsiao.  Columbia University Press, 1971.

THE DISTRICT MAGISTRATE IN LATE IMPERIAL CHINA, by John R. Watt.
Columbia University Press, 1972.

LAW AND POLICY IN CHINA'S FOREIGN RELATIONS:  A STUDY OF ATTITUDES
AND PRACTICE, by James C. Hsiung.  Columbia University Press,
1972.

PEARL HARBOR AS HISTORY:  JAPANESE-AMERICAN RELATIONS, 1931-1941,
eidted by Dorothy Borg and Shumpei Okamoto, with the assistance
of Dale K. A. Finlayson.  Columbia University Press, 1973.

JAPANESE CULTURE:  A SHORT HISTORY, by H. Paul Varley.  Praeger,
1973.

246

JAPAN'S FOREIGN POLICY, 1868-1941: A RESEARCH GUIDE, edited by James William Morley. Columbia University Press, 1973.

DOCTORS IN POLITICS: THE POLITICAL LIFE OF THE JAPAN MEDICAL ASSOCIATION, by William E. Steslicke. Praeger, 1973.

THE JAPAN TEACHERS UNION: A RADICAL INTEREST GROUP IN JAPANESE POLITICS, by Donald Ray Thurston. Princeton University Press, 1973.

PALACE AND POLITICS IN PREWAR JAPAN, by David Anson Titus. Columbia University Press, 1974.

THE IDEA OF CHINA: ESSAYS IN GEOGRAPHIC MYTH AND THEORY, by Andrew March. David and Charles, 1974.

ORIGINS OF THE CULTURAL REVOLUTION, by Roderick MacFarquhar. Columbia University Press, 1974.

SHIBA KŌKAN: ARTIST, INNOVATOR, AND PIONEER IN THE WESTERNIZATIOI OF JAPAN, by Calvin L. French. Weatherhill, 1974.

EMBASSY AT WAR, by Harold Joyce Noble, edited with an introduction by Frank Baldwin, Jr. University of Washington Press, 1975.

REBELS AND BUREAUCRATS: CHINA'S DECEMBER 9ERS, by John Israel and Donald W. Klein. University of California Press, 1975.

HOUSE UNITED, HOUSE DIVIDED: THE CHINESE FAMILY IN TAIWAN, by Myron L. Cohen. Columbia University Press, 1976.

INSEI: ABDICATED SOVEREIGNS IN THE POLITICS OF LATE HEIAN JAPAN, by G. Cameron Hurst. Columbia University Press, 1976.

DETERRENT DIPLOMACY, edited by James William Morley. Columbia University Press, 1976.

CADRES, COMMANDERS AND COMMISSARS: THE TRAINING OF THE CHINESE COMMUNIST LEADERSHIP, 1920-1945, by Jane L. Price. Westview Press, 1976.

SUN YAT-SEN: FRUSTRATED PATRIOT, by C. Marin Wilbur. Columbia University Press, 1976.

JAPANESE INTERNATIONAL NEGOTIATING STYLE, by Michael Blaker. Columbia University Press, 1977.

CONTEMPORARY JAPANESE BUDGET POLITICS, by John Creighton Campbell. University of California Press, 1977.

THE MEDIEVAL CHINESE OLIGARCHY, by David Johnson. Westview Press, 1977.

247

ESCAPE FROM PREDICAMENT:  NEO-CONFUCIANISM AND CHINA'S EVOLVING
POLITICAL CULTURE, by Thomas A. Metzger.  Columbia University
Press, 1977.

THE ARMS OF KIANGNAN:  MODERNIZATION IN THE CHINESE ORDNANCE
INDUSTRY, 1860-1895, by Thomas L. Kennedy.  Westview Press, 1978.

THE CHINESE CONNECTION, by Warren Cohen.  Columbia University
Press, 1978.